Praise for *Happy at Last*

"Many self-help books are wildly unrealistic and not grounded in any kind of scientific evidence about how the mind actually works. Not so with Richard O'Connor's book. The author provides a clear road map through the opportunities, obstacles, and complexities of happiness, drawing on the latest scientific research as well as his long and compassionate experience as a therapist. This is a book that leaves you wiser and better equipped to face the future."

> —Daniel Nettle, Newcastle University, author of
> *Happiness: The Science Behind Your Smile*

"Richard O'Connor, having already helped us to undo depression and chronic stress, now helps us to do happiness. Filled with humor and humanity, this book gives an up-to-date summary of the best of what research and clinical experience have to tell us about being happy. O'Connor is an engaging writer who holds the reader's attention while providing real substance." —Bill O'Hanlon, author of *Change 101*

"[A] graceful blend of philosophy, research, and practical advice ... substantive yet accessible and engaging." —*Library Journal*

"After such a frenetic year, this book is rather a small pleasure."
> —*Winston-Salem Journal*

ALSO BY RICHARD O'CONNOR, M.S.W., PH.D.

Undoing Depression
Active Treatment of Depression
Undoing Perpetual Stress

happy at last

THE THINKING PERSON'S
GUIDE TO FINDING JOY

Richard O'Connor, M.S.W., Ph.D.

ST. MARTIN'S GRIFFIN
NEW YORK

www.stmartins.com

The Library of Congress has catalogued the hardcover edition as follows:

O'Connor, Richard, Ph.D.
    Happy at last : the thinking person's guide to finding joy / Richard
O'Connor. — 1st ed.
        p. cm.
    Includes bibliographical references.
    ISBN 978-0-312-36906-4
1. Happiness. I. Title.
    BF575.H27026 2008
    158—dc22   2008025263

            ISBN 978-0-312-36907-1 (trade paperback)

        First St. Martin's Griffin Edition: January 2010

        10 9 8 7 6 5 4 3 2 1

for sally

YES, IT *IS* MARVELOUS.

CONTENTS

ACKNOWLEDGMENTS

To my patients, who have let me be a part of their courageous journeys, and have taught me so much in the process.

To Bill O'Hanlon, for being such a spark plug.

To Paul Lippmann, for his wise and persistently skeptical advice all these years.

To my wife, Robin, for being herself. For patiently and consistently encouraging me, for being so positive when I've needed it. For the title. For brainstorming, editing, listening. For always knowing somehow when I need unqualified support and when I need objective feedback.

happy at last

Happiness is at a dead end. For centuries, one of the basic operating principles of Western society has been the belief that increasing prosperity will lead automatically to greater happiness. But now, for the first time,
we have the data to prove that's just not so. In the USA and Europe, in the
last fifty years since scientists started measuring personal happiness reliably,
people continue to report that they are less and less happy every year—
although personal wealth continues to increase. As other nations become
more Westernized and prosperity spreads around the globe, happiness declines as well. This theory that most of us unconsciously buy into—*If I get
rich, then I'll be happy*—doesn't work. In fact, what seems to work is the
opposite—*If I get rich, I'll be depressed and anxious.* Rates of depression
and anxiety disorders are zooming into the stratosphere in Western countries. Other social indicators we can assume are linked with unhappiness are
climbing as well—divorce, illegal drug use, incarceration rates, poor educa-
tional performance, violence, obesity.

So wealth is not the answer. Maybe it's a good thing to face that now, be-cause those of us in the West are probably at the very pinnacle of personal wealth, looking downhill from here on. In fact, it's likely that the United States passed the peak of personal wealth without much fanfare about twenty-five years ago, because ever since then, we've been working longer and longer hours to maintain the same standard of living. Still, whether the peak is in the recent past or the near future, the long-term outlook is tough simply because the global economy means there's a great leveling coming. All the billions of people in China, India, and Africa want our standard of living, too; and because energy and other resources are finite, as their slices of pie get larger, ours will get smaller. Look at the cost of gasoline in the United States over the past five years—sure, some of the increase comes from profit taking and price gouging, but most of it is due to the fact that there's some newly wealthy guy in Shanghai who wants gas, too.

It's not bad enough that wealth doesn't bring happiness. Wealth itself is going to be harder and harder to get. It's time for a revolution.

This is going to be a small revolution, however. Although the govern-ment could do a much better job than it does, government can't provide the solution to happiness. The revolution in happiness has to come at a personal level—mostly at an individual level—although our relationships with others can help, too.

If you've read any of my previous books, you know that I've identified myself as someone with clinical depression. While someone with clinical depression might seem to be the last person qualified to write a guide to happiness, that's not actually the case. Here's why—my patients and I, other fellow depression-sufferers, are your canaries in the coal mine. We suffer from what's known as depressive realism—the tendency to see things with-out comforting illusions. We've been facing the realities of life for a long time, and we can help you as those realities become sharper and tougher, as they are going to do. Besides that, depressed people know that the ability to experience happiness again is the very last symptom of depression to lift, and we've had to work hard to get there. I've done my share of that hard work, and at this point, I feel more joyful and content with my lot than I ever have before. I've learned a lot along the way, and I want to share it with you.

If I can make it, with one metaphorical hand tied behind my back, so can you.

I've also helped some very unhappy people. I've been a therapist for almost thirty years, and I've seen a lot: People who were raised by, or married to, sadists or sons of bitches. People who've been raped, abused, bullied, discriminated against, and tortured. People who were there at 9/11. People who've had cancer, stroke, heart attack, chronic pain. People who live in a permanent state of fear. People who seem never to have felt good—for no reason that we could ever find. I'm not saying that working with me has turned them all into dancing forest sprites, but most of them have come to feel a lot better. In the process, I've learned a lot from them, as well.

So—there are some unpleasant new realities that interfere with happiness. (There are plenty of old ones, too, which we'll discuss.) Fortunately, there have been some truly revolutionary developments in psychology and brain science in the past few years—and more on the way—that can help us immensely. Psychology is moving from simply alleviating distress to helping people live richer and more satisfying lives. We know now that focused attention and practice, such as accomplished musicians experience, change the brain; the neural circuits that correspond to the motions of Eric Clapton's fingers or Pavarotti's discrimination of tone become enlarged and enriched with time. However, Western psychology is only beginning to investigate whether that kind of intentional, focused practice can change something like feelings of happiness, relatedness, or empathy. We've operated on the—largely untested—assumption that those are fixed traits, determined by our genes and perhaps influenced by childhood experience, certainly not changeable by any kind of adult experiences other than, perhaps, severe trauma. Now there's evidence to suggest that practicing happiness skills can change your brain circuits as well. If you can learn to type, you can learn to be happy.

It may surprise you that achieving happiness takes effort, at least for most of us. It doesn't come naturally. We can—hopefully—feel good when a good thing happens, but the feeling doesn't last. Soon we go back to our normal state, which for most people is one of vague discontent. In this book, we're going to talk about achieving a deeper and more sustained kind of happiness.

Maybe you're not surprised that happiness is in big trouble. Maybe you already suspect that society is headed in the wrong direction. After all, why else would we be such suckers for exotic martinis, lotto, fashion, plastic surgery, and all the other nostrums that promise ecstasy and fulfillment? Our culture has promised us that the secret to happiness is making enough money so that you can buy the right things, with the right labels, so you can belong to the elite and feel really good about yourself. The fact that it just doesn't work that way is not an expression of values, like me wagging my finger at you to say you should be above worldly things; it's a scientific fact. Psychologists and economists have known for twenty years about the hedonic treadmill—a fancy way of saying that no matter how much you have right now, you want more; and when you get more, you will want more still. It's also a proven fact that sudden wealth won't make you happy, and a catastrophic illness won't necessarily make you miserable. Much of happiness depends on your attitude toward what life hands you.

Here's the good news: <u>We can change our own brains.</u> And here's the bad news: <u>It takes longer than we want it to.</u> Some researchers recently taught a group of college students to juggle and, using the latest high-tech neuroimaging equipment, observed their brains as they learned. After observing three months of daily practice, the researchers could identify measurable growth in gray matter in certain areas of their subjects' brains; after three months of no practice, the growth disappeared. <u>Life experience changes the structure of the brain itself</u>. Just like juggling, happiness is a set of skills you can learn; and, just like juggling, <u>learning</u> to be happy is work that requires dedication and practice. Science and experience have taught us that the ways of acting, thinking, feeling, and relating that lead to greater happiness do not come naturally to most people. It takes conscious, sustained effort to overcome the habits that keep us unhappy and learn new habits to replace them. But after you've done that work, actually <u>being</u> happy is not much work at all. Once you've learned to ride a bicycle, or type, or juggle, it doesn't take much conscious effort to maintain your ability. If you practice regularly, your brain will incorporate your new skills so that it gets to be easier and easier to be happy.

So if what comes looks daunting to you, try not to be daunted. This is a complete program for restructuring your life and rewiring the brain, it covers a lot of territory, and you won't learn it all overnight. In fact, you won't learn it at all just by reading the book. You will have to practice much of my advice consistently. But give it time, and your daily attention. If it takes three months for the skills of juggling to be imprinted on your brain, surely you ought to give the skills of happiness three months. This is no idle promise. This is the real thing. Give it a try.

It's useful to have a framework for what we're learning, so here's a little guide about what's to come in this book:

- An introductory chapter to discuss just what happiness is and isn't.
- Three chapters about the reasons why it's so difficult for us to be happy.
- A chapter about mindfulness and emotional receptivity, the core skills we need in order to feel happiness in today's world.
- Three chapters on strategies for increasing happiness: reducing unnecessary misery, feeling more joy, and feeling greater satisfaction.
- A brief chapter on coping with unhappiness, since that's an inevitable part of life.
- A chapter modestly titled "The Meaning of Life," about the need to have our lives make sense.
- A final chapter of review.

I hope you will enjoy this journey we're about to take together. Writing any book is hard work, and this one is no exception, but I've allowed myself to be playful at times. There's a lot of science here, but a book on happiness shouldn't be dry as dust. I hope that it brings out a smile once in a while.

learning happiness

Everyone wants to be happy, but most of us don't know how to do it. We tend to assume that happiness should be an easy, natural thing. The bluebird of happiness is supposed to land at your window of its own volition, and if you try to hold on to it, it'll fly away. There is something to that bluebird myth, because if you attack happiness too directly, it will slip away from you. Happiness is, in a way, a by-product of how we live our lives. The latest research in psychology and neurology is proving the ancient wisdom that happiness is an art, a process, a way of living day to day that has very little to do with how much money or status we have, whether we've "reached our goals" in life, or even how much misery and pain we've suffered. Science is teaching us very concrete methods we can use to increase our happiness. A famous study compared lottery winners and accident victims a year later. The researchers found that people in both groups had pretty much returned to the individual levels of overall happiness that they'd had before their good or ill fortune. If you were a grump, winning the lottery just made you a rich grump; if you were pretty contented, pain and disability didn't have much impact on your overall positive outlook.

But there are a few people who have a life-changing accident or illness that forces them to take stock of their lives and make some changes that lead to more happiness, permanently. One of the things they realize is that happiness is a lot smaller than we think, often found in the details and moments when we're not looking. A really good grilled cheese sandwich can go a long way toward making your day, if you have the right outlook. <u>Happiness is smaller than you think.</u>

Assuming that happiness should come naturally is likely to make us less happy, because the assumption sets us up to blame ourselves or curse our fates when we're not feeling great. That blaming only adds another useless layer to our problems and distracts us from what we really need to do. Though it's true that we have a natural capacity to experience joy when good things happen, that state quickly fades. When you think about it, that's the nature of being human. If our normal background state wasn't one of mild anxiety or dissatisfaction, we'd lose our motivation to make things better. We might still be in the Stone Age. Evolution has made us alert, tense, acquisitive, jealous, competitive, and never satisfied for long. Those traits are bred into us; our ancestors who were more laid back were more likely to get eaten, and didn't pass those laid-back genes on to us. Although we may never feel completely comfortable, we can certainly change the joy-to-misery ratio of our existence—both by changing how we live, our pursuits and values and use of time, and by changing how we think and see the world. Our happiness is as much about the attitude we bring <u>to</u> our lives as about what happens <u>in</u> our lives.

don't: ASSUME THAT HAPPINESS SHOULD BE EASY.

Not only does happiness not come naturally, but our brains are not terrifically adept at figuring out what will make us happy. Human beings are really quite good at subsistence, at scrambling and scratching and elbowing, but abundance and comfort bring us a whole set of problems our brains don't know what to do with. We have a constant *I want . . .* down deep in our souls where evolution put it, but now that our basic needs are taken care of, we don't know what we want. We have lots of little circuits that keep telling us that we need <u>more</u>—money, drugs, room, sex, salvation, protection. The commodity almost doesn't matter; we're hard-wired to be jealous and competitive, and to believe that you can't have too much of a good thing. We have a million ways of distorting reality so that we can rationalize, for instance, working harder and longer hours despite our New Year's resolution to spend more time with the kids.

Fortunately for us all, psychology has made significant progress in understanding the mental mechanisms that prevent and destroy happiness. Add in the new brain technology that allows us to see for the first time how the physical structure of the brain affects and is affected by life events and mental processes, and you have the past decade or so of astounding discovery. Much like the Hubble telescope allows us to see deeper into the universe, in wonderful detail, new instruments allow us to see a whole new world right now, inside our own heads. The brain (and its connection to the rest of the body) is no longer off-limits to us, and new, vitally important discoveries are being made every day.

rewire your brain

Those juggling college students are just one example among hundreds of studies that have shown us how life experience changes the physical structure of the brain. You were probably taught that each of us is born with a fixed number of brain cells, and we keep losing them as we age. That was the governing belief for decades, but it was impeached just ten years ago. Now we know that the brain is constantly forming new brain cells—stem cells, which have the potential to replace any specialized cell in the brain. Those new cells can migrate outward to areas like the higher cortex. Learning stimulates that cell division, and learning takes place by growing and enriching the connections between nerve cells. Practicing a task seals the connections between the new cells and the existing ones. Studies have revealed:

- The brains of London cabbies are enlarged and enriched in the areas associated with navigation and orientation.
- The area of the brain that controls the left hand is greatly enlarged in violin and other string players—even those who take up the instrument in adulthood.
- Successful psychotherapy results in brain changes that are visible on PET scans.
- Merely rehearsing a task mentally results in the same kind of brain changes that actual practice does.
- People who are hopeful have better health after heart transplants, recover more quickly from bypass surgery, have less anginal pain, do better and live longer with HIV treatment, and have generally better functioning immune systems.
- <u>Simply reading this sentence has changed your brain.</u> Every experience changes the brain a little; but <u>you can control how much change</u> takes place by controlling your focus and attention.

Time has taught each of us many skills. We can't all juggle, but long ago we learned to read and write and do some math. Now we don't have to think about how to do those things; they've become part of us. Most of our mental processes—making decisions, handling emotions, comparing ourselves to others—are automatic, but that doesn't mean we were born with them or that we can't change them. Although we hopefully adapt our thinking to the unique realities of the situation we're facing, nevertheless we tend to think, feel, and behave in characteristic habits. I like to call those habits <u>skills</u> because it emphasizes that you've learned those things. They are skills that life experience has taught you over time; they didn't just appear in your brain like mildew. Now each of them has a physical manifestation in the circuitry of your brain.

We have some skills that make us more happy, and others that make us more miserable. Whenever we think about ourselves in a systematic and objective way, we try to stop practicing some of the habits that obviously make us miserable: gambling, drinking, eating too much; isolating ourselves, being a grouch, focusing on the negative. What we don't realize (because science is just finding out about it) is that we have a lot of other habits, traits, and ways of thinking that seem perfectly fine and normal to us, but add substantially to our misery index.

We don't normally pay attention to our happiness habits systematically and objectively, because we tend to assume that we will naturally do more of what makes us feel good. Unfortunately, that is not a safe assumption. Often, our choices result in a mix of pain and pleasure—and far too often, the prospect of a little short-term pain interferes with our long-term happiness. Exercise is the classic example: Of course, we'd all feel better if we worked out every day, but sometimes staying in bed feels too good. Or we go for the quick pleasure, and we neglect what would make us much happier later on— buying an expensive trinket instead of investing the money. Besides, we can be very unobservant and jump to mistaken conclusions about what's actually making us happy; we can think it's the lovely lady we just met at the bar, when it's really the martini talking.

Before we go too much further, let's define our terms.

what is happiness?

Recently I took a test that measures how happy you are, and flunked miserably. That surprised me, because I was really feeling pretty good. Maybe I only <u>thought</u> I was happy. But in actuality, this test was measuring only one aspect of happiness, and Western psychology talks about three:

1. Happy people have a preponderance of positive feelings. They experience emotions like joy, enthusiasm, contentment, peace, and love frequently and deeply. (In the rest of this book, I'm going to use <u>joy</u> as a shortcut word to describe that constellation of positive feelings.)

2. They also have a relative absence of negative feelings. Sadness, depression, bitterness, negativity, jealousy are rare. (I'll use the word <u>misery</u> henceforth in the text to refer to that group of unpleasant feelings.) Surprisingly, this pattern is somewhat inde-

pendent of the presence of positive feelings. Some people feel a lot of both; some people don't feel much of either.

3. Finally, happy people are generally satisfied with their lives. They aren't disturbed by a lot of wants or feelings that they've missed out on important things or failed in important areas. They feel they have most of the things they need, they're happy with the relationships they've got, and they tend to be optimistic about the future.

Naturally, all those factors are interdependent. Although it is possible to swing between extremes of both joy and misery, that's the exception, and when it goes too far, it is an indication of a bipolar-type disorder. For most of us, the more joy you feel, the less misery you feel. People who have the capacity to experience positive emotions are more likely to experience their lives as satisfactory, and it's harder for people who are dissatisfied with their lives to feel a lot of positive emotions. Still, those qualities are distinct enough that the differences are important. The test that told me I was really miserable when I thought I was pretty happy was a test of only positive feelings. I do much better on measures of life satisfaction, where I'm usually found to be in the upper 25 percent.* And that squares with my own experience: I've accomplished some things that are important to me, and I'm generally happy with what I do every day, but I know I have a tendency to be a grouchy pessimist and have trouble feeling excited or joyful. As for the third factor, controlling or eliminating unnecessary misery, that is the everyday discipline of dealing with depression; I work hard at it, and have been gradually getting better over the course of my life.

I see those distinctions in the people I work with. Despite severe episodes of depression, Susan is a naturally buoyant, bubbly person who makes others happy to be around her. Stanley feels extremes of both positive and negative emotions, but is never satisfied with his life. Joe is an artistic, creative person who is largely satisfied with what he's done with

---

* If you're interested, the two tests are in Lykken (p. 35) and in Peterson (p. 89). I do much better on the second, the life-satisfaction scale, rather than Lykken's well-being (bubbliness) scale, where I'm pretty low. I've never been noted for fizz.

his life, but rarely feels much intense emotion of any kind. Peter feels a preponderance of negative emotions, chiefly anger and anxiety, and rarely
feels good, despite being realistically proud of what he's achieved. Grace's
chief problem is her inability to feel proud of anything she accomplishes.
Howard can feel good only when he's intoxicated. Walt is very dissatisfied
with the way his life has turned out, yet he puts up a good fight against negative feelings.

Three Strategies

If our goal is to help you be happier, psychology suggests three major
strategies: to try to feel more positive emotions at the same time as feeling
fewer negative emotions, and to work on feeling greater satisfaction with
your life. And obviously none of those is easy, nor can they happen
overnight. Trying to gain control of our emotions is a constant for most of
us, one that we've been practicing since we were two years old, and one
that we should never hope to master completely. Greater life satisfaction
clearly has two separate components: One is calibrating our standards,
making sure that we're not being too hard on ourselves or expecting the
impossible. The other has to do with how you live your life, and that has
two further subcomponents. The first is being sure that pursuing your
goals and values will indeed lead to greater happiness—because many
people find themselves disappointed when they get what they want, realizing that they are no better off at all. The second is about being sure you
are, in fact, using the best strategies, making the wisest decisions, to pursue your goals.

There's also the matter of the grasshopper and the ant. In order for us
to have happiness in the future, we have to trade off a little happiness now.
If we spend our twenties partying and chasing after sex, we're probably
not going to learn a set of skills that will bring us financial security. We
have to give up some current pleasure for some future satisfaction. Experience tells us there are no rules for making decisions about that, but one
does best following a middle way. While you probably shouldn't spend
your twenties stoned to the gills, you can also spend those years working

far too hard and perhaps programming yourself out of the ability to experience pleasure. Every day we face smaller examples of decisions like that, some personally very difficult. *Work all my evenings for a promotion or go home and play with the kids?* Learning to make such wise decisions is probably one of the most challenging tasks of greater happiness.

WHO'S HAPPIER? THE GRASSHOPPER OR THE ANT?

The new neuroscience is showing us that we can deliberately change the wiring and structure of our brains to raise our happiness quotient. If that sounds impossible, consider that it happens to us all the time—it's just that the changes are unplanned and usually make us more unhappy. Depression and anxiety are now understood to be brain malfunctions, but malfunctions that result from a lifetime of stress, hurt, and pain. Too much stress can burn out the brain receptors for good feelings and keep us in a constant state of fight or flight. But in the same way, by choosing what kinds of experiences we feed our brains, and by being careful how we interpret events, we can change our brains in a positive direction. We can experience a greater degree of joy, more of the time, than we've ever done before. We can achieve a greater degree of satisfaction with ourselves and our lives, and at the same time, we can control and reduce the amount of misery we feel.

It's important that I make one major disclaimer: Don't expect this book to make you immune from sadness. Sadness and other unpleasant feelings are a part of life, and it's a good thing. We're wired to feel the pain of loss of love, guilt when we let ourselves or others down, jealousy when we feel excluded. If we didn't feel those things, we'd be incapable of love and aspiration. We have to accept that some misery is just a part of life, but there is necessary misery—associated with grief or illness, for example—and unnecessary misery, the kind we bring on ourselves. This book will help you avoid unnecessary misery.

Meaning

Besides the three components of happiness we've discussed—presence of joy, absence of misery, and life satisfaction—there is another dimension to happiness that, for want of a better word, I'll call <u>meaning</u>. For instance: I'm sitting here at my laptop at 9 P.M. on a beautiful summer evening, writing this book, and it's close to torture. There are lots of feelings associated with misery for any writer—frustration, anxiety, insecurity, a state of tension that does unpleasant things to your muscles and digestion. About three times a day, you become convinced you're losing your mind. Yet I freely choose to do this, instead of fixing a nice meal, reading a good mystery, or playing with the dogs, all of which would bring me more immediate joy. While it's true that I expect that choosing to do this now will lead to a state of greater satisfaction later—so perhaps I am betting that by the end of my life, I will have garnered more joy units in all because I'm miserable tonight—that still doesn't explain fully why I choose to write. Nor does the fact that accomplishing something difficult brings us pleasure. I could be advancing up the levels in *Zelda* or *Halo* or another video game, which is difficult and frustrating and provides a sense of accomplishment, but surely we'd all agree that writing is "better" somehow—deeper, more important. This other dimension of happiness has got something to do with self-expression, with making a contribution, with creating something that will last. This "meaning" dimension of happiness complicates everything, and science certainly doesn't know very much about it, but at this point, I just want to introduce the idea and then leave it alone until we get to Part II: Practicing Happiness.

The Philosophers

Historically, there are at least three important ways of understanding happiness. Two date back to the Greeks. <u>Hedonism</u> is the simple pursuit of pleasure. Hedonism has a bad reputation in our work-ethic world; the hedonist is usually considered selfish and shortsighted, living only for the sensual pleasure of the moment. That isn't necessarily so. Epicurus, a hedonist if there ever was one, developed the concept of ethical hedonism—do no harm when seeking your own pleasure, and the world works out for the best. And hedonism is the basis for the utilitarianism of Jeremy Bentham and John Stuart Mill, which is still perhaps the best way to think of social policy—try to do the greatest good for the greatest number of people. But hedonism, of course, faces the problem of adaptation—the fact that we quickly get used to any pleasure we've got, and need more to give us the same kick. After the tenth orgy, they get a little boring.

The other theory of happiness is referred to as <u>eudaimonia</u>—living in accordance with one's individual strengths and virtues, living up to one's true potential—credited to Aristotle. The positive psychologists (see Chapter 10) believe they have research showing that eudaimonia trumps hedonism in terms of life satisfaction, and so most of their effort is to help people find eudaimonia. In doing so, sometimes they emphasize things that are assumed to be good for you rather than make you feel good. Of course, the two are not at all mutually exclusive, and generally things that are good for you <u>do</u> make you feel good, but not all the time. We have to be careful not to add unnecessary misery in the pursuit of virtue.

Still, eudaimonia seems to take into account that "meaning" dimension of happiness, while hedonism doesn't. The goal of this book is to help you find a balance—a lot of joy, minimal misery, and plenty of life satisfaction, with some attention to the problem of meaning. Some people might not want this, and that's not necessarily wrongheaded of them. For instance, many people might choose to lead more challenging lives (artists, writers, and musicians come to mind) with less subjective well-being and more creativity or achievement, and some creative torment as an acceptable part of the bargain. Yet as far as I know, creativity doesn't <u>require</u> suffering. And there are far too many people who are unhappy, and could be a lot happier, if they didn't make some of the mistakes I'm going to describe.

There is also an Eastern approach to happiness, which is very different from the Western. Buddha taught of Four Noble Truths. The first is that life means suffering, the second is that suffering is caused by attachment. The third Noble Truth is that the end of suffering is within our reach. And the fourth is the path toward the end of suffering, what Buddha called the Eightfold Path. It emphasizes that there are "correct" (healthy, constructive, objective) ways of seeing, thinking, behaving, which can reduce our earthly suffering. The Eightfold Path is often called "the Middle Way," the path between blind hedonism and an ascetic life of withdrawal. Learning the Middle Way requires developing the skill of mindfulness, a central concept we will emphasize throughout this book.

Here are three traditions, which neatly dovetail with our threefold path toward more happiness: Buddhism can help us reduce misery, Hedonism teaches about joy, and Eudaimonia gives us a way to think about bringing greater satisfaction into our lives.

who's happy?

Despite my gloomy news on the opening page about the decline of happiness worldwide, when people are asked directly to rate their happiness on a ten-point scale, almost everyone considers themselves well above average. More than half rate themselves at eight or above.* (You have to look at other, less subjective measures to see the negative trends.) It's the Lake Wobegon effect: All the children are better than average. These results are found, with some slight variation from country to country, all over the world. Not only that, but everyone also expects to be happier still in the future, and the happier you are now, the happier you expect to be. Is everyone really so happy?

Just think about this question: *How happy are you?* In most cultures, it's considered a weakness or sign of failure to admit unhappiness. If you're not happy, you're a loser in the horse race of life. Additionally, we generally assume that people get what they deserve, so if you're not happy, it's probably your own fault. Those assumptions are totally wrong, of course, and contribute to much unnecessary misery, but they provide powerful motivation to put on a happy face for the pollster. In addition, the question *How happy are you?* demands that we think about happiness experiences, and that probably skews our report. If we asked, *Compared to the average person,*

---

* It's even more skewed for intelligence: Only 2 percent of responders will rate themselves below average in intelligence (Schumaker, p. 26).

how sad are you? we might get slightly different responses, because the question requires us to think of sad experiences.

When we ask someone about their overall happiness, we're not asking them whether their lives are full of joy. We're asking a question that requires a little reflection, and it seems safe to assume that most people are taking into account all three of the factors that I just described: presence of positive feelings, relative absence of negative feelings, and overall satisfaction with life. The answer is often called subjective well-being (SWB) by psychologists.

But our feelings about our own well-being are enormously sensitive to influence. If I remind you about 9/11, Darfur, the Middle East; cancer and heart disease; all your insecurities about your job; your worries about your children and your parents—your sense of well-being might get whittled down a few pegs. In one of those fiendish little social psych studies that keep exposing our foibles, the experimenters arranged to have half of a group of subjects find a dime in a copy machine just before taking the SWB quiz; those who had found the dime reported themselves to be significantly happier with their lives overall. Happiness self-report is also highly influenced by comparison. Olympic bronze medalists report higher satisfaction than silver medalists. Presumably the silver winners are comparing themselves to gold medalists, while bronze medalists are pleased to have won anything at all. Overall, researchers have found that two things consistently influence our self-reports of happiness: One is the human tendency to see ourselves as better than average; the other is our mood at the time we're asked. Still, for all its variability, subjective well-being is worth talking about because the same person will tend to answer the same way fairly consistently over time. If Jane tends to score higher on SWB than Joe, then for our purposes, Jane is a happier person than Joe.

If you're interested, on the next page is a commonly used scale of SWB, this one obviously tapping life satisfaction more than immediate feelings of joy or misery. You can take the test and score yourself. Credit goes to Ed Diener, the pioneer of SWB research, who generously makes this available without copyright.

Below are five statements that you may agree or disagree with. Using the 1–7 scale below, indicate your agreement with each item by placing the appropriate number on the line preceding that item. Please be open and honest in your responding.

7—Strongly agree

6—Agree

5—Slightly agree

4—Neither agree nor disagree

3—Slightly disagree

2—Disagree

1—Strongly disagree

_____ In most ways, my life is close to my ideal.

_____ The conditions of my life are excellent.

_____ I am satisfied with my life.

_____ So far I have gotten the important things I want in life.

_____ If I could live my life over, I would change almost nothing.

Scoring:

35–31 Extremely satisfied

26–30 Satisfied

21–25 Slightly satisfied

20 Neutral

15–19 Slightly dissatisfied

10–14 Dissatisfied

5–9 Extremely dissatisfied.

After you get your score, I think there are going to be a good number of readers who will just be confused. *I scored a 27. I <u>should</u> be happy, but I feel miserable a lot of the time. What's wrong with me?* The next three chapters are going to explain why happiness is not always so self-evident as Dr. Diener's test suggests. For now, let's just explore one more question:

can we be happier?

If you take that test every year, your scores are going to be pretty similar every time. That finding, and a great deal of other research data, suggests that each of us has a "set point" for happiness, like a thermostat: a self-regulating mechanism that returns us to our own characteristic subjective well-being point after the ups and downs of immediate joy and misery have worn off. If so, can we adjust it? If my thermostat is set for a relatively cool 65 degrees, can I turn it up to a warmer 72? Or is the set point something that's determined so much by our genes and our early life experiences that adults should not try to change it but put on sweaters instead? That's what at least one happiness researcher suggested when he said people might as well try to be taller as to change their subjective well-being—but thoughtful reflection made him withdraw that opinion.

There's much exciting research going on right now about how our genes work, which ends up in the newspapers and television as "finding the gene for" happiness, baldness, shyness—just about anything. That's an enormously oversimplified view of how genes operate. As far as happiness is concerned, this oversimplified gene theory suggests that some of us are constitutionally bubbly, while others are genetic sourpusses—and it's in our genes and there's nothing we can do about it. Things are not really so dismal: Though we obviously have basic temperamental differences, there is good reason to believe that the set point is changeable, especially through some of the mindfulness techniques we're going to talk about. Nor is it necessarily the case that the set point is determined by our genes alone; by the time we reach adulthood, life has treated some of us well and some of us badly, and it would be foolish to argue that those experiences don't influence our level of happiness. As we continue to age, our set points will continue to change because of our experiences. Fortunately, we have some power to choose what kinds of experience we will have.

Resetting Your Thermostat

It remains true that some people are naturally happier than others. Some of us are lucky enough to be perky under almost any circumstances, while others radiate gloom. These are reasonably stable traits. Studies have followed people through changing life circumstances and ups and downs in income, and still found that the best predictor of an individual's level of happiness at the end of the study was his happiness at the beginning of the study. A grumpy old man was probably a teenager with a bad attitude; the high school cheerleader is probably a pretty ebullient old lady. David Lykken and Auke Tellegen identified sixty-nine sets of identical twins raised apart in the United States, and tested them for happiness twice, at an interval of nine years. They found that one twin's score on happiness was very closely related to the other's, both at Time 1 and Time 2. Further, they found that Twin A's happiness score at Time 1 was a good predictor of Twin B's score at Time 2, almost as good as Twin B's own score.

Note that I said a twin's happiness score is a good (not an excellent) predictor of her sibling's score. These twins, raised by different adoptive parents, had a correlation of .53 on adult happiness; non-identical twins reared apart had a correlation of .13. Without getting deep into a discussion of how those statistics work, you can say that genes apparently account for about 50 percent of the happiness set point. On the other hand, these people are genetically identical; if biology were the major component of happiness, you might expect a correlation in the .90s, as you get with height. Looked at in that way, you might feel it's somewhat surprising that identical twins' happiness set points are so widely different, all because of what's happened to them over the course of their lives.

In the most recent, respected research articles that I can find, the authors estimate that about half of an individual's subjective well-being set point is determined by genetic heritage. Another 10 percent, they estimate, is due to the relatively unchangeable circumstances of their lives (health, marital, and occupational status). That leaves a substantial 40 percent of your happiness level that's subject to things you can control much more easily than drastically changing the circumstances of your life.

Even if some of the happiness set point is determined by your genetic heritage, it's a vast oversimplification to think of genes as an inevitable blueprint. Genes control much more of our being than we generally imagine, but they do it only by being "turned on" by experience. Genes in brain cells (neurons) manufacture the basic cellular material that, when turned on by a signal from another cell, makes the cell adapt and change. A nerve cell that has repeatedly sent a "worry" signal on to the next neuron has been changed by that experience, so it is more ready to send the alarm signal next time. The same process of change occurs in the cell if it repeatedly sends "enjoy" signals; it's easier for this cell to send the enjoyment signal again. That is how circuits—chains of cells—get built up in the brain that make us more likely to worry or enjoy.

Building Better Roads

Consider the brain circuits as millions of tiny footpaths. As more and more traffic travels down a particular footpath, it gets widened and deepened. The grass dies away from wear; travelers break off the interfering branches of shrubs, and the path gets easier. In New England, many of the old roads follow Indian footpaths, which themselves followed game trails. They developed gradually from footpaths to horse trails to wagon trails to paved roads. In the same way, every time a particular brain circuit is used, it widens and deepens its own path, making it easier to use in the future. Some of our circuits become highways. For depressives, there's a direct four-lane expressway from disappointment to self-blame. For extraverts, there's a nice little highway from thinking of a party to feeling excitement and joy.

Thus, the brain gets changed by experience. A neuron on the receiving end of a transmission from another neuron will turn on its little genetic factory in the nucleus <u>and change itself.</u> Not only does each neuron transmit a message to the next, but the neuron itself is changed a little in the process. That's just the way genes work; it's the genes in the nucleus that prepare the neuron to transmit its message, and as they do so, they change the neuron itself a little bit. <u>Every future event affects a brain that has been changed by previous events.</u> Every time you smile, you make it a little more likely you'll smile more; same goes for frowning. When we get to talking about will power, it will be very important to keep in mind that you have the ability to change your own brain circuitry. Over time, with focused practice, you may even be able to change some of that 50 percent of your happiness level that comes from your genetic heritage.

Happiness doesn't come naturally, though we assume it should. We have to be willing to make some real changes in our thoughts, feelings, and actions if we want to reset our happiness thermostat, because, unless we have a life-changing event that wakes us up, we're highly likely to keep doing what we've always done, keep feeling as we've always felt. We've established default circuits in the brain that lead to automatic, mindless behavior. If we want to be happier, we have to establish new circuits through deliberate effort. Fortunately, the new brain science shows this is not hard to do, with deliberate attention and dedicated practice. In the next section, we're going to explore the obstacles that interfere with our attention and practice.

PART ONE

good
at being
miserable

There's a lot of brush to be cleared before we can be happier, far too many bad habits and false assumptions that each of us has learned through the course of our experience. The fact that so many of the things that make us miserable have been recurring issues in our lives for such a long time—depression, overeating, unhappy relationships, self-defeating behavior, disorganization, too much worry—is enough in itself to suggest that normal problem-solving skills aren't going to help. Much of the time, our brain has learned <u>skills of misery</u>—for good reasons, from painful experiences. Some of them we just seem to have been born with. Others are our attempts to adapt to a difficult world. In what's to come, I've divided our sources of misery into three sections:

1. *Contemporary Insanity.* Our society and culture contribute mightily to our misery. We live in conditions our brains and nervous systems weren't designed for—depriving ourselves of natural sleep with artificial light, expecting ourselves to stay focused on one task eight or ten hours a day for years, isolating ourselves from the natural world, cutting ourselves off from our families and tribes. Those conditions cause enormous stress on the brain and body. Obviously we can't entirely go back to the old ways, and there are many great things about the new ways: but we must adapt ourselves thoughtfully to contemporary life in order to reduce our misery. However—as if current reality weren't bad enough in itself—we're also being brainwashed to believe we should like everything new and different. Business, government, and media all would have us believe that the fifty-hour workweek is natural, that happiness comes from possessions, that it's a good thing that both parents of small children are working now—and that in any case, there's nothing anyone can do about it. We have to free ourselves as much as possible from those destructive myths.

2. *Innate Foolishness.* Our genetic heritage inclines us to do a lot of things that might aid in our survival as a species but actually interfere with individual happiness. The drive to acquire, to win, to be on top, for instance, has its uses, but making us happier isn't one of them. Psychologists and economists have also unearthed some interesting ways we consistently lie to ourselves about how happy we are—for instance, by believing that getting what we want will make us happy—which make it all the more difficult for us to gain genuine happiness. The brain is the focus of attention here, all the little leftovers of our genetic heritage that keep tricking us into doing things that may have evolutionary value (or had it once upon a time) but don't make us happier at all.

3. *Unnecessary Misery.* None of us is totally secure or without fear. No one never feels anger, guilt, or shame. Those emotions are normal, but they can literally be crippling. In order to get by, we learn ways of distorting reality so that the unpleasant emotions can get to seem more manageable. Some of those distorting skills are harmless, but experience has shown that you can't really be happy if your reality is so skewed you're living in la-la land. For instance, if you depend on denial so that you can not see the effects of some of your self-destructive behavior, the real reality has a way of coming back to get you. Here the focus is on the mind, what we've come to believe about how life works, and how dazzlingly wrong some of those beliefs are.

contemporary insanity

THE CULTURE

Much of the basic reality of contemporary life is enough all by it-self to make us depressed, anxious, sick, or dead, let alone unhappy. That news may surprise you. After all, we're so much better off than our ances-tors were, in so many ways. And it's true we have greater freedom, better health, many more choices open to us. But there's a drastic downside to the course of recent history. Although we tend to take our living conditions for granted as the natural order of things, in truth life has changed so drastically since the Industrial Revolution—and the pace of change keeps on accelerat-ing with no end in sight—that the effect of all that change is to stress us out in devastating ways we are rarely even aware of.

Since the Enlightenment, Western society has been operating on the as-sumption that eliminating the causes of suffering will result in greater happi-ness. It seemed eminently sensible to believe that eliminating or controlling disease, early death, and hunger at the same time as increasing wealth, leisure time, and opportunities for advancement would inevitably lead to a utopian society wherein all could pursue their own specific happiness. Now, it's becoming apparent that this assumption has been a cruel hoax. There is no reason to believe that we as individuals are any happier than our forebears three hundred years ago; in fact, ever since scientists have been measuring it reliably (about fifty years), happiness seems to be declining.

the culture of stress

In a nutshell, living conditions have changed so drastically in the past few hundred years that our bodies, minds, and nervous systems are trying to adapt to conditions we were never genetically or culturally designed for. The result is a wholly new kind of stress, something we've never seen before. We all know the stress of working too hard and juggling too many priorities, but there is a deeper, more pervasive stress we're largely unaware of that gets right into our bodies—our nervous and immune systems, our digestion and heart, our skin and bones. In a difficult, complicated, and exotic world, we're constantly on the alert for danger—and that is killing us.

Humans, like all animals, have a complex set of innate responses to danger that is extremely efficient at keeping us safe. If you're walking down the street and suddenly get threatened by a mugger, your body will automatically go into fight-or-flight mode, with no thought or feeling at all; only afterwards do you feel the emotion we call fear. What gets us to move so quickly is a complex cascade of hormones and neurotransmitters that starts in the _amygdala,_ the central danger-sensing area in the brain, and ends with the adrenal glands secreting the emergency transmitters of adrenaline and cortisol, which activate the body, mind, and senses to deal with a threat. That is the stress response system, the fight-or-flight response. It will increase your heart rate and blood pressure, redirect energy to the muscular and sensory systems, shut down digestion and reproduction, send immune cells into storage depots, deploy steroids to help you heal from wounds, focus your vision—all kinds of good things to help you escape from danger. If the guy you thought was a mugger turns out to be only asking for directions, another part of your brain, the _hippocampus,_ sends a "slow down" signal to the body. The adrenal glands stop sending out the emergency transmitters, your heart rate and blood pressure decrease, your muscles relax, and systems return to normal.

The Proverbial Dark Alley

Now let's imagine you in a nightmare: You're in a dark alley from the New York of *Taxi Driver,* surrounded by muggers with guns, knives, clubs—you name it. Wherever you run, there's another threat. You are evading them, but you know you can't keep it up. Under those conditions, your stress response system will not slow down or turn off. You'll be stuck in fight-or-flight mode, and we know that if you stay in that state long enough, you'll eventually have all kinds of bad outcomes—exhaustion, cardiac strain, kidney stress, muscle fatigue, damage to the digestive and circulatory system, chronic high blood pressure. You won't be able to eat, and your bowels will be damaged. Your immune system will be impaired; you'll both be more vulnerable to infection and at the same time you'll overreact to minor irritations. Worst of all, you'll suffer brain damage; when you look at the PET scans of people who suffer chronic stress, you see big white spaces where there used to be brain tissue. Eventually you may "learn helplessness"—just give up and stop trying. Thank God it's only a nightmare, and you'll wake up.

Or will you? The catch is, it doesn't matter if your nightmare is real or imaginary, whether the threat is to your life or your livelihood. Working in an office with eight different bosses, each of whom can tell you what to do, and knowing there are five people knocking on the door wanting your job is not all that different from being surrounded by muggers. Except that you can't escape. Whether you are constantly threatened, or only <u>feel</u> constantly threatened, the effects on your brain, mind, and body are the same. One thing brain scientists have discovered is that, with enough stress, we wear out our brakes. The hippocampus can't send out that "slow down" signal any longer. With enough stress, the receiving ends of nerve cells in the hippocampus begin to shrivel up; with more, the nerve cells themselves begin to die. Victims of child abuse and combat veterans have shrunken hippocampi. Continued stress interferes with the hippocampus's ability to consolidate memory, so we get confused and can't tell the difference between a memory and a nightmare. Then stress gets into our very bones—when tissue cells all through our body become overwhelmed by too many stress hormones, they close down receptor sites to try to compensate. But that just makes the endocrine system pump out even more stress hormones. Awash in neurotransmitters telling us there is constant danger, our immune systems, muscles, bones, guts, and hearts wear out. Our brains become rewired by stress, our neural circuitry restricted to firing along preconditioned pathways, so that we are literally unable to think of new solutions, unable to come up with creative responses.

Happiness is out of the question if you're living in too much stress; your brain and body are overwhelmed with merely keeping you alive and functioning. That's exactly where twenty-first-century life has us, doing our best to stay afloat. Today, eight out of ten of the most commonly used medications in the United States treat conditions directly related to stress: antidepressants, tranquilizers and sleeping pills, medications for gastric problems and high blood pressure. But these are only addressing symptoms, not causes. It's like taking painkillers so we can continue to play football with a broken leg. We need to pay attention to what our bodies and minds are telling us: back off, give ourselves time to heal, then learn how to protect ourselves from stress and how to cope with it effectively. If we don't, we will die early, in unnecessary pain and unnecessary disability.

Think about how society has changed in 160,000 years, since the first human appeared. It's wonderful, for the most part, how the human race has advanced. But we're still getting by with the same nervous system our earliest ancestors used. For them, there was never any evolutionary pressure to temper the long-term effects of stress, because few people lived past thirty-five. Now our longer life spans are showing us exactly what a lifetime of stress will do to your body and mind.

The biggest obstacle to happiness is that we're just not wired for the kinds of stress we face today. Our bodies and brains evolved over a million years for certain conditions, which never really changed very much until three hundred years ago. We were certainly not designed for the breakdown of the family and community, the absence of purpose and connectedness in our daily activities, the ten- or twelve-hour workday, the loss of contact with nature, the absence of physical activity, of a natural sleep–wake cycle.

Neither were we designed for stressors like cell phones, traffic jams, personal debt, eight bosses, and HMOs. Unlike our ancestors, we can't run away to escape those problems, or get together with others with sticks and rocks to beat them to death—but that's the natural response. That's the meaning of "fight or flight"; but whether we fight or flee, our bodies were designed for a quick resolution, and with it the quick emptying of the flood of stress hormones. Now we have constant stress. It's possible to learn to modulate the stress response through mindfulness, but it's not easy and doesn't come naturally to us. However, modulation is not really enough. If we really want to escape and not just manage stress, we're going to have to make some tough choices about how we live.

Elephants, Rats, and People

Worse yet, stress is transmitted through generations. A mother who has been traumatized will pass trauma on to her children. It's happening to elephants. Young male elephants, traumatized by witnessing their elders "culled" by poachers, without the guidance of older bulls, are raping and murdering rhinos, and senselessly attacking SUVs. Young mother elephants, deprived of the presence of elders, don't know how to soothe and protect their babies. We know that infant rats who receive more licking and grooming from their mothers are less fearful and more intelligent as adults, have better immune systems, and are more attentive mothers themselves. All it takes is for us to stress a mother rat out for a while to turn her into an ineffective and inattentive mother. There's not much research yet about human mothers and children, but it's coming, and it won't be good news. A recent UNICEF survey ranked the United States next to the bottom of all wealthy countries in terms of overall child well-being, dead last in family and peer relationships and in risky behavior.

the culture of overwork

One of the greatest sources of stress in our lives is work itself. Of course, work can also be a source of great fulfillment and joy, too—we're going to get to that aspect of it in time. But the demands of work have been accelerating recently, and that's proving more difficult to adjust to than we want to recognize.

Life for the average family three hundred years ago wasn't so different from that of a family three thousand, or even thirty thousand, years earlier. Things were predictable and preordained. Most people lived in small villages, and got their bread and the necessities of life through a system of barter within the community. Work was done communally (hunting, farming) or in the home. People knew almost everyone they were likely to ever meet, and the occasional traveler was a big deal. They knew what they were going to be when they grew up, because they were going to be whatever their parents were. People were pretty sure about whom they'd marry, because there were only two or three choices. They went to bed when it was dark and got up when it was light. They lived in harmony with the cycles of the seasons. They had daily interactions with birth and death, partly through their intimate contact with other species. They were connected to the natural world.

The Affluent Society

A contemporary example of the natural way of life is the Bushmen of the Kalahari, a living hunter-gatherer society. Robert Sapolsky, the renowned neuroscientist and stress expert who spends half of each year in Africa, refers to the Bushmen as the original affluent society—partly because they work only two to four hours per day, as is the norm in hunter-gatherer societies. That's enough time to provide for their needs, and they don't "want" any more. The rest of the day is spent in communal activities—mostly just talking, but also a lot of time spent developing artistic skills, singing, and dancing. They have almost zero stress. What we look down on as a primitive society, a subsistence economy, is really a society free from want. We can't go back and undo history, but we can learn from the contrast.

Consider how things have changed in the West since the Industrial Revolution, the spread of a money-based economy, the invention of the clock, artificial light, and now instant communication. The whole notion of "work"— the exchange of labor for wages—first had to be invented, and then people had to be forced or brainwashed into believing it made sense to leave your family, friends, and neighbors—initially for twelve hours a day, six days a week. That was a time of immense social upheaval—well documented in Britain, where the wealthy began to buy up and enclose what had for centuries been "common" land, forcing families off the farm and into the cities. We tend to think of the Luddites—the machine breakers, textile workers who sabotaged powered looms—as ignorant peasants standing in the way of progress, but in fact, there were many people asking if progress was really all it was cracked up to be. Those voices were drowned out by history. Read Dickens's *A Christmas Carol* carefully; there's a radical message inside. Dickens makes it clear that the poor are poor not because of bad luck or temporary economic hard times, but because the economy needed cheap labor.

Idle Hands . . .

Tom Hodgkinson, in his brilliantly subversive *How to Be Idle,* points out that the "Protestant work ethic" is not an empty cliché; that the Protestant leaders in eighteenth- and nineteenth-century England enthusiastically supported the social industrial revolution by preaching that idle hands are the devil's playground and that it was man's natural place to work himself to death. There was a moral justification in keeping wages low, because it coerced people into working by necessity rather than by force, preventing civil unrest. As the Rev. Andrew Townsend, a nineteenth-century management consultant, wrote, trying to force people to work

> gives too much trouble, requires too much violence, and makes too much noise. . . . Hunger, on the contrary, is not only a pressure which is peaceful, silent, and incessant, but as it is the most natural motive for work and industry, it also provokes the most peaceful efforts.

Even today we are brainwashed into thinking of unemployment as a temporary result of bad times, instead of realizing that a market economy relies on a certain amount of unemployment to keep wages low. The specter economists raise against full employment is that it would mean inflation, as wages would rise, and then magically prices would rise as well. Imagine if wages rose and prices didn't—but that would mean regulating markets and depriving investors of the opportunity to make just as much money as possible, a capitalist taboo.

From the standpoint of personal happiness, these changes have been exceptionally destructive. Instead of a cooperative society where life's value is defined by how well you contribute to your community, we have a competitive society that has a hard time defining just how a life is valued. Instead of a world of social ritual that fit the individual like a glove, we have a world of uncertainty. Instead of the security of the community, we have the anxiety of unemployment and homelessness. The result: for the past twenty-five years in the United States and Europe, rates of anxiety, depression, and stress-related disorders have been accelerating every year. Stressful jobs lead to a marked increase in major depression and anxiety disorders in previously healthy young people. In 2004, 45 percent of college students reported feeling depressed to the point of having trouble functioning; 94 percent reported feeling overwhelmed at times. In 2006, Americans spent an estimated $76 billion a year on antidepressants. Now the World Bank and the World Health Organization predict that soon depression will be the world's single biggest public health problem. At the same time, society continues to get wealthier, and we have more and more ways to keep ourselves distracted. Diener and Seligman point out that gross domestic product was a meaningful measure of social value as countries were emerging from poverty; but now that everyone in the West is wealthy, it makes more sense to look at more sensitive social indicators. *The Economist,* analyzing the world country by country, finds that material well-being remains the single largest factor in determining quality of life—but that lower ratings in family life, in community life, and in job security result in reduced national happiness in the United States and United Kingdom.

National happiness seems to decline in each country as it becomes Westernized. In China during the period of 1994 to 2005, average real income rose by an astounding 250 percent, but the percentage of those reporting themselves happier with their lives decreased, and unhappiness increased. Books like Robert Putnam's *Bowling Alone* and Robert Lane's *The Loss of Happiness in Market Democracies* describe how alienation and stress grow, and happiness declines, as economic conditions have improved in the USA. If you graph GDP per capita against the percentage of people who say they are "very happy" over the last fifty years, you get two fairly straight lines: GDP keeps rising as happiness keeps heading south. Increasingly, we find ourselves isolated and mistrustful of others. We leave our air-conditioned homes in our gated communities and drive in our air-conditioned cars to the air-conditioned mall, and back home again with our purchases, but without human interaction.* Or we can go online and buy electronics and games that will mean we never have to leave the house. We have less and less contact with neighbors, and less and less trust of each other, of the government, of schools, religion, medicine, the media. At the same time as social scientists have been demonstrating that intimacy, community, and trust are the basic elements of human happiness, those elements are disappearing from our society.

That close-knit social support we were meant to have probably insulated us from depression; it certainly insulated us from loneliness. But since the 1950s, the neighborhood has been slowly dying. Average hours worked and time spent commuting have greatly increased—and now both spouses are doing it. So membership in churches, civic organizations, bowling leagues, PTAs—you name it—has been declining steadily. Golf clubs are in trouble because people don't have time for golf anymore. All of which means we have fewer opportunities or means to define ourselves—we are only workers, not workers and Rotarians and Presbyterians and members of the bridge club. So we have less identity to fall back on if there is trouble at work.

One more thing about life in small communities: There was no room for fakery. If someone didn't do what he promised, word got around. Trust was an absolute necessity; if you weren't trustworthy, you were an outcast. Eric Weiner, in *The Geography of Bliss,* his account of his travels in the world's happiest countries, makes the point over and over. Whether in Switzerland, where if a train is late, it prompts a crisis of faith, or in Bhutan, where it's

---

* There's a new SUV out called the Enclave. What's next? The Redoubt? The Bunker? The M1A1 Abrams Tank?

impossible not to be trustworthy—happiness is linked with trust. If we can't trust each other, or our leaders, or our institutions, we can't feel safe, we feel compelled to be selfish and competitive, and it's going to be hard to have a happy life.

Let's All Hurry More

Meanwhile, the pace of life keeps accelerating. Literally. Across thirty-two cities worldwide, people in 2006 were walking an average 10 percent faster than they were in 1994.

In America over the past twenty-five years, the average citizen has increased his working hours from forty to fifty—more than any other country in the world, including Japan. Remember when we used to condescend to Japan, where those nameless, faceless, "salarymen" were supposed to be pitiable wage slaves, exploited by their employers? Funny, you don't hear those remarks so much anymore, because Americans are now working about three and a half weeks longer than the Japanese each year (six weeks more than the British, twelve weeks more than the Germans). And French workers, whom we love to sneer at for their short workweeks and long vacations, are actually more productive per hour than Americans, giving a full dollar's-worth more value per hour. New immigrants to America undergo an automatic rise in blood pressure. Americans have to work 25 percent more hours, and have 25 percent fewer hours for leisure, just to maintain the same standard of living we had twenty-five years ago.* In 2005, Americans experienced the fifth year in a row of stagnant median household income—while corporate profits doubled. Labor unions, which used to provide some sanity, reminding people that there were other priorities than work, have been neutered by the changing economy. Americans are so intimidated by the prospect of unemployment that we take less vacation time off than we actually earn, which is anyhow less than any other industrialized country.

---

* "Why is this," you ask, "when GDP keeps climbing?" Please keep in mind that all that growth in national wealth has not been evenly distributed. In 1976, the richest 10 percent of Americans controlled 49 percent of all wealth; in 1999, it was 73 percent (Collins and Yeskel, 2000). CEOs in the United States in 2004 were earning approximately five hundred times what their average worker makes; in 1980 it was only forty times (Reuters, 2004).

Remember there are five guys down the hall who want your job. So it's no wonder that 34 percent of us check in with the office so much on vacation that we come back just as stressed as when we left, if not more. It's not surprising that those of us who have "time affluence" rather than material affluence report greater overall life satisfaction.

do: TAKE ALL YOUR VACATION TIME.

Those changes in our time priorities are wreaking havoc on family life. Some joke that the feminist revolution has earned women the right to be treated as badly as men. We take it for granted now that both partners in a marriage work, and that the children are in day care. Somehow I don't remember that we planned for that back in the sixties. Now four out of ten Americans work nontraditional shifts, so it's rarer still for both parents to be home at the same time. The *Leave It to Beaver* family, where Dad is the sole breadwinner and Mom is at home waiting for the school bus, is now down to about 5 percent of the population, while 49 percent of marriages end in divorce. More than twice as many children of divorce, compared with those from intact families, will need mental health services during their lifetimes.

Knowing all this, there's a good question why more companies don't offer their employees the choice of a more flexible and less intense work schedule. It doesn't seem that it would affect the bottom line and it might result in a happier and more stable workforce. One survey found that half of Americans would gladly trade a day's pay for the opportunity of a four-day week.

The Happiness Gap
Now we find that there's a growing worldwide happiness gap between men and women. Back in the seventies, women were generally found to be a little happier than men. Since then, men report their overall happiness to have increased, while women's has declined, so that now the genders have switched places. That is difficult to understand because most of the social changes (autonomy, higher pay, more education) for women since the seventies are associated with greater happiness. A time-sample study found that men are spending less time in things they don't enjoy (like work) and more in things

they do (like leisure) while for women, the opposite is true. It suggests that women's to-do lists have gotten longer, while men haven't taken up the slack. Most women today are working but still take primary responsibility for housekeeping, minding the children, and caring for aging parents (including their in-laws). If this is the case, it suggests that the feminist revolution still has some work to do, and men aren't going to like it. Or women may have to reset their expectations and not try to hold down two full-time jobs—one at home and one at work.

The American Dream

Suburban living, the American dream, turns out to destroy the American family. Suburban sprawl leaves everyone dependent on automobile travel, adds to obesity and health problems, and leads to isolation. If you chart the trend in frequent visiting with neighbors over the past forty years, you'll see that it's a straight line down into isolation. Why borrow a cup of sugar from a neighbor, risking an actual interaction with someone you might have to talk to, when you can drive to the "convenience" store? Another result of suburban life is that parents don't have neighbors or grandparents to help them with parenting. When it used to be that the whole community was involved in child rearing, now there is no community. The task falls solely on parents and professionals, who seem to be more and more at odds. School administrators now have to be sensitive to gender discrimination, bullying, social ostracism, Facebook hazing, and kids coming to school with automatic weapons, at the same time as being expected to show continuous improvement in standardized test scores, all without any budget increase. Kids aren't getting the help they need from parents to deal with all the issues they're facing—because parents are overworked and overstretched. Parents and children alike are overwhelmed by mass culture, without a support system to reinforce any alternatives.

Look at the world around us. We've made our air dangerous to breathe and our water dangerous to drink. We've overfished the oceans, so that many species are in danger of dying out. We've damaged the ozone layer so that it's become dangerous for us to get a suntan, the glaciers are receding, plant and animal habitats are changing. Our diets have become full of artificial fats, carbohydrates, and flavor enhancers, resulting in an epidemic of obesity. Allergies are out of control because we've both damaged our own immune systems and polluted the air; people show up at the doctor's office today allergic to the world. We squander oil and gas supplies that can never be restored. We go everywhere nowadays in our SUVs and ATVs, scattering our trash behind us, leaving nothing natural. Our work and our leisure have become monotonous and sedentary, depriving us of the opportunity to have regular exercise and stretching as a natural part of the day. Our bodies cramp up, our muscles atrophy, our joints turn to stone. Yet we can't find the time to just be still—to rest on the hoe while we look at the sunset, daydream waiting for the fish to bite—essential to nourish the right brain, the creative side of our natures. Cubicle culture deprives us of the opportunity for transcendent experiences when we can be in touch with something larger than ourselves—the sea, the sky, the mountains, the grass growing, the wind blowing, the leaves falling.

affluenza

Set against this dismal picture, we have consumer society. That really is the basic message of our culture today—*Sure, there are some things to worry about, like global warming and the divorce rate, but we can tackle those and at the same time go about our business. The world has a lot to offer us, lots of ways to enjoy ourselves, and it's easy to pursue happiness. Don't worry; be happy.* Let me be clear: Worry! There is a great deal about contemporary culture that inherently, structurally, gets in the way of our ability to lead joyful and satisfying lives. We need to be aware of all that and make our life choices accordingly.

We've all been trained to believe that consumerism is the path to happiness, but we're finally learning that it only adds to stress. True to the principles of the hedonic treadmill, that brass ring is always just a little out of reach. Last year's luxury becomes this year's necessity. Last year, you couldn't afford a flat-screen TV (iPhone, cappuccino maker); this year, you can't get by without it. If you ask Americans what it takes to have a comfortable income, it's always just a little bit more than what they have at the time. In 1985, the average worker was making twenty-seven thousand dollars a year, and believed that thirty thousand dollars would make him happy. Two years later, he was making his thirty thousand dollars, but he wasn't happy yet. He believed if he just had a couple of more thousand a year, <u>then</u> he'd be happy. And so on, year after year. What does it take for us to begin to see the pattern? Our wants always exceed our resources, and we believe that's the source of our unhappiness. Not so. Never was. No wonder we always feel stressed out and inadequate; we never make enough money to afford what we tell ourselves we need.

The power of brainwashing can't be underestimated. Sixty-six percent of Americans report that they enjoy shopping as a leisure activity. There's a whole magazine devoted to shopping now; it's called *Lucky*. It sponsors a shopping contest, in which readers nominate their favorite stores. The prize is a shopping trip. "Destination shopping" is a new trend; places like the L.L. Bean store or the Mall of America or big outlet centers are thought to be worth planning a trip around. By the way, if you use your credit card instead of cash when you go, you're likely to be willing to spend twice as much on each purchase. The American worker can go to the mall and buy cheap clothes, toys, and electronics, because they're made by slave labor and imported, and feel pleased with himself, without noticing that his overall standard of living compared to hours worked is declining—or that his job is in jeopardy because of outsourcing.

I don't want to come across as some kind of cultural snob; it's not only that I <u>believe</u> that consumerism is empty; there's all kinds of evidence that it just makes us more miserable. It's relatively accepted among happiness researchers that people with materialistic values tend to be less happy, unless they are rich (and even then, they are not necessarily happier than average). In the lab, people who've watched a sad movie are willing to pay up to four times more for a small item—yet they deny that their sad feelings have anything to do with their decision. "Depressed shopping" is something therapists see all the time. People go shopping because they feel lonely, empty, bored, and they hope that buying something new will relieve those distressing feelings. In the process, they experience a little thrill of acquisition, but then they get buyer's remorse and feel worse. Most likely they've spent money they didn't have and added to their indebtedness to get something they really didn't need in the first place.

More _Things, Please!_

In a consumer culture, feeling good is the only purpose in life. We've lost sight of the fact that feeling good is a by-product of how we live. We don't get to feel good by mouthing self-affirmations, by having all the children win, by wearing the right clothes, even by climbing the corporate ladder. Happiness, pride, self-respect are accomplishments we earn by working hard and making difficult choices. Feeling good is not a right, but an achievement. My own profession has contributed to this mess by suggesting that, if you don't feel good, it's because you're sick, and we can cure you. Take this pill, go to that retreat, guide your life by this workbook. Of course, there is a lot of unnecessary misery in the world, and I'm glad we can help those who suffer. But there are many more people who are trying to feel good without accepting the fact that life is hard work, that we're constantly faced with difficult decisions, that we're responsible for how we treat others.

Remember what we said about adaptation and the hedonic treadmill. It's easy for us to get used to all this, to accept it as the natural order of things and not be aware of the damage it does to us and the rest of the world. It's wonderful that we are so adaptable, <u>but there are some things we should not adapt to.</u> Some things we can't let happen. These are losses that are so profound that we must heighten our awareness of what is happening to us as a result. Our brains and nervous systems were designed by nature to be part of nature. To live in an artificial world makes us exotic, fragile, easily damaged. It puts enormous strain on our systems—strain that gets expressed as emotional disturbance, physical symptoms, a reliance on pills, a calcification of the self into something ugly and brittle.

I don't mean to paint an overly idyllic picture of the past; there are many wonderful things about life today. Our world is safer and much more interesting. We can go where we want and do what we want, within a much wider range of choices than was available to our grandparents, let alone our medieval ancestors. Sometimes, though, it was comforting to have predictability and structure. There are an awful lot of single young women in their thirties out there who haven't found a partner and are now desperate, depressed, and blaming themselves—young women who thirty years ago would have married young and raised children. There are a lot of young people flipping burgers because the factory where Dad worked has closed up and moved to Mexico. Sometimes the range of choices itself can seem like a burden. How many kinds of soup can Campbell's make? You get tired just looking at the shelves.

the value of money

Please don't assume that I'm saying society is so sick, we should renounce all and go meditate on a mountaintop. Most of us can be far happier living in the world, not retreating from it, but we have to be smart about it. So since prosperity is at a dead end and consumerism is the root of so much stress, let's look at what money really can do for us.

There are two situations where an increase in income will reliably make you happier: One is if it lifts you out of poverty. If you're at the bottom of the income ladder, life is grim. You have to work much harder just to make the necessities. You have no leisure time, and no money to spend on enjoying yourself. You have a great deal of real stress, just trying to make ends meet and worrying about homelessness. Your health will suffer because you'll scrimp on medical care. When you're making $300K a year, a thirty-thousand-dollar raise will not mean much to you. But if you're making only thirty thousand dollars to start with, another thirty thousand dollars will really make you feel wealthy, and will genuinely resolve a lot of the stress and anxiety you feel every day.

Until relatively recently, that effect of wealth on poverty was the standard economic model. Economists assumed that wealth equals happiness, that the purpose of business was to increase wealth, and that the purpose of government was to support business in making wealth (mostly by staying out of its way). Now we know that the relation between wealth and happiness is more complex, affected not only by the law of diminishing returns but by human psychology as well. In fact, Americans, who have the highest per capita income in the world, rank only in the middle on personal happiness compared with other industrialized countries, and only slightly higher than Colombia, Brazil, and the Philippines, where personal income is only a small fraction of that in the United States. It's interesting to see that the Latin American countries in general, where the pace of life is slower and family ties are strong, are pretty high on personal happiness despite relatively low personal income. Among the highest are most northern European countries, where income inequality is low and social security is high. By contrast, the countries of the former Soviet Union are the most unhappy of all—perhaps because of the social and political instability they have been so subject to. In addition, over the last fifty years, rates of depression, alcoholism, and crime have increased dramatically in almost all Westernized countries, trends that go contrary to the idea that increased wealth leads to greater security and happiness.*

Although prosperity doesn't bring happiness, the belief that it does is hard to kill. Most people, when asked what they need to be happier, answer first that they need more money. And that brings us to the second scenario where more money can really make a difference. If you (like most people today) are deep in debt, paying heftily on credit card interest and finding it hard to pay your monthly bills with your current income, that causes a lot of stress and worry. You know you're only a couple of paychecks away from serious financial trouble. So it's true that if you suddenly got a bequest that would pay off your bills, or your salary jumped enough that you could get out of debt in the near future, you'd feel a lot better. The fly in the ointment is that it's extremely likely you'll get into the same trouble again. If you're like most people, your spending will increase proportionally to your increased income. It's guaranteed to go up somewhat, because of inflation, energy prices, and so forth, but it's very likely that you'll spend more besides, because of that human itch to have more—the hedonic treadmill, the addiction to things.

Research shows that perceived wealth is much more important than actual wealth. If we're content with our income, no matter how much it is,

* Bhutan isn't on the chart yet. It will be interesting to see how that country tracks in coming years, because its rulers have decided to measure national happiness and design policy to raise it.

we're likely to be happy. But there's only a slight tendency for the actually wealthier to be actually happier.* If you want to get happy through wealth, you've got to work hard to stay ahead of the curve. If you're the first person in your social circle to get a BMW, you're going to feel pretty good for a while. If you're the fifteenth, not so much. And that first guy's joy is dissipated when fifteen others in his reference group are driving Beemers. He'd better jump ahead and buy a Mercedes. That is the habituation effect of the hedonic treadmill, combined with the effects of social comparison, otherwise known as the rat race.

In fact, there's good reason to compare the desire for wealth to an addiction. Because of adaptation and the hedonic treadmill, we will quickly get accustomed to whatever goods we have now, and it will take more in the future to give us the same buzz. The platform keeps rising. If you get a raise of ten thousand dollars this year, you'll be happy. But next year another ten thousand dollars won't mean as much; scientists estimate you'll need fourteen thousand dollars more next year to experience the same pleasure as ten thousand dollars this year. And so on for the coming years—you'll keep on needing more, plus.

Just One More, I Promise!
In Buddhist wisdom:

> We think, "I know it's endless. I know it's painful. I know what you're saying. I believe you. But I've got one more thing, just one little thing."
> We can go to the grave saying this. That is *samsara* [the fruitless quest for permanence and relief from suffering]. "Just one more" is the binding factor of the cycle of suffering.

There's lots of experimental evidence to suggest that the happiest people are those who work part-time, set their own goals, get involved in their communities, and participate in active leisure. Most of us don't do that—largely

---

* The wealthier are also healthier, but interestingly, one's own perception of wealth status is more strongly associated with health than more objective indicators of wealth (Singh-Manoux, Marmot, and Adler, 2005). Perhaps having fewer wants decreases stress and improves health.

out of fear. Today, more and more college students are stating that their chief life goals are to make a lot of money, rather than to have an impact on the world or even just be involved in politics and organizations. That's a fear-based position: They want security.

They're on to something. Because money does buy some things that are associated with happiness. One of them is security. One of the benefits of my job is that you get to see what life is really like for people from widely varied backgrounds. In my experience with patients rich and poor, the really good things that money can get you are autonomy, security, and the time to enjoy life. If you're financially comfortable, you have greater freedom to do what you want—to take a year off from work to travel the world—and greater opportunity to educate yourself and enrich your life. And security means a certain amount of insulation from stress. You don't worry if the plumber's bill is five hundred dollars when you have a family trust that gives you $250K a year. "Personal control"—the belief that we're in charge of our lives—is much more closely associated with happiness than money is. Although the wealthy are slightly more likely to feel they have personal control, those on the bottom rungs of the economic ladder who feel they have greater personal control are much happier than those at the top without it. So the freedom and security that can come with wealth can directly affect your happiness, but only if you're smart about it, if you let it buy you the time to enjoy your life. It's an ironic reflection on what we've lost through social change that part of the reason we pursue wealth today is that it can buy us many of the things that society once provided for free—the time to engage in social pursuits, time to relax and enjoy the sunset, time to just sit around and chew the fat.

do: SAVE MONEY FOR AUTONOMY AND SECURITY, TO INSULATE YOURSELF FROM STRESS.

The question is, Will you use your money to build security and take advantage of your freedom? The answer is, contrary to your own conviction that you are wise and prudent, no. Here's a really scary experimental result: Researchers asked people if they'd rather make $50K a year when everyone else was averaging $25K, or $100K when everyone else was averaging $250K (the dollar buys exactly the same amount of goods in both cases). The vast majority of people decided they'd like to make more than average, even though it meant they'd have a lot less.* So apparently, being able to save for retirement or college or health care or travel—gaining independence—wasn't worth as much as the feeling of keeping up with the Joneses. Many other studies have found similar results. It makes you cringe a little to be human and certainly suggests that relative wealth is more important to us than absolute wealth, and that one of the basic functions of wealth in our society is a way of keeping score. But there's <u>always</u> going to be someone richer than you, someone who has something you don't—so can you gain happiness by chasing wealth? Only if you deliberately choose to swim against the flow by saving instead of spending. Otherwise trying to get rich is just another way of burning yourself out on the quest for happiness.

HOW DOES $100,000 A YEAR SOUND TO YOU? HOW ABOUT $50,000?

Another example: Real income per capita in the United States has nearly doubled in the last fifty years, but the proportion of people who say they are satisfied with their income has actually fallen. The most likely explanation is that, although average income kept rising over the past decade, the gap between the rich and poor was rising even faster. It truly was a new Gilded Age. As we've just seen, relative income seems more important than actual income when it comes to happiness. Mr. and Mrs. Doe, who make a decent household living of $150,000 ("decent" depends on where you live; I'm going by New York standards), are surrounded by other people driving the latest Lexus, adding wings to their houses (or buying a second home), and sending their kids to the most prestigious private schools. If they look around too much, the Does are likely to be dissatisfied with their "measly" $150K. We are bound by our reference group. If we feel we are doing better than the people we compare ourselves

* What makes this worse is that this study was conducted among students in the Harvard School of Public Health, who we might have thought were less materialistic than, say, students in the Business School.

to, we are happy with our economic situation; if we feel we're doing worse, we feel pretty lousy. That's why bus drivers are more content than stockbrokers. All bus drivers make roughly the same, and the rules about who makes more (seniority, overtime) are clear-cut. But stockbrokers always have someone much wealthier than themselves to compare to, and how you get to the most exalted level is much more a matter of luck and chance than hard work. Another way of saying the same ugly fact: If everyone's income goes up, we're all happier, but if my income goes up more than others, I'm more happier.

things you never knew you wanted

So—chasing the bucks and overloading on toys and status symbols is not the road to happiness. Not a huge surprise, is it? Philosophers, sages, religious leaders, even some psychologists have been telling us that for centuries. So why is it so hard for us to change our values and choices accordingly? Part of the answer is competition—we get seduced by the wish to do better than the other guy, and lose sight of our more fundamental values. Most of us now consider competition as a huge, all-consuming instinct. Don't forget that for most of history, societies were much more cooperative and interdependent than ours is. Capitalist culture is designed to bring out our competitive urges. And competition is by no means all of the answer. Much of it has to do with the values messages our society immerses us in so deeply that we're like a fish in water, not likely to notice that he's wet. I call it brainwashing; others call it advertising.

The strange result of genetic programming is that it makes us—and all other animals—act as if we want the things associated with evolutionary success. In this, humans are just like wolves or baboons or any other social, territorial animal. In order for wolfish genes to survive, the male wolf will select a healthy female wolf that displays the traits associated with childbearing success. The female wolf will select a male wolf that can hunt successfully and defend their den from predators. Human males tend to be attracted to younger women with perky breasts and tight skin; women tend to be attracted to men with power and status. Those are the traits associated with evolutionary success for humans. So men are programmed to seek power and status, women programmed to worry about their physical appearance. We think those things will make us happy, but they don't (more of this in the next chapter); nevertheless, they remain powerful motivators. Then advertising takes those desires and insecurities and turns up the volume to an earsplitting pitch.

Advertisers know as much as—maybe more than—psychologists about how the human brain works. Advertising tells us the product will make us more popular, prettier, sexier, more powerful (and suggests that we're defective without it) and that these things will automatically lead to happiness. *If we just buy the right things, we'll be happy.* The result is the highest rate of consumer debt in the United States in history. We're getting richer and more miserable all the time. Consumer culture has provided us the freedom to choose from seventy-two varieties of yogurt and have lousy medical care. In the last thirty years, the varieties of Pop-Tarts available have increased from 3 to 29, Frito-Lay chips from 10 to 78, running shoe styles from 5 to 285. Nine hundred channels of nothing to watch. The amazing range of choices is meant to distract us from the fact that the choices themselves are meaningless.

do: GET VERY CYNICAL ABOUT ADVERTISING.

Advertising has a tough job, because its basic purpose is to get us to buy things we don't need. (We'll buy what we really need with or without advertising.) The best way to make us want what we don't need is to associate it with things that we really crave—wealth, beauty, popularity, breeding, or status. By their very nature, those are low-end values. You can't sell a product by pretending it links you to high-end values like wisdom or kindness or bravery—everyone can see through that. So advertising has to appeal to our weaknesses, our doubts about ourselves. Since it's streamed into our homes around the clock, we're continually reminded of how insecure and needy we are.

Consumers "know," without being told or convinced, that they are not adequate as they are. They appear to be fully aware that they are inadequate, unattractive, incompetent, or inconsequential and must be transformed into different people in order to be happy, loved, and fulfilled.

From the standpoint of happiness, a real problem is that consumer culture in general, television in particular, and commercials above all give us the message that happiness should be easy. Just buy the right things.* But if you do that and are still unhappy, the unspoken corollary is that it's your fault. I think back to my grandparents, born around the turn of the last century. They knew, and I'll bet your grandparents knew also, that life was not supposed to be easy, that happiness was largely a matter of attitude. My grandfathers were factory workers who were grateful to have jobs that provided for their families. My grandmothers worked from dawn to dusk: I can remember wringers on washing machines and

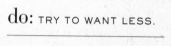

do: TRY TO WANT LESS.

ber wringers on washing machines and hanging the clothes on the line, making pies from scratch, putting up preserves. My grandparents knew how to enjoy themselves, but they didn't <u>expect</u> to be enjoying themselves all the time.

buyer's remorse

By the way, the more television you watch, the more you see people who are richer than you. The result is that you overestimate the income of real people, and rate your own income unrealistically lower. So the more television you watch, the less happy you become. You also spend more money; by one estimate, you'll spend an extra four dollars per week for every hour of television you watch. You also are more likely to overestimate the frequency of violence, drug abuse, divorce, and infidelity in real life. So you tend to see social conditions as worse than they actually are, and you're more likely to stay home and keep watching television because you believe that the world is

---

* To give yourself a laugh, please check out Havidol.com—"When more is not enough." (I hope it's still up when this book goes to press.) It's the first and only treatment for Dysphoric Social Attention Consumption Deficit Anxiety Disorder (DSACDAD). While you're on the Web, check out the Adbusters Web site, www.adbusters.org. Thank god for satire.

not safe. Maybe television contributes to the lack of safety. When Bhutan began to allow television in 1999, it experienced a crime wave. Marijuana—formerly used only to feed pigs—became a drug to abuse. Boys began mugging strangers for money; girls began prostituting themselves. The national bank experienced its first embezzlement.

There's experimental evidence to show that both men and women exposed to repeated images of attractive members of the opposite sex feel that their commitment to their own spouse has lessened. Repeated exposure to images of attractive or powerful members of your own sex makes you feel worse about yourself.

don't: READ FASHION (OR "LAD") MAGAZINES.

But what do television, movies, and magazines give us? In the old days, when the world was small, we all had a chance to be the best at something—the best hunter, the best knife-maker, the best baker, the best at finding berries. Now when we try to play baseball, we're not comparing ourselves to the firehouse team from the next town; we're comparing ourselves to steroid-enhanced freaks. Why try?

Television and consumer culture are not the only factors at work in giving us a distorted image of reality; so is the news business. If you watched the network news over the past fifteen years or so, you couldn't escape the impression that the economy was booming, with the occasional blip, and that everyone (except for disaster victims, the darlings of the news business) was benefiting. That simply wasn't true; only the wealthiest saw any growth in real income over that period. Virtually all income growth has gone to the richest fifth of the population, while real wages for the bottom three-fifths have stagnated or fallen. In 1976, the richest 10 percent of Americans controlled 49 percent of all wealth; in 1999, it was 73 percent—not much left over for the rest of us. There's good evidence to worry that, for most Americans, prosperity had maxed out even before the new upheavals in the economy. The middle class is disappearing; there are no new skilled jobs, because all manufacturing is now done overseas. Only McJobs are left—but you don't see that reality reflected in the media, the cheering section for unbridled capitalism.

EXERCISE 1:
DOES CONSUMERISM MAKE YOU HAPPY?

Don't buy anything for a week. Before you start, go to the store and stock up on perishables—vegetables, eggs, bread. Top off your gas tank. Then, for a week, don't go to a single store, don't order anything online or by phone. Don't eat out. Try not even to buy a coffee or a candy bar or a newspaper. Fix your coffee at home; get your news from the Web or radio. When you think you need something, start a shopping list to use later.

At the end of the week, think about a few things: Did you go through withdrawal? Did you get bored, irritable, anxious, depressed? Chances are good that you did, and that if you did, it was not because you missed something you really needed, but because you missed the habit of buying things. Buying things, even a newspaper or coffee, gives us a little kick. It makes us feel a little powerful. It gives us a little present when we're feeling down.

But it's likely that you also felt some good feelings. Pride, empowerment, freedom. When we resist temptation, we're building will power skills.

Look at your list of things you felt you needed. How many do you really need? There are probably some real necessities there (you're out of lightbulbs), but many things you wanted you can still do without. Notice how many of those desires were triggered by external cues—commercials, billboards, magazine ads, catalogs, and now e-mail pitches. But if you stayed out of stores you avoided many of the cues that prompt you to buy more. Fifty percent off! Two for one sale!

How much money did you save? How much could you save in a year if you followed this practice all the time? I'll bet it's more than a few thousand dollars, which can translate into a Caribbean vacation or a healthy investment.

McJobs and McCredit

Recently it's become normal to be in debt in America. That is a huge change from earlier times; we tended to be a nation of savers. Despite the fact that their continued employment is very uncertain, Americans have built up more indebtedness now than at any time in our history. In 1952, household indebtedness (mortgages, bank loans, and the like) was equal to 36 percent of income. That fraction has steadily grown to the point where, in 1997, indebtedness was 95 percent of income, which meant that households were spending 17 percent of their income merely to pay off debt, interest, and late fees. Much of the increase is due to the easy availability of personal credit cards (though borrowing for college has also added to the problem as tuitions have skyrocketed and the student loan market corrupted). Many Americans feel they are managing their money well if they are merely making the minimum monthly payment on their charge cards. It seems to me that capitalism couldn't ask for a better labor market: everyone in debt, deathly afraid of losing their jobs, willing to work longer and longer hours for less and less money, very little job protection—yet unable to mobilize against the unfairness of such a system because we have been so conditioned to believe it's the only way and that we really can be happy after all if we only buy more. We've been such perfect consumers that we've forgotten how to produce.

The latest economic news has us poised, if not in a recession, then on the very brink. Many people fear that it will be a bad one, because of some of the factors I've just mentioned—the high level of personal debt, the lack of real value in American industry, the economy dependent on consumer spending. Some regulation in the market in order to control greed a little, rather than simply trying to stimulate more spending, would seem to be the answer, but that's a political decision, anathema for the past thirty years. If the recession takes hold, it's likely to make personal happiness even more difficult, because most Americans will have to cut back on spending—and as we've said, spending in pursuit of happiness has become an addiction. The job market will be tighter so that people will feel even more stuck where they are, exploited and working too hard, because nobody's happy on unemployment.

Short of a drastic social revolution, change has to come on an individual basis. As someone said, "One way to be rich is to get more; the other is to want less." If we want to gain real happiness, we have to learn to protect ourselves from rampant consumerism and insulate ourselves from the effects of recession. We have to tune out the commercials. We have to spot the product placements and learn to make fun of them. Ridicule is a great defense against brainwashing. And it can feel <u>really good</u> to realize that you are becoming more and more independent and inner-directed. That may lead to more saving and wiser spending, the only protection from recession.

Finally, we have to stop thinking that happiness comes on a trip to Disney World, or on the weekend, or with a Bud. Happiness is smaller than we think. It's here in sitting in the sun with the dog, or listening to Mozart or the Beatles, or watching Jon Stewart. It can be woven into the fabric of our daily lives, if we live deliberately. It has no price tag at all.

conclusion

Here's how contemporary society interferes with happiness and contributes to our misery:

- It puts us into a constant state of stress, which damages our health and makes it difficult for us to make wise decisions, as well as causing brain damage in the areas associated with good feelings.
- It tells us that overwork is a good thing, that we should be proud of how many commitments we can juggle, instead of reminding us that we were probably designed to work only three or four hours a day.
- It interferes with leisure time, family time, nature time, God time, other-people time—all things that would lead to more happiness.
- It tells us that we can be happy by merely buying the right things. This is simply a lie, but there's so much social force behind it that we feel strange if we don't believe it.
- It tells us that wealth is the ultimate value in life—when, in fact, wealth is a very relative, conditional thing.

innate foolishness

THE BRAIN

*It is quite possible that people could get so preoccupied
with wanting things that they could forget to do things they enjoy.*
—*Daniel Nettle*

Pleasure and desire are altogether different things in the brain.
There is a system for feelings of pleasure up there, modulated by neurotransmitters called opioids, including those famous endorphins. The purpose of the pleasure system seems to be to help us tune out other stimuli and
let us focus on our immediate feelings. When we're making love, we ought
to be able to forget for a while that our back itches. (If you can't, it may be
telling you something about your relationship.) When you're running a
marathon and you're in that endorphin rush called the runner's high, your
awareness of the pain in your leg muscles is suppressed. Endorphins slow
time for us as well, making pleasurable experiences seem to last.

Then there is a system of desire, modulated by another neurotransmit-
ter, dopamine. It tells us what we want, and enables us to work very hard to
get it. It makes us feel "motivated, optimistic, and full of self-confidence."
But dopamine is a trickster—it makes us believe that we'll be happy if we get
what we want, even though that's often not the case at all. Or if we do get

happy, we quickly adapt. Getting what we want gives us relief from desire, but that's only temporary. Pretty soon we'll desire something else. There's pleasure in scratching an itch, though there ought to be more to life than that. There's also pleasure in mastering desire.

why do you think they call it <u>dopamine</u>?

Dopamine used to be thought of as part of the happiness system. When it was found that rats would give themselves a mild shock to the brain that was so addictive, they would forsake food and sex for more shocks, that was dopamine being released. At first, researchers thought dopamine was producing pleasure, but the rats never <u>looked</u> like they were enjoying themselves.* There have been many other indications to suggest that dopamine doesn't make rats or people happy at all, but it gets them activated and craving. Many of the drugs of abuse, like alcohol and nicotine, activate dopamine; that's what makes them so addictive.

It makes sense to believe that the evolutionary purpose of good feelings is not to make us happy but to keep us wanting to be happier. We should never really be satisfied for very long, or else we'll get eliminated by natural selection. Psychologists believe that this is the way the "happiness system" is supposed to work. It's always on

> YOUR BRAIN DOESN'T CARE IF YOU'RE HAPPY OR NOT.

the lookout for something better, and it makes us pursue those things. It doesn't give us much time to stop and smell the roses. That, we have to do for ourselves.

Dopamine and opioids are deep systems that flow not only in our family members, but the family dog as well—and in the fleas on his back. We have this in common with the lowliest worm: We like what we like based on the secretion of the same chemicals in the brain. Does that mean the worm experiences pleasure? No, because by definition you need a cerebrum to experience pleasure.

---

*Believe it or not, rats show a whole range of emotions, which scientists who've spent too much time in the lab have become good at reading. Rats even giggle when tickled, though at a frequency too high for us to hear. See for yourself at www.youtube.com/watch?v=myuceywaOUs.

What it means is that what we experience as pleasure is programmed into us because it's good for our survival. Or: our genes train us to do what's good for their survival by giving us a shot of pleasure. Our genes, like the worm's genes, program us to seek some kinds of experiences and avoid others, so that we can stay alive and pass our genetic material on to another generation.

Contentment and desire are like the ends of a seesaw; when one is up, the other must be down. Happiness is some of each. When we're in a state of great desire, we experience the pleasure of anticipation, imagining how we'll feel when we get what we want—but

LIFE'S BIGGEST FALLACY: *I'LL BE HAPPY IF I GET WHAT I WANT*

that's a restless craving, very different from the contented satisfaction of pleasure. When we are in that highly satisfied place, we can't stay long; we begin to crave something else. Pleasure is a message, and once the message is delivered, the messenger departs.

Think of it as training your dog. You give him a little piece of biscuit every time he sits, and pretty soon he sits on command. Your brain gives you a little squirt of joy juice (endorphins) every time you do what it wants (something good for species survival). Pretty soon you're doing what your genes want, and you think it'll make you happy. It will, in the short run, but in the long run, it may have you competing against your friends or chasing women, activities that may well interfere with long-term happiness.

fooling ourselves about happiness

Daniel Nettle, in his brilliant little book *Happiness: The Science Behind Your Smile*, points out that most of the primary emotions initiate a specific hard-wired program in our brains and bodies. Fear? Run away. Anger? Defend yourself. Disgust? Spit it out. Positive feelings don't really work in that way. If there were a happiness program, we should expect that it would drive us to seek out and linger with things that are good for us in some evolutionary sense—attractive sex partners, pleasant environments. But we seem to be a little too restless to really settle down, probably because the contented Cro-Magnon was more likely to get eaten, and less likely to be our ancestor. If the happiness program were truly effective, we should expect that we would accurately remember how good or bad certain experiences make us feel, and we should be able to predict how much more or less happy we will be when we choose among familiar alternatives. Yet science, over the last few years, keeps coming up with more and more examples of how we fool ourselves about happiness.

Adaptation

The hedonic treadmill is one example of the common human trait of adaptation. Studies of human response to positive and negative events have shown that we are very adaptable creatures. When things around us change, we get used to it pretty quickly, and return to near our individual set point of happiness. This ability of ours definitely has its good side—it helps us get through difficult experiences like jail, disability, and grief. We would probably not want to be less adaptable than we are. But from the viewpoint of happiness, the problem is that we return to our set point pretty quickly after good things happen to us, too—which leaves us always wanting more. That raise that we thought would make the difference between feeling poor and feeling rich?—guess what: We got it, and we still don't feel rich. What we once found thrilling, we now take for granted—exotic foods, illicit drugs, attractive sex partners. The more you get, the more you want. So things that make us feel good in the moment are doomed to lose some of their luster. Although there's nothing inherently wrong with feeling good in the moment, continually seeking more is obviously not the best path to happiness.

Misery Units

Worse yet, <u>the pain of losing something that makes us feel good outweighs the joy of getting it in the first place.</u> If you like a good imported beer, the first time you try it, you get five happiness units in your pleasure system. But after a while, the novelty wears off and you don't appreciate it so much—it brings only two happiness units, which isn't great. But what's worse, if your budget gets tight and you have to go back to the brand with the Clydesdales, you may actually feel ten misery units—worse off than you were before. Although nobody has come up with a reliable way yet to measure happiness and misery units, some studies suggest that losses have more than twice the impact of equivalent gains. You get a 10 percent raise at the end of the year, and you're elated at first. But your spending quickly increases so that after a few months, you take for granted the effects of the raise. Then if the company gets bought out, and you're forced to take a 15 percent salary reduction, you'll really howl. You'll have to cut back on the satellite radio, the fine wines, maybe take the kids out of private school—much more misery than the joy you gained in the first place. <u>Losing money or status will make you feel like a bigger failure than getting it made you feel a success.</u> The hedonic treadmill suggests that we are not only voracious consumers of the new and improved, but also very jealous and protective of our prizes, even though they don't bring us much happiness. With a recession upon us, we are likely to see a great many newly miserable people, unless they can change their values quickly.

If this business of happiness and misery units still is confusing, let me give you another example, this one from Barry Schwartz. We're gambling, and I give you a choice: I'll give you one hundred dollars right now, no questions asked, or you can have a coin toss. If you win the coin toss, you get two hundred dollars; if you lose, you get nothing. Almost everyone takes the sure hundred bucks—because we experience less joy getting the second hundred than the first. In fact, people start to be tempted only when the stakes go up to about $240. So you could say that if each dollar of the first hundred brings one happiness unit, each dollar in the second hundred brings only about 0.7 happiness units.

Now let's reverse the conditions. You give me a hundred dollars right now, or you can have the coin toss. I'll either take away two hundred dollars, or nothing. Here, most people choose the coin toss. Why? Our brains make us hope we won't lose, because deep inside, the brain knows that if you lose a hundred, losing a hundred more feels only a little worse. Again, considering that each dollar in the first hundred is worth one misery unit, the dollars in the second hundred are devalued in comparison.

It's Very Special to Me

Yet another example of adaptation, this known as the "endowment effect": People were given a choice between receiving a coffee mug or some money, and asked how much money they'd need to choose money over mug. The answer was about $3.50. But when given the mug to keep, then asked how much cash they'd want to give it back, the answer averaged $7.12. Apparently the fact that it becomes my mug endows it with some special quality that makes it more than twice as valuable as a mug off the shelf. The idea of giving up our stuff makes for more misery units than all the happiness they brought us.

don't: GET ON THE HEDONIC TREADMILL.

A scary recent study found that consumers served the same wine at different prices liked it better the more it cost. What's scary is that the researchers were looking into the brain: They found that the pleasure circuits in the brain did indeed light up more when the subjects were sampling the wine at higher prices. At the same time, the taste centers in the brain were staying steady. The wine tasted the same, but the subjects enjoyed it more as it rose in price. So the brain itself was tricking the subjects. If marketers learn about this study, and they will, it provides them with an incentive to raise prices, and plenty of rationale for never lowering them.

So we continue to believe that things will make us happy, but they reliably don't; in fact, they just give us *agita*. Here's Daniel Nettle again:

> The things we want in life are the things that the evolved mind tells us to want, and it doesn't give a fig about our happiness. All the evidence suggests that you would probably be happier not caring about your promotion and going and building boats or doing volunteer work instead. Moreover, the more important people believe financial success is, the more dissatisfied with both work and family life they are.

People who judge their success by material goods are generally found to be less happy than others, and are often disappointed when they have made their purchases. That may be because they are hoping acquisition will mean self-actualization or the feeling of having finally made it. Inevitably, they find that material goods can provide the outward trappings, but not the feeling. Every Friday afternoon, I see a different Land Rover or Hummer or Leviathan with lightbars and little cages around the headlights to protect from rhinos, driven by a guy in khakis and boots looking like he's going on safari—stuck in traffic on the West Side Highway with the kids whining in the backseat. He's driving something that cost four times what my car did—is he four times as happy? He certainly doesn't look it.

Yet, I'm human. I'm intrigued by the Land Rover. If I'm brutally honest with myself, I have to acknowledge I'm just a touch envious. Why do we envy people with more money? Why do we assume that we'd be happier in their shoes? It's the dopamine system tricking us—it's got nothing to do with happiness at all, though we feel like it does. There may actually be a circuit in the brain that makes us forget about the effects of adaptation; certainly we seem to be suckers for the myth of success. But there are other ways our brains fool us about happiness.

what do a colonoscopy and a funny movie have in common?

The peak-end rule, another way our brains trick us, was tested first in connection with colon exams. One of the first observations was that subjects preferred a longer colonoscopy that had a relatively painless interval at the end, compared with a shorter one that was painful all the way through. Doctors simply left the probe in without moving it, and people rated that as a less unpleasant experience even though it was just extra time—as much as twenty minutes' extra time. Findings like that have been repeated in many other situations, like watching funny movies. If it ends well, we loved it; if it starts out good but ends up flat, it's a bomb. The total number of laughs doesn't matter. We consistently skew our happiness judgments based on factors like how things wind up. Overall duration seems not to matter much. Subjects prefer to keep their hand in ice water <u>longer</u> if the temperature is raised (unbeknownst to them) in the last seconds, over a shorter time at a steady cold temperature. Same with pleasurable experiences. We prefer experiences that end on a high note even if a longer experience might have given us more total happiness units. Daniel Gilbert sums up the research:

> Whether we hear a series of sounds, read a series of letters, see a series of pictures, smell a series of odors, or meet a series of people, we show a pronounced tendency to recall the items at the end of the series far better than the items at the beginning or in the middle. As such, when we look back on the entire series, our impression is strongly influenced by its final items.

There are things you can do with this knowledge, like always save room for dessert. Seriously, imagine planning a vacation with the peak-end rule in mind. Your overall pleasure will be enhanced if you end it on a high note. It's certainly something for me to keep in mind in planning my workshops. Maybe people will believe the whole presentation was terrific if I end with something especially compelling. You should also keep in mind that here is a way your brain consistently distorts your perception of your own happiness and misery. Politicians use this principle all the time—that's why they propose their most audacious policies just after they're elected, assuming that we'll be lulled into not caring, as we adapt to their new reality. Remember GWB's attempt at social security reform?

tricks with time

The peak-end rule is only one of the ways we get fooled by time when making decisions. Imagine this: You're given a restaurant menu and asked to pick out a different meal to have once every month for a year. As you look through the selections, you can droolingly imagine each delicious experience you'll have every month to come. Unfortunately, you'll actually experience fewer happiness units than your experimental partner, who is asked to pick out the same meal to have every month. You'll have some great meals and some mediocre meals, because you'll have been forced to stretch beyond your favorites. It turns out that for your partner, a month is enough time to allow the novelty and anticipation of his favorite meal to regenerate.

But if you and your partner went to the restaurant every night for twelve days, you having different meals and him always having the same, you'd be the happier person for it. For him, habituation and boredom would set in. As Daniel Gilbert says, "time and variety are two ways to avoid habituation, and if you have one, then you don't need the other."

$19 Right Now, or $20 Tomorrow?

Another example: If I stop you on the street and offer you the choice of nineteen dollars right now, or meeting me back here tomorrow for twenty, you're likely to take the bird in the hand, thinking no doubt of what you can do with the money right now—a nice lunch, a taxi home, a special dessert tonight. But most people would rather have twenty dollars a year from now than nineteen in a year less a day because, at a distance, the delay seems trivial. Apparently the near future is intensely colored by feelings like greed or impatience, while the distant future seems abstract. Objectively, we're better off with twenty dollars tomorrow than nineteen today, as we would all see instantly if we were talking in thousands.

the Coolidge effect

President and Mrs. Calvin Coolidge were being given a tour of a farm. Mrs. Coolidge happened to be alone with the farmer in the chicken coop when the rooster was mounting a hen. The First Lady asked how often the rooster accomplished that, and seemed impressed that the answer was dozens of times a day. "Please tell that to Mr. Coolidge," she said.

Later, the farmer told the president about the rooster's accomplishments. "Really," said Mr. Coolidge. "Always with the same hen?" The farmer replied that the rooster picked a different hen every time. "Please tell that to Mrs. Coolidge," said the president.

When a male rat sees a new female behind a pane of glass, his dopamine level rises by 44 percent. If he's allowed access to her, his dopamine level will continue to rise as they begin courtship, doubling as he approaches orgasm. Each successive time they mate, however, the increase in dopamine level will diminish, until it's hardly more than normal. But let him see a new female behind that pane of glass, and his dopamine level will shoot up again.

Men are a little more evolved than roosters and rats (we believe), and the comparable studies haven't been done yet in females, but loss of interest in sex partners after years of marriage is often a serious problem. It's difficult for wives to understand why their husbands might enjoy pornography or strip clubs—but that just seems to be the nature of the beast, so to speak. Again, dopamine is associated with craving, with novelty and the chase, while happiness and pleasure are something else again.

competition

Getting involved in a contest is a great way to lose sight of what really makes you happy. We're genetically programmed to want to win, so all our concentrated competitive juices get flowing if we're in a zero-sum game. Indeed, winning does feel better than losing, and under most circumstances is better than losing, at least from our selfish point of view. But pushing too hard to win can have lots of hidden costs. For instance, now that baby boomers are aging, but fighting it, sports-related injuries are the second-most common reason for visits to the doctor. That weekend softball game or tennis match can result in crippling injuries if the desire to win makes us push ourselves beyond our body's limits. Of course, trying too hard to win can strain relationships and make friends keep their distance.

Business schools know that competition is a great way to make people work harder. The idea of a "stable workforce" bit the dust some time ago, along with GM's pension plan. Nowadays employers limit the number of jobs available, and make it a real contest to get them and keep them. That's one of the reasons why Americans work longer hours and take fewer vacation days than workers in any other country. Some fields, like television or publishing, are considered prestigious, and they work their junior staff like galley slaves. In a competitive workplace, just holding on to your job can seem like a triumph. But it's a shortsighted kind of happiness if it means working sixty hours a week. It keeps you away from your family, afraid of change, and unable to relax. Losing is better than winning if you have to kill yourself in order to win.

making ourselves look good to ourselves

We regret inaction more than action, though we think just the opposite. Say you own stock in Time-Warner, and during the past year you thought about switching your stock to Upstart Ventures Inc., but decided against it. If you learn later that if you'd invested in Upstart you'd have made $1,200, you'll regret it. On the other hand, say you own stock in GE, and during the past year switched your stock to Flybynight Travel. But if you later learn that if you'd kept your shares in GE you would have earned $1,200 more, you'll regret that, too. Almost everyone believes that they'll regret more taking that foolish chance on Flybynight than they will passing up the opportunity with Upstart; but they're wrong. "In the long run, people of every age and in every walk of life seem to regret <u>not</u> having done things much more than they regret things they <u>did.</u>" And of course, that is the folklore of the deathbed: No one dies wishing they'd spent more time at the office, but they do regret not having been up in a balloon, not seeing the Pyramids, not having pursued the girl. Gilbert argues that the reason we regret inaction more is that it's easy for us to rationalize taking action, if only because we can say we learned something from the experience. We prefer to think of ourselves as courageous, if foolish, rather than cowardly and also foolish.

thinking about happiness

So if there is a "happiness program" in the brain, it's a very inefficient one. We're just not very good at predicting how good or bad things will make us feel. We consistently overestimate the impact on happiness of money, success, and power. We have a kind of selective memory loss about the adaptation effect, because we will always quickly get used to and take for granted our new and improved circumstances, and they will always cease to bring us joy, but we will always forget that. Then there are things like the peak-end rule, which makes us notoriously defective at remembering how good or bad experiences made us feel in the past. And the happiness program is also subject to influence by our current mood, the weather, finding a dime in the copy machine, and so on.

I can't say it better than Daniel Nettle: When we try to figure out what will make us happy,

> We make a kind of best guess . . . biased by things like the peak-end rule, our current mood, the standard of comparison we are making, and our failure to predict our own adaptation. This means we may end up with an inaccurate picture of the net effects of our behaviour on our happiness, and choose things that don't in fact make us happier. . . . These effects are probably not faults in the happiness programme; they are the way that it is designed. That is, <u>the purpose of the happiness programme in the human mind is not to increase human happiness; it is to keep us striving</u> [emphasis added].

It's that old dopamine black magic, keeping us very busy chasing things we don't need.

Your brain couldn't care less if you're happy or not. It just wants to keep you alive. It does that by making you believe you'll be happy if you keep striving, driving, competing, winning. If you want to be happy, you have to outsmart your own genes.

EXERCISE 2:
THINKING ABOUT HAPPINESS

These are merely some questions to get you thinking. We'll be getting into these subjects in coming chapters.

- Think about yesterday. Try to remember three things that made you feel good.

- How many of the things that made you feel good involved sensual pleasure—food, sex, comfort, beauty, physical activity? How many involved accomplishment, pride? How many involved spending money or buying material things? How many involved watching television?
- What are you looking forward to next week? What—if anything— do you imagine with pleasurable anticipation?
- Think back over the past year. What were your major purchases? How much joy are they bringing you? How many do you regret?
- Try to think of two or three occasions in the past year when you felt very happy or content. Did any of those involve purchases? Money?
- What <u>did</u> those things involve? Can you do them again?
- Did you take a vacation last year? How long? Did you plan it well? Did you enjoy it?
- What's the last thing that made you laugh out loud?
- How do you know if you're relaxing? How can you tell if you're enjoying yourself?
- Who's the happiest person (adult) you know? What's their secret?
- Are you drinking—or using other drugs—more than you feel right about?
- How many hours are you working? How many hours do you have for reading, hobbies, exercise, socializing?
- What's your workplace atmosphere like? Are people there friendly and supportive? Is the boss reasonable?
- Does what you do for a living make a contribution to people's lives?
- Is your work stimulating or challenging?
- How much time do you spend with your significant other, just talking?
- How much do you exercise?
- How much debt are you carrying? Over the past few years, has it increased or decreased?
- Has your take-home pay increased, stayed flat, or declined relative to inflation?

- Have your benefits (health insurance, sick time, vacation pay, comp time) increased or diminished over the past five years?
- How much time of your day goes into television? The research suggests that heavy viewers (four or more hours per day) actually enjoy their TV watching <u>less</u> than light viewers (under two hours per day).
- Are you concerned about changing values in American life—more vulgarity, less respect for others, more distrust or apathy, deeper political divisions?
- Do you go to religious services? Do you consider yourself a religious person? Does that contribute to your happiness?
- What are your greatest sources of stress or worry? If you could make yourself take time, could you make a dent in those problems? Or are they just facts of life you must accept?
- How many pills are you taking regularly?
- Compared to ten years ago, how's your medical care?
- Do you think you and your contemporaries are happier than your grandparents when they were your age?
- Do you think your children will have less, more, or the same amount of stress in their lives as you do?

unnecessary misery

THE MIND

As if it weren't bad enough that your brain—the physical organ in your head that is so governed by evolutionary programming—doesn't really want to make you happy, it often seems as if your mind (the thoughts and feelings produced by your brain) doesn't either—or else why all the self-defeating behavior that humans seem to be such masters of? From suicide and addictions to procrastination and lack of assertiveness, it's these miserable mental habits that keep therapists like me busy—and make it seem almost impossible for us to change our happiness set point.

We all have bad habits we'd like to stop, habits that get in the way of our success or happiness. Yours may be simply procrastinating, eating too much ice cream, or not exercising enough. It may be more handicapping than that—not making your needs clear, not getting out of a bad job or relationship. It may be a more serious problem: abusing drugs or alcohol, going deeper and deeper in debt, taking foolish chances with your life. Whatever your particular situation is, simple will power is not enough to make you stop, and you probably don't understand why. You know very well what you <u>should</u> do. You probably lecture yourself about it incessantly. You beat yourself up every time you fail a new resolution: *Why did I say such a stupid thing? When am I ever going to get over my self-consciousness? My laziness? My overeating? My lack of organization?* The problem, whatever it is, is taking up a lot of space in your brain. It seems so clear: you can choose A, the "good" choice, or B, the "bad" choice. You want to choose A, but it seems like you always choose B. <u>Why in the world can't you simply do what will make you happy?</u>

Well—it shouldn't surprise us that there's no easy answer to that question, or else we'd all be in a state of healthy bliss, always perfectly doing what's best for us. Scientists, religious figures, philosophers, have debated this since history was first written. In fact, it's the subject of the Western creation myth, the story of Genesis—why <u>do</u> Adam and Eve choose to disobey God? It's not like he didn't warn them.

The answers to those questions are complex, and will lead us into some dark corners that you won't find in most happiness books. In my opinion, your mind itself is the source of most of your unnecessary misery, and if we ever want to really be happy, we have to understand that.

the psychodynamic way

Let's start with Freud. He was the original master at understanding common human self-destructive behavior, and he had to create "the unconscious" to do it. It's difficult today for us to understand what a revolutionary concept that was, because nowadays we take for granted the idea that we might have motives we're unaware of, that there are hidden payoffs for things we protest. The whole idea of denial—that we can literally <u>not see</u> what's perfectly obvious to everyone else, like the effects of our drinking—rests on the idea of unconscious motivation. Freud forever lifted what was a kind of cultural collective denial, but he was only pointing out what we commonly accept today—the idea of <u>mixed motives.</u> If you're sabotaging yourself, if you're not doing what would obviously make you happy, it's likely that you have some reasons, some motivations, for self-sabotage, which you're not totally aware of. They're unconscious. Defense mechanisms

are the tools your mind uses to keep unwelcome ideas out of your consciousness.

defenses

One reason why it's so easy to sabotage ourselves is that our minds have some
wonderful ways of adapting to a difficult reality, skills that we use every day,
largely for constructive purposes. But we can use them also to lie to ourselves,
to make it seem perfectly fine—for the moment—to do what we'll only regret
later, when reality sets in. We call those skills defenses. Defenses help keep
our internal conflicts out of awareness, and we're full of conflicts. We want to
be good, and we want to be bad. We want to take it easy, and we want to get
rich. We are always trying to find a balance between what the animal brain
makes us want (*pleasure right now!*), what our conscience tells us we should
want (*sorry, duty first*), and what reality will let us have (*oops—no money*).
Sudden change in any area upsets the balance. Defenses distort reality to re-
store the balance temporarily. We'll start to deny or rationalize, or any of a
hundred other defenses. *It probably would have rained in Cancún. Those
grapes were probably sour, anyway.* When our desires are in conflict—for instance, being attracted to someone who's off-limits to us—we may transmute
the desire into a wish for someone else, turn it into hate, intellectualize it, or
any of a number of other possibilities. Defenses are like art: a creative syn-
thesis. The mind unconsciously creates something that was not there before.

   In the early 1960s, researchers discovered for the first time that people
under stress—students entering college for the first time, for example—had
elevated levels of cortisol, a stress hormone, in their urine. That finding naturally led them to check the cortisol levels of soldiers in Vietnam. First they
went to forward firebases, where men were pinned down under enemy ar-
tillery attack. The researchers collected the soldiers' urine and flew it back
to Washington for analysis, where they got a surprise—no elevation in cortisol. The GIs explained that because they were able to dig into their bunkers
and protect themselves, they really didn't feel any danger at all. But they
said, *If you want guys under stress, check out those helicopter pilots and crews.
There's nothing but aluminum skin between them and enemy fire.*

So the researchers dutifully collected the urine of some helicopter crews after combat missions, and analyzed that; again, no elevated cortisol. The pilots and crews said, *We feel fine up here—we can bob and weave and evade anything that comes at us. The guys who are really under stress are those poor SOBs pinned down at the firebases.*

"Each group denied that they were experiencing stress, and their bodies believed them." That is how defense mechanisms work—in this case, denial and rationalization. We can distort reality so that we don't feel its effects on our emotions, even to the extent of temporarily fooling the adrenal glands. Defenses can be extremely beneficial—soldiers in combat can temporarily turn off their fear, ER surgeons can turn off their horror. In anger, we can control our blind rage and turn it into the fuel for logical argument. We can sublimate our own grief by taking care of others. We can just say, *I'll think about that tomorrow,* and get a good night's sleep.

Defense mechanisms themselves are necessary for human existence. They are often creative, adaptive strategies for dealing with difficult situations or people. But they all distort reality to some extent, some more than others. By distorting reality, they can blind us to the effects of our own self-defeating behavior. Denial is the classic defense, though the name is deceptive. It's not that the alcoholic sees the truth and denies it. He literally doesn't see how his drinking is getting him in trouble at work, making his wife and kids uncomfortable, and making him behave like a jackass sometimes. "Selective blindness" might be a better term than denial. Projection is another defense mechanism. When we feel guilty about something, we can try to make the other guy the guilty party. A husband promised his wife he'd be home at eight thirty. When he came in at quarter past nine, the first words out of his mouth were, *Are you going to ruin our evening because I'm a little late?* That wasn't a conscious manipulation, a deliberate guilt trip; it was his unconscious attempt to shift the blame. By the time he arrived home late, he had already created in his head the image of her as an unreasonably demanding shrew. Defenses like these lead to unnecessary misery for us, whether it's sinking into alcoholism or aggravating your spouse. A major task in stopping self-defeating behavior—and thereby freeing ourselves up for happiness—involves learning about how we use defenses to allow us to keep on hurting ourselves.

The defenses that distort reality in a big way always get you in the end; there are always unintended negative consequences, both in the mind and body. Not only does the negative emotion we're trying to avoid usually surface in some other, perhaps disguised, way, but the use of defenses like these shapes our personality. Instead of simply wrestling with a painful experience, we become someone who denies reality. Instead of accepting responsibility, we become a blamer and accuser. If we do an injury to someone we love, our defenses can go to work on our guilt—we might rationalize that we were simply too busy. But our guilt, now unconscious, might make us avoid that person or even blame him for the uncomfortable way we feel when we're around him. We might not realize it, but our body may tense up when he's nearby, our stomach acid churn, our blood pressure rise—and we can forget that we caused all this in the first place, and rationalize that he is just a difficult guy.

Use of defenses to deny reality is lying to ourselves, and just as what happens when we start lying to others, we gradually build more and more elaborate lies to buttress the first one. Those elaborate lies blind us to more and more of our own experience, so that our perception becomes more and more distorted, the blind spots become bigger and bigger, our character armor more cumbersome and restricting.

The metaphor of "character armor" comes from Wilhelm Reich, an early psychoanalyst, years ago. It's our own individual pattern of defenses, rationalizations, paradigms—our ways of responding to anything that threatens our comfort. Unless we're careful to remain open to experience, we can put on more and more character armor

do: PERIODICALLY INSPECT YOURSELF FOR CHARACTER ARMOR: PREJUDICES, RIGID THINKING, AUTOMATIC JUDGMENTS, DIFFICULTY LISTENING.

throughout our life, until we become prisoners in our own armor. We're like a tank driving down an Iraqi street, unable to see except through tiny portholes, unable to hear, to communicate, unable to respond to anything except by shooting at it.

trauma

Over the course of a hundred years of psychotherapy, the concept of defense has remained very useful, but the idea of just what it is that we defend against has changed a lot. Freud originally thought defenses were used to blind us to forbidden impulses and the internal conflicts they cause. Nowadays we think of defenses as helping us with any emotion that we feel is dangerous or too upsetting. We also recognize that, while defenses may be temporarily helpful in the mind, damage—from the out-of-control effects of the chemistry of emotions—may still be taking place in the brain and body.

We've changed our thinking about the purpose of defenses largely because of Freud's greatest error. Most of his patients were Viennese women from nice, conventional families, who had unexplained symptoms like hysterical paralysis. When they began suggesting to him through their dreams and associations that their respectable families were hotbeds of twisted sexuality—that, in fact, sometimes these young women had been sexually abused by male relatives or trusted family friends—Freud was horrified. At first he took his patients' stories at face value, and developed a treatment approach to deal with repressed trauma as we would today—that is, to bring it into consciousness in a safe and supporting setting. To Freud's great disgrace, however, he later gave in to the immense social pressure to deny his patients' reality, and developed the entire Oedipal theory in response: It's not that parents are seductive or abusive to their children; rather, children have a natural sex drive that focuses on the opposite-sexed parent. The attraction is so shameful to them that they have to repress their desires below the level of consciousness, though they continue to experience unconscious guilt. So Freud concluded that his patients were projecting their own forbidden sexual desires on their innocent fathers, uncles, and brothers. Nowadays, now that we know how common childhood sexual abuse is, now that we no longer think of women as inherently weak and untruthful, most analytic gurus believe that probably many of Freud's patients were, in fact, sexual abuse victims. In fact, children do have a sex drive, and we do experience unconscious guilt, but generations of women (and men) in analytic treatment were told to deny their memories of abuse and blame themselves for their own incestuous wishes.

A book about happiness may not seem like the best place to go into a discussion about child abuse, neglect, and trauma, but we need to talk about those subjects somewhat because they are so common and they are the source of so much adult misery.

Remember those soldiers in Vietnam whose defenses were working so well that there was no excess cortisol in their bloodstream? It didn't work out all that well for them in the end. The Department of Veterans Affairs now estimates that more than 30 percent of the men who served in the Vietnam theater experienced full-blown post-traumatic stress disorder (PTSD) in later life. But they're not alone—10 percent of women and 5 percent of men in the United States general population also suffer from PTSD. More women than men because women are more vulnerable to victimization, and that's a huge risk factor, because helplessness to change the outcome may make the difference between acute PTSD and normal stress reactions. Feeling powerless to change events, people try to change their emotional reactions instead—by dissociation, by turning to alcohol or drugs, by lashing out in violence.

PTSD is a complicated body–mind–brain condition caused by our exposure to acute, severe stress. Formally, it means that you've been exposed to a situation that you believed threatened death or serious injury to yourself or others, and that your emotional response at the time was intense fear, helplessness, or horror. The hallmark symptom of PTSD is that the traumatic event then lives on as intrusive memories or symptoms. PTSD occurs even among those who choose to expose themselves to trauma, such as rescue workers.

People with PTSD are in a chronic state of stress. There's a significant increase in adrenaline levels throughout the body, resulting in hypervigilance, a hair-trigger startle response, and flashbacks. The amygdala's danger-sensing system is stuck in the "on" position, and we see danger everywhere. The hippocampus, which normally helps us tell the difference between real danger and safety, is damaged by all that adrenaline, and is unable to switch off the amygdala. Thus people with PTSD are always anxious and always on the alert; they overreact to daily events in ways that may appear irrational or antisocial, and just scare the daylights out of their loved ones in the process.

Messy Memories

PTSD also messes with your memory. With PTSD, we keep <u>reliving</u> the experience, with all its sounds, smells, physical sensations, panic, fear, and confusion. Normally, memories get processed and stored by the brain as a narrative that captures the essence of what happened; some of the details get lost, yet there's a coherent story. But if you ask a PTSD survivor to tell you what happened, she can't do it very well; her story is confused and incoherent. The details are all there, but she's lost in them. You won't be able to understand the sequence of events and their effect on her, because the hippocampus was so flooded with stress hormones during and after the trauma that it was unable to perform its normal function of consolidating memory, knitting the emotional memory and the actual events into a coherent form that can be filed away in long-term memory. The PTSD experience is like the distinction between remembering and dreaming. When I remember an experience, I remain conscious that I am in the present,

do: KEEP IN MIND THAT
FEELINGS ALWAYS HAVE A
CAUSE. THERE'S ALWAYS
A REASON WHY YOU'RE
FEELING WHAT YOU DO.

looking back on the past. But when I dream, I'm not conscious of dreaming; whatever "I" exists is in the dream. That is the experience of reliving in PTSD—you have nightmares while you're awake.

Then there are the side effects of living with a condition like acute PTSD, which are somewhat different from the effects of the trauma itself. Since you're reliving instead of remembering, you're likely to blame trivial current events for your anxiety, and alienate the people who care about you. You experience yourself as being out of control, perhaps a little dangerous. You don't understand where the nightmares, blackouts, and outbursts are coming from, so you may fear you're going crazy or that you have a brain tumor. You feel separated from your own past, and your memory problems mean that the whole story of your life—your own identity—is disrupted and no longer trustworthy. You may rely more and more on dissociation as a defense, which makes you dreamy, spacey, and detached; it's hard to concentrate or focus or learn. Because you're unable to calm yourself, you may turn to substance abuse or other pathological self-soothing mechanisms like muti-lation or bingeing and purging. You also are likely to be highly suspicious of others, guarded and untrusting—and of course, in a self-fulfilling prophecy, you will continue to find that others fail the tests you set up for them. Your world becomes one of vigilance, mistrust, and fear.

PTSD was probably much more common among our ancestors, who were exposed to physical danger all the time; but since no one lived past thirty-five anyway, they never suffered too much in the way of long-term consequences. There was no evolutionary pressure to change the stress re-sponse. Besides, being in a hypervigilant state when danger is all around you is a good thing. Being hypervigilant when you're stuck in traffic or at home trying to play with the kids is a very bad thing.

chronic stress

So PTSD is a really horrible condition shared by almost 8 percent of us. But PTSD is not an all-or-nothing condition. There are a lot of people who have been deeply affected by past trauma yet don't meet all the formal criteria for PTSD. You can have nightmares, flashbacks, intrusive memories, be con-stantly suspicious and on the alert, but because your experiences are caused by the cumulative effects of stress instead of a single life-threatening event, you're not in that 8 percent. You're in the uncounted numbers—I estimate somewhere around 30 percent of Americans—who have chronic trauma syndrome.

Chronic trauma syndrome—the term for the effects of living for ex-tended periods of time in conditions that create fear and helplessness—is worse than acute PTSD because it takes all the symptoms and multiplies them. It gets so far into your bones and your brain that you are deformed in ways that seem so much a part of you that you can't be aware. It's very, very common. The incidence of battering by an intimate partner—a surefire route to chronic trauma—may range from 25 to 50 percent of women. In a well-known study of seventeen thousand largely white, middle-class people, 22 percent reported that they'd been sexually abused as children. More than a quarter reported regular parental substance abuse, which implies child neglect. In my experience with all my patients over the years, most have had experiences of being abused or neglected as children. It's not usually the horror stories of beatings or incest, although those are frequent enough. Much more often, it's emotional abuse: One or both parents seem to undermine the child by criticizing harshly or cruelly, name-calling, emotionally battering the child as a form of discipline, having arbitrary rules for conduct, yelling at the child just because the parent is in a bad mood (or intoxicated, or hungover), or withholding attention or affection because the child has displeased the parent. And then, perhaps, acting like a perfectly good parent the next day, as if nothing had happened. That <u>unpredictability</u> may be the worst thing for the child's emotional health. But those patterns are so common that most of my patients are surprised when I point out that their experience amounts to abuse.

An Epidemic of Stress

Many of us also suffered some form of emotional neglect, though we don't think of using that label. Neglect can simply mean paying more attention to the television than the child, being emotionally unavailable when the child needs you, preferring one child over another, or not taking an interest in the child's schoolwork. It can result from not recognizing trauma when it happens, when a child is being picked on by others or abused by adults; there are always changes in behavior that an attentive parent can catch. But who can be attentive enough nowadays? Parents who neglect

A LESS STRESSED PARENT IS A BETTER PARENT.

their children like this all believe they love their children, and though many feel a pang of guilt at times, they also believe they are good parents. They may be better parents than their parents were, but they are not good parents. We need to raise standards for parenting in this country. People must understand that humiliating or scaring your child is cruel, that being emotionally unavailable is heartless.

Emotional abuse and neglect of children are extremely common in today's culture. It's estimated that only a slight majority of American youth now grow up feeling safe and secure. But what's especially tragic is that no one <u>wants</u> to abuse or neglect their child. These patterns are simply the usual result of parents being overworked and overstressed, coping with their own problems, and feeling isolated. Abuse and neglect are much less common when children are part of an extended family. It does indeed take a community to raise a child, and community is collapsing around us.

It's possible that childhood neglect may have more destructive impact on adult character than occasional abuse does. Sometimes parents who love their children can lose control under pressure; that may be better than indifference. Treatment can help victims of sexual or physical abuse, if they had enough early experience of being cared for. Some neglected children had no such experience; there is nothing to build on, no trust, and no connecting. The child's very self has been abandoned or undermined by the person who should have been helping to build it.

Chronic trauma syndrome doesn't have to be the result of a difficult childhood. Everyday living conditions for many people can pile up so much stress that the effect is traumatic. Many people know that simply working a tough job can be enough. Too much pressure, too many bosses, too long hours, changing and irrational expectations, backbiting among the staff, or the threat of layoff. It's like the frog in the pot: The heat is raised so gradually that you don't notice you're starting to boil. You start to believe that the way you feel is normal, and maybe you're just weak to complain about it. But when you can't sleep at night, when your digestion is shot, when you can't wait for a drink after work, when you forget how to enjoy yourself—that's chronic trauma syndrome. It creeps up on you so gradually, you don't notice how bad it is until it stops.

People with chronic trauma syndrome tend to avoid or control emotions, because any emotion can trigger a meltdown. One result is the flatness and joylessness of depression. Another, more subtle but more devastating result is paralysis of the will: People lose the capacity to experience motivation, to want something, to wish for something, to care for somebody. That's one reason there are so many people out there who feel stuck in soul-destroying jobs.

PTSD, exposure to trauma, can produce symptoms that are devastating and dramatic. Chronic trauma syndrome results from an ongoing, more subtle pattern of neglect or abuse that undermines personal security and sense of safety. Or from being stuck in a situation where too much is demanded and conditions are inhumane. Talking about happiness in the context of people with these problems may seem insensitive, to put it mildly. But I'm taking us in a progression here; now we need to talk about the effects of parenting style on the adult's capacity for happiness. Besides that, the millions of people with PTSD and chronic trauma syndrome need the most help finding happiness, and chances are good that you, dear reader, are one of them.

childhood and a good-enough brain

The bottom line is both reassuring and scary for today's parents. All you have to do is be a "good-enough" mother—or father, or grandparent (whoever the child's primary caregiver is). A good-enough mother is simply one who's interested in her child, wants to do a good job, and <u>is able to ride out the child's emotional storms with a certain degree of calmness.</u> Unfortunately, that last quality is harder and harder to achieve.

Most developmental psychologists now accept that the very first year or two of life lays down the foundation for the future adult's temperament, specifically how he will handle emotions. This takes place both in the child's mind and in the physical structure of the brain, and it's the primary caregiver who does the molding process. Mothers who are sufficiently attuned to the child's emotional state help the child calm down when overstimulated, perk up when apathetic, and regain a sense of safety when frightened, and the child builds a good-enough brain in the process. However, many parents are either unresponsive to the child's needs, or inconsistent, stimulating the child when they feel like it, unresponsive at other times. Other parent–child combinations are just a "bad fit"—an energetic, demanding child paired with a mildly depressed mother; a quiet, undemanding child of an overworked, distracted mother.

Bonding

But when things are going well between mother and child, when mother can lose herself in the baby's world, they can get deep into a primitive instinctual state that is the human equivalent of cats licking their newborns. It's a union of two emotional brains, the mother <u>imprinting</u> herself on the child's brain, "a very rapid form of learning that irreversibly stamps early experience upon the developing nervous system." In that way, the mother imprints her own emotional style on the child. If she's anxious, she's likely to raise an anxious or avoidant child; if she's calm enough, she'll have a calm enough child. All of this does <u>not</u> mean that the mother, or whoever's doing the mothering, has to be perfect. She doesn't even have to be happy. She doesn't have to be carefree, or able to solve all her own problems, or available around the clock for the infant. She does need to be able to get into that deep merged state and adapt as the child's emotional needs for her change.*

In today's world, that ability becomes more and more scarce. Mothers are expected to go back to work far too soon after their child's birth. When they do return, their attention is divided. Women are expected to balance career and family today, and that's a very stressful thing. It leaves them distracted and guilty, and makes it difficult to find the bonding time that children desperately need. A disturbing recent study found that mothers ranked child care as one of their least preferred, most frustrating activities, right down there with commuting. The researchers noted by way of explanation that those mothers were likely engaged in other activities and found child care distracting.

There was an interesting natural experiment that took place a few years ago, when a tribe of Cherokees began to receive an average of twelve thousand dollars each per year from a new casino on the reservation. Their children's behavioral problems improved significantly after these families became relatively more affluent. (Actually, they just barely moved over the poverty line.) The only variable that the researchers could find to explain the finding was that the parents simply had more time to supervise their children. In the wider world, you don't have to be poor not to have time to supervise the kids. All you need are both spouses working, and school dismissing at two thirty.

do: MAKE IT A PRIORITY TO GIVE YOUR KIDS YOUR UNDIVIDED ATTENTION.

* If the child misses out on this experience at the appropriate developmental stage, all is not necessarily lost. Psychologists are conducting important research into the concept of "resiliency"—the fact that some children can overcome those lost opportunities while others can't. Nevertheless, missing out on the opportunity of bonding puts the child at a serious disadvantage.

As we said at the outset, we know now that the brain is a lot more change-able than we ever thought before, and that gives us great reason for opti-mism: You can train yourself to be happier, and it'll become a habit. But the downside is that we can see also how negative life experiences have lasting consequences. Put simply and directly: If you were lucky enough to have a secure, consistent relationship with a caregiver who had a stable and healthy identity, you have a better chance of having a happy and satisfying adult life. That's because we need to have that kind of soil to grow a brain that works. Thanks to all our new technology that allows us to see the human brain as it develops, we know now that negative childhood experiences cause brain damage. Allan Schore and Daniel Siegel, the leading researchers in this growing field, agree: <u>It doesn't take outright abuse or neglect, but simply a poor relationship between parent and child, to result in damage to the struc-ture of the brain that persists into adulthood.</u> This results in adults who have trouble feeling and controlling their emotions, trouble focusing, con-centrating, and learning, trouble in trusting and understanding others, trou-ble with self-esteem, and trouble with self-control. We know now that, in mice, attentive mothering leads to better survival of new neurons in the hippocampus—the area that's so important in regulating emotion and stress; I don't think it will be long before we know the same about human mother-ing. Good mothering leads to stronger, more resilient brains.

Meanwhile, we can see the effects of mindless parenting, television, video games, and overstimulation in our schools today. More and more child and adolescent depression, school phobia and other anxiety problems, learning disabilities, ADHD, conduct disorders, Asperger's syndrome, drug abuse at younger and younger ages. Kids go to school today not wired up correctly, so they literally can't sit still and pay attention. They don't have emotional con-trol. Every taxpayer is up in arms about the skyrocketing cost of the school's special ed budget. Don't we want to think about why it is that there are so many more kids who need special ed services?

This may seem scary, but let me reassure parents again. You don't need to know a lot or have any special expertise to be a good-enough parent. What you really need is <u>time</u> with your child, time when you aren't distracted by the idea that you should be working. Good parenting is an easy and natural thing. Even if you had lousy parents yourself, if you can remember what you needed and didn't get as a child, give your child that. If you can be undistracted enough to empathize with your child, to understand what he or she is feeling, then you know what to do. The empathy itself may be the most important thing.

back to happiness

Bottom line: PTSD, chronic trauma syndrome, and even not-good-enough parenting result in brain damage. Not the gross damage we see from a stroke, but a subtle damage that means we're just not wired up correctly. So many of us are wounded today in these ways that talking about happiness as a goal can seem like a big stretch. But we are remarkable, resilient creatures. Our brains can repair themselves, given the right conditions. And I've never known a patient who was never happy, except during crisis phases that might last a few weeks at most. People tend to bounce back after that. Even the most depressed, the most anxious, have moments during the day when they will smile and feel good. Simple pleasures—the sunshine, a butterfly, the wind on your face, a beautiful flower—never seem to lose their magic. As damaged as we can be, we never seem to lose the capacity for joy for very long.

Joy is good for us, too. Barbara Fredrickson and her colleagues have been investigating the effect of positive emotions on coping and thinking. They've shown that positive emotions broaden our thinking about solutions to problems, and over time build our confidence and coping skills. Feelings of joy and contentment can quickly reverse the narrowing, defensive thinking style that's induced by stress. Over a period of weeks, people who experience more positive emotions become more creative in their coping skills and more resilient in the face of stress. And, in an example of a virtuous circle, better coping and greater resilience lead to more positive emotions. So it's vital that we be willing to take on our own minds and find ways to minimize the damage we do to ourselves, limit our self-defeating behavior, and learn that we don't need to deny, or intellectualize, or project our own emotions.

> IF YOU'RE FEELING BLOCKED OR STUCK, GO SEE A FUNNY MOVIE, OR FIND SOME OTHER SOURCE OF QUICK POSITIVE FEELINGS.

Let's return to defenses. You know that you may be using denial or dissociation when you are in an uncomfortable emotional situation. If you're a trauma victim, you probably have a deep unconscious fear that your own feelings are dangerous. In the next chapter, we're going to address how to deal with that fear. For now, how do you know when your defenses are operating? Table 1 is a list of some very common defenses with their definitions and their bite-you-in-the-butt effects: the ironic unintended negative consequences. See if you recognize yourself (or your spouse, your boss, or others close to you) here:

table 1. defense mechanisms

DEFENSE	DEFINITION	UNINTENDED NEGATIVE CONSEQUENCES
Denial	Simply not feeling your feelings, and thereby not seeing the consequences of the event (often your own behavior).	You drink. You spend money you don't have. You don't exercise. And so on; you may not feel the results now, but you will.
Dissociation	"Going away"—we experience a temporary lapse in consciousness with upsetting feelings or situations; or traumatic memories come as flashbacks without context or meaning.	You may not recognize when you are in real danger. You may not be able to assert yourself. Dissociation can also become a part of our character: spacey, inattentive, disconnected.
Projection	Attributing your own feelings to someone else.	Makes for difficult, if not crazy, interpersonal relations. Absolves you of responsibility. *I'm not angry; you're the one who's angry here, Buster!*

(*continued*)

DEFENSE	DEFINITION	UNINTENDED NEGATIVE CONSEQUENCES
Passive aggression	Getting others to express your own anger; inviting anger by being controlling, negligent, lazy.	If you keep making messes for others to pick up, but have no idea why they're upset with you, they will eventually give up on you.
Isolation of affect, intellectualization	Feelings are experienced in a very impersonal, intellectualized way.	If you express your feelings at all, it will be only through sudden outbursts. Leads to coldness, rigidity, loneliness.
Rationalizing	Using faulty reasoning to justify unacceptable behavior, attitudes, or beliefs—*Everyone does it. One more won't hurt.*	Makes you dishonest with yourself and morally lazy; supports bad habits. Besides that, more people see through you than you suspect.
Procrastination	Putting things off till the last minute gives you an excuse from really trying.	Leads to poor results, sense of being out of control, anger at the self, depression.
Somatization	Emotions are not felt in the conscious mind but expressed by the body.	Anger becomes back pain, the wish for attention becomes an incurable "illness." A quick way to alienate people that can also have very destructive effects on the body.

EXERCISE 3:
LEARNING YOUR OWN DEFENSES

Think about something you've been wanting for a while. It could be something you daydream about, like a trip abroad. Or maybe something that nags at you, like losing weight. Something you've been procrastinating about. The wish to reorganize your life, or spend more quality time with your spouse. For the purposes of this exercise, we want something that's just outside your grasp—not something impossible or terribly guilt-inducing, just something that you'd really like.

Now think about what's in the way. Listen to the voices in your head that are explaining why you can't have it. *I can't save money. It's too much trouble. There's no time. It's in my genes.*

Treat those voices with respect; they are important parts of you. But listen for the subtext, for the emotional message underneath. They are the voices of your defenses, and they are there to protect you. They're usually protecting you from the fear that goes with taking a risk, with trying to change. They're protecting your self-esteem because they don't make you face the fact that fear holds you back. If it's not fear, it may be an expression of anger. *Why should I be the one to change?* Your defenses may be protecting you from feeling grief or desire—*Those grapes are probably sour anyway.* There's a desire—something you wish for—and a defense, the reason you tell yourself why you can't have it. The defense helps take the itch out of the desire and may even drive it out of consciousness. It turns off the dopamine valve.

Once you've identified a defense, reflect on how it affects your life. Do you feel any of the unintended negative consequences from the defense mechanism table on pages 83–84? Does it distort your character, make you less of a person than you want to be?

Reflect on the feelings the defense protects you from—fear, grief, anger, desire. If you give yourself time, the memory of the first traumatic time you felt that way will bubble up to your consciousness.

Chances are good that it's related to a big disappointment in your life. You lost someone or something important to you, or didn't get something you really needed. Since then you've been protecting yourself by trying not to feel those feelings. But now, is there really anything to be afraid of? Or are you hurting yourself more by not going after what you want?

When you hear those voices in the future, rationalizing or projecting or denying, see if you can get to the feelings underneath—the fear, anger, grief. Then try your best to do what you know you should do without being mindlessly controlled by those unconscious emotions.

Some obviously self-defeating behavior serves the same purpose as defenses: to regulate emotions. If you ask people who cut, or binge, or purge, they are likely to tell you, *I was feeling too tense, and the cutting let it out*. Or else the opposite: *I was feeling dead inside, too depressed to live, and bingeing made me feel real again*. People who abuse alcohol or drugs, or gamble, usually have too many rationalizations and excuses to be so honest, but at bottom their habits serve the same purpose: to soothe them when upset, or excite them when bored or empty. Little bad habits like procrastination or overwork or overspending do just the same thing: bring excitement to a dull life. Television and Internet addiction and overeating can numb us out.

The big reason why self-defeating habits like those are so hard to break is that they are extremely effective at what they do, and no substitute behavior we try is going to be able to provide the same instantaneous control of scary feelings. If we diet, or abstain, or refrain from cutting, or turn off the TV, we're bound to feel that unpleasant state we've avoided for so long. In extreme cases, drugs can help us through the transition: a tranquilizer while going through alcohol withdrawal (though they're addictive, too), an antidepressant for eating disorders or self-mutilation. Researchers are at work on new drugs that are targeted directly at the dopamine system, the mechanism behind craving. But drugs are a temporary measure; eventually, we're going to have to turn around and face our demons.

Which turn out not to be demons at all, but only parts of ourselves, emotions we've avoided for so long that they've mutated in our subconscious into personal bogeymen.

max and stella

I have two standard poodles at home, Max and Stella. We got Max when he was just a puppy. He is a ninety-pound goofball who loves everyone, and expects everyone to love him. He approaches people with his head up, tail wagging, a smile on his face. He gets a lot of petting and love. When we have friends over, we sometimes have to put him outside, because he'll make himself a nuisance, wanting attention.

Stella is a different story. We got her at eight months, after she'd already been adopted out to one home (with her brother) but returned to the kennel—because they couldn't handle two dogs, we were told. But maybe Stella was difficult from birth, or maybe she was abused there. She's afraid of everyone and everything. Her immediate response to people at the door is a danger bark (which sounds, even to people who don't know dogs, very different from a friendly bark, and they feel nervous around her). If they come in, she'll skulk away and growl. The tragedy is, she wants attention. When we're alone, she's our lapdog. When we have guests, she appears at the edge of the room, then does an approach/avoidance dance with people that is the essence of neurotic conflict. If she decides someone is safe enough, she'll come close and sniff but is always ready to flee at any big gesture or loud noise.

Max and Stella see the world in completely different ways; they have different paradigms. "Paradigm" is a word from science that describes an overarching theory. Paradigms determine how we interpret the world, and often determine directly what we see. When astronomers held the paradigm that there were canals on Mars, they looked through their telescopes and saw canals. They didn't tell themselves there were canals there and then imagine them; their visual organs registered the presence of canals. When psychologists held the paradigm that depression required a certain level of maturity, they didn't see that children could become depressed. The legend is that when

Cortez sailed up to Mexico, the Native Americans couldn't see his ships. They saw strange men dressed in metal coming out of the water, but they couldn't see the ships that had brought them. Their minds had never been trained to conceive of large wooden objects in the water; they lacked a paradigm. Max's paradigm is that new people are friends; Stella's is that they're a threat.

The Interstates of Our Minds

Paradigms are the interstate highways of our minds. The quickest way from New York to Miami is I-95 all the way, about twenty hours of driving. But you miss Chesapeake Bay, the Shenandoah Valley, the Great Smokies, Savannah, and all the richness of the South. You get to eat at McDonald's the whole trip, and miss out on barbecue, fried green tomatoes, fried chicken, and grits. Paradigms are very efficient, but they can take all the richness and joy out of life. In a hurry-up world, we're always called on to use our quickest paradigms.

Human beings naturally create theories to help us make sense of the world. You probably have a theory that the sun will rise in the morning—it's a well-founded theory, based on lots of experience, but it's still a theory. You may have a theory that your mother-in-law hates you, or that your neighbor is a busybody, or that if you just owned a Harley-Davidson Fat Boy, you'd be a total stud. On the subject of happiness, you may believe that wealth will bring it (though I hope I've disabused you of that notion), or having many friends, or enjoying your vacations. Being logical creatures, we try to have theories that are internally consistent with each other, to organize our experience and help us make decisions. Everyone is a theoretician, and our theories, interwoven, become paradigms. A paradigmatic sequence of theories that depressed people often have is *Life stinks, life will always stink,* and *it's my own fault that life will always stink.* On the other hand, extraverts and optimists tend to believe that most people like them, that they will probably be successful in what they do, and that they will probably have fun at it. You can see already that paradigms like those are self-fulfilling prophecies. The depressive is more likely to have experiences that confirm his belief that life stinks, just because he believes it, while the extravert will find that most people do indeed like him because they have a good time with him.

Paradigms are meant to give us the power to predict the future and make sense of the past, help keep us out of danger and our nightmares under control. If we were perfectly logical creatures, we would always be changing our paradigms in light of experience.

When I'm kind and thoughtful with my wife, she's usually kind and thoughtful with me. I guess it would be good if I were always kind and thoughtful.

But we're not perfectly logical:

I tried to be kind and thoughtful today, but she was too busy with the kids to notice. Screw this "kind and thoughtful" crap. I'll show her! Our anger and hurt sneak in and make us forget that kindness and thoughtfulness usually pay off.

changing paradigms

Paradigms are hard to change, but it's possible. Racism and sexism are classic paradigms. Racism is still pervasive, but it's lost a lot of its vitriol, and it's no longer publicly accepted. There are still a lot of sexist attitudes toward women like Nancy Pelosi and Hillary Clinton, but those women and others have achieved more power than would have been conceivable fifty years ago. Social paradigms can change over time. Our own individual paradigms can change, too. That's what any kind of good psychotherapy does. That's what "life-changing" experiences do—serving in war, becoming a parent. It dawns on us that the interstate we drive every day is taking us some places we shouldn't go. Deeply held beliefs and values can change. We can change our paradigms deliberately, too, through some of the techniques we'll describe later. The real trick is learning to recognize when our own paradigms are interfering with our happiness.

Some time ago, I woke up one morning feeling lousy. I'd had way too much to eat and drink the night before—and that usually happened at least once a week, and had been going on for a long time. I beat myself up emotionally, as I always did—*You're weak, you have no self-discipline, you're doomed to be fat and you're on the way to alcoholism. Why the hell are you so self-destructive? Isn't it time to grow up?* It was extremely painful, as it always was.

As I took my morning shower, I made a resolution. *Starting today, I'm going on a program—diet, exercise, abstaining. I'll feel great.* Almost immediately,

I started feeling better. Instead of hating myself, I started feeling proud of the new me that was going to change all my old bad habits. It was a dramatic change in mood.

Then reality hit me for the first time. How many times had I been through exactly that sequence—a thousand? How many times had I really followed through? <u>I realized that I was simply making empty promises to myself in order to get relief from feeling so bad</u>. It was just a cheap and easy escape. I might stick with my reforms for a day or two, but they were not serious commitments, just rationalizations, a way of escaping from an unpleasant reality. By making promises to myself that I wouldn't follow through on, I was being truly self-destructive, undermining my own ability to believe in myself.

Since that day, I no longer lie to myself (at least, about this). I catch myself starting, and it doesn't work anymore. Because I take my word to myself a little more seriously, I'm careful about what I tell myself. And I think because I have more self-respect, my bad habits are less compelling. It's been a while since I've overindulged like that.

An especially pernicious paradigm, very common in today's culture, is that feelings are dangerous. Many of us have reached that unconscious conclusion, and we put a lot of effort into avoiding, denying, or controlling our own emotions. All of us were conditioned by our parents to believe that certain feelings or desires were unacceptable or ugly. Depressed parents may have inadvertently quashed excitement or exuberance in their child. A frequent subtle message is that too much pride or self-love is not okay. Anger is almost always condemned, though it's absolutely necessary in its place. Overly harsh or critical parents may have taught the child that ambition and goals are pointless. My own periodic overindulging comes from an effort to regulate emotion, to calm myself or soothe myself when things get rough inside my head. That kind of conditioning continues in adulthood, too. Our spouses, our bosses, our social groups are continually letting us know what they approve of and what they don't. In some work situations, open competition and ambition are encouraged, while in other groups, those feelings are frowned on. Some wives

do: LEARN YOUR BIASES: YOUR BASIC ASSUMPTIONS ABOUT THE WORLD, PEOPLE, AND YOURSELF.

will reinforce their husband's healthy sexual self-image, while others won't. Some husbands will support their wife's desire to succeed in her career; others will subtly put her down. When others disapprove of our feelings, we'll try not to feel that way. We can't help that; it's a reflex.

But when we try not to feel our feelings, we're in trouble. Feelings give us important information about the world, often on a deep unconscious level. There is a part of our brain that makes instantaneous evaluations of faces: safe or dangerous. Men who are unable to feel fear (because of brain tumors) trust everyone and get taken advantage of, while normal people register fear with their bodies before they are consciously aware of it. Those kinds of feelings are the vague hunches and gut feelings we really should pay attention to. We need to be able to feel anger, too, when we or our loved ones are being threatened. And of course, not being able to feel joyful or proud or sexy takes all the fun out of life.

Avoiding or overcontrolling or fearing feelings is a particularly vicious paradigm. We try to avoid the unpleasant feelings, but most of us can't do that without shutting down positive feelings, too. We become emotionally numb and stunted, cold and withdrawn. We may experience emotional storms that seem to come out of nowhere, merely because we've been stuffing so much that we have to let off steam. When that happens, we feel embarrassed and out of control, and our belief that feelings are dangerous is only reconfirmed. We may try to overmedicate ourselves with legal or illegal drugs, but that just leads us down the rabbit hole. The next chapter will present a plan for how to get emotional richness back into your life.

Our minds are truly wonderful things, but unfortunately life can hurt them, make them overly self-protective, make us fear or distrust our own feelings. Contemporary life requires us to be very organized, logical, competitive, on top of things. There's a lot of pressure to think quickly. Get on that interstate and zip by life at 75 mph. Unfortunately, doing so deprives us of essential information about ourselves and the world that we really must have in order to guide ourselves

don't: TRY TO CONTROL THE EXPERIENCE OF EMOTIONS.

wisely and find genuine happiness. In what's to come, we'll learn a lot about how to rediscover the lost pieces of our selves.

EXERCISE 4:
MY BIOGRAPHY

Here is an exercise to get you thinking about yourself from a fresh perspective. Spend a few minutes on it now, because we'll be referring to it later.

Take a pad of paper, notebook, or your word processing program. At the top of each page write your name. Then on the first page, write "Age 5"; on the second write "Age 10," then a new sheet of paper for each five-year increment up to your present age.

Now, for each age, simply describe yourself. Get into a mindful state. Think about yourself with compassionate curiosity, with affection and respect; this attitude is very important, and it may take some work to get yourself in that frame of mind. If the exercise becomes boring or taxing, put it aside for a while until you can regain affection and respect for yourself. As you write, since you can now look back and place yourself in the context of other five-year-olds, twenty-year-olds, and the like, think about what made you different. Were you curious, energetic, serious, shy, happy, worried? Write a little about what you liked to do—ride your bike, study, hang out with friends, cook dinner for the family, close a deal. Write a little about the most important people in your life at that time—your parents, teachers, lovers, bosses—and how they made you feel.

That's the hard part of the exercise, the part you should spend the most time on, but once you've completed it, I want you to go back to each age and answer some questions:

Was there trouble? Was there something that was making you unhappy or worried? What was making you think badly of yourself? Were you getting the message that you were unimportant, or that people didn't like you, or that you were incompetent? Did you think you were different because you were fat, or clumsy, or anxious? Were you feeling unsafe?

What would you tell yourself? What was life trying to tell you that you weren't getting? Now that you have the benefit of hindsight, how could you go back and help yourself with whatever the trouble was?

Think about your fears. Fear is the heart of the matter. Too many of us secretly fear that no one loves us, that our lives have no meaning, that we're incompetent, that we're only faking it and will be found out one day. In one sense, these fears are an artifact of the stress of contemporary life, like a dog in a learned-helplessness experiment, never knowing when he'll get shocked and without any means of control. Free-floating anxiety is the natural response. But in another sense, the content of those fears is very real, and we must eventually stop pretending and face our demons.

Think about what you didn't like about yourself. Most of the things that you're unhappy with yourself about now go back a long way. See if you can trace those things to their origin.

Think about what made you happy. Think of your most pleasant memories. Are they about family, love, accomplishment, discovery, excitement?

Now here's the point of the exercise. Look back at the development of fears over the course of your life. As you think about childish fears, think about their connection to what you're afraid of now. Like a figure-ground optical illusion, in which you can see either the vase or the two faces but can't see both at once, I'll bet that you can alternately dismiss your childish fears as silly or experience their continued hold over you in their current terrifying form. That's the conflict between the logical and the emotional parts of our brains. But I want you to develop a new attitude, one of tolerance for yourself.

The things you didn't like about yourself also have their childish roots: ideas about yourself that you learned from experiences—like being rejected for a date or chewed out by your father—that seemed all-important then but in the grand scheme of things are rather trivial.

Remember that you are thinking of yourself with affection and respect now. You can see how your fears developed when you were young—they weren't silly or childish; they had a real basis. You can't think of yourself with affection and dismiss that fear. Nor can you think of yourself with respect and be completely overwhelmed with fear in the present. You can learn to tolerate the fact that there are things that scare you, but that doesn't make you inadequate or bad. In so doing, you begin to heal the rift between how you think and how you feel about yourself.

Likewise, you can see that the things you don't like about yourself now have grown like weeds with the passage of time from things that you used to think were important, but really aren't. Probably they would not have grown except that you were paying too much attention to them. Like the splinter in your finger that burns and throbs; you're so aware of it, you think everyone can see it. When you look at it objectively, you're surprised how small it is.

Think about what made you happy. Are you cut off from some of those feelings now? How did that happen? Is there a way to bring them back into your life?

PART TWO

practicing happiness

There are three huge obstacles to happiness: the culture we've built for ourselves, our own brains, and our own minds.

- Our society, built on the premise that prosperity leads to happiness, has now had enough experience with prosperity to know that idea's a chimera, a mirage that leads us off only to the mall. We have it drummed into us that happiness just comes from buying the right things. So when we buy those things and are still unhappy, we blame ourselves. Besides that, we're being brainwashed into believing that overwork, multitasking, and debt are normal and desirable.
- Our brains, valuing survival over happiness, have all kinds of ways of tricking us into believing that if we just do what's good for the species, we'll be happy. Primarily that means making us believe that happiness comes from getting what we want. Getting what we want may give us some relief from craving, but that's only temporary, because very soon we'll be wanting something else.
- Our minds, trying to cope with a reality that is sometimes just too confusing and stressful to manage, distort that reality in all kinds of ways. This is natural and normal and helps get us through the night, but often those distortions lead to self-destructive or self-sabotaging behavior. We avoid risks, we comfort ourselves with drugs, we rationalize taking the easy way out when we know we'll regret it in the long run.

Clearly, there's a lot to do before we can be happy. The next chapter talks about developing what I call a new pilot, a new, more objective, less easily influenced orientation toward society, the whims of our brains, the automatic responses of our minds. We gain that new perspective primarily by learning to be mindful. Practicing mindfulness regularly is our best hope at resetting the happiness thermostat. Subsequent chapters focus in on more specific methods for decreasing unnecessary misery in our lives, and finding how to provide more joy and satisfaction. Then, after a brief detour about coping with unavoidable pain, we get to talk about that last, mysterious dimension of happiness, putting meaning into our lives.

a new pilot

Knowing intellectually that happiness isn't easy doesn't take away our deep faith that it should be. So we look around for someone to blame for this state of affairs, and 90 percent of us will settle on the usual suspect: ourselves.

EXERCISE 5:
YOUR DIRTY LAUNDRY

Take a piece of paper and make a list of everything that's wrong with you. All the parts of yourself that you like the least, that embarrass you or make you ashamed. Bad habits from nose-picking to yelling at the dog to things that actually hurt others. Weaknesses and character flaws like being anxious or letting others walk all over you. The things that make you grimace or give you a sudden sinking feeling when you think about them—social awkwardness; can't catch a fly ball; pimples; all the things you think are wrong with your body. Even things that other people have accused you of but you're not sure you're guilty of—but keep you wondering—your old girlfriend who said you were selfish; the work colleague who seems to think you don't pull your weight. Give this a good ten minutes; we want you to get everything out there. Please don't read the next paragraph until you've finished your ten minutes; we don't want to give the gimmick away.

Okay? Now think about how many years you've struggled with those issues. If you're like everyone else, most of them have probably been there since adolescence or early adulthood, when we first become socially aware enough to realize that we're different from others. Some have probably been there since childhood. In any case, these issues have been around a good long time.

Can you step back and simply listen to the voice that's criticizing you? Does it remind you of someone? Is it a family member or a character on TV or in the movies?

How many ways have you tried to change these things you dislike about yourself? Resolutions, therapy, self-help books, confession, pledges, groups, or drugs. How often have you tried? Does the thought of trying again seem unbearable, or are you still willing to fight?

Out of all your efforts, how often have you succeeded? Obviously not very many, or those things wouldn't still be on your list. You've probably tried everything you know. Are you willing to consider the idea that maybe you don't know how to change those things? That maybe the conventional powers of the mind aren't the right tools?

What if I suggest you stop fighting? What if the fighting is actually making the problem worse, or at least keeping it alive?

Put the list away for later. Put it somewhere where you won't think about it until you need to.

Steven Hayes, the architect of Acceptance and Commitment Therapy, makes a fascinating point. We have marvelous minds that are very good at solving problems, but some problems can't be solved—hurt, pain, loss, disappointment, rejection, illness, fear, anger, jealousy, to name a few. When we turn our minds loose on these things and get nowhere, we make matters worse for ourselves because we feel frustrated that we can't change them, and then feel inadequate and self-blaming. Depressed people, for instance, are naturally enough going to believe that thinking intensely about their problems will help their situation. It turns out that's exactly the wrong approach; all that rumination just perpetuates the feeling state of depression, so they feel worse, more immobilized and helpless. Most of us think, at times, *What's wrong with me? Other people don't seem to worry like I do. Other people seem to be in control of their lives. Other people don't yell at their kids.* We want to solve all the problems associated with merely being human, and we can't. We expect ourselves to master a world we simply weren't designed for, a world where we're always in fight-or-flight mode, and we can't do that, either. But we can't give up. This is the stuff of obsessions, of waking up at 4 A.M. and not being able to get back to sleep, spiraling downward in vague self-focused recriminations.

Other psychologists have come up with a concept they call the "fundamental attribution error." It means that when we think about events in our lives, we exaggerate our own importance in those events so that it's far out of proportion. We can't help this; it's automatic. It's only natural that we are the central characters in the stories we tell about our own lives. We don't like to think about the essential randomness and indifference of the universe, so we assume things have to do with us when maybe we're really just extras in a crowd scene. Someone is rude to us, and we wonder what we did to cause it. Maybe they're just thinking about their sick wife. There's an accident on the highway and traffic is backed up for miles; we can't help thinking mostly of our own inconvenience when we're stuck with thousands of others. So when we're thinking about a problem we can't solve—how to be happy, for instance—we inevitably assume that it's got to do with us and what we're doing or not doing. So we redouble our efforts at improving ourselves. That might just make matters worse. All that self-directed attention may not be good for us. It feeds what I call the Inner Critic, it sets us up against impossibly high standards, it puts blinders on us so that we're seeing only a small part of the world. It puts us on the defensive and piles on more character armor.

Picking on Yourself

Here's a relevant story about fear. When I was in my twenties and lived in Chicago, I developed a fear of high buildings and bridges. I was very depressed and had some real self-destructive impulses, and that was the seed of the phobia. But as everyone who's ever had one knows, a phobia takes on a life of its own. I spent years in therapy and analysis getting help for my depression but getting nowhere with my fear of heights. It was the source of great shame for me—and some realistic fears about my future because as I was becoming more successful, there were more and more occasions where I was expected to go to meetings or work in tall buildings. On such occasions, I would be tortured with anxiety and indecision and obsession for days in advance. *Is there a way to get out of this? How many tranquilizers should I take? What if they don't work? What if I have to run from the room? I'll never live it down.*

I found a serendipitous solution, in the form of a great job offer out in the countryside in Connecticut. As we drove across country, I planned the route to avoid bridges as much as possible. After we got here, with no tall buildings and no bridges, <u>I wasn't given the opportunity to fear, and to hate myself because of my fear.</u> I had a couple of years of doing well at my job and not facing the daily degradation of feeling like a wimp. After a while, when we went to New York, I avoided the Empire State Building, but I found I could enjoy looking out the seventh-floor window where we stayed. And that's about where things have remained. I'm fine now with bridges and going up about fifteen stories, but if I go higher, I'm going to get vertigo—and I can live with that. I'm not going to beat myself up anymore just because my brain hiccups at precipices. I stopped picking at myself, and I healed.

That is the way it is with most of the things you put on your list of what you believe is wrong with you. You struggle mightily with them, and they get stronger. Hercules had to wrestle the giant Antaeus, the son of Gaia, mother Earth. Each time Hercules threw him to the ground, his mother would only make him stronger. We make our merely human weaknesses seem like giants because we devote so much of our mental energy to them. We reinjure ourselves in a vain attempt to rush the healing process. Hayes is saying the same thing that Genesis, Freud, and the Buddha pointed out—it is our own minds that cause us most of our misery. Our unwillingness to accept that things can't be the way we want them to be, and our fruitless attempts to do the impossible.

In all my thirty years of doing therapy, it has <u>never happened</u> that therapy eliminates someone's fears, self-doubts, self-consciousness, whatever, and then they go out and change their lives. That's what everyone wants, but they don't get it. Instead, they start to change their lives, and their fears and doubts turn out not to be so crippling. They get something out of talking about their fears with me; they feel a lot less shame, they understand their issues from a much more objective, less critical point of view, and that makes the fear more manageable, but it doesn't totally go away. They have to face their fears in real life, and then they start to feel real relief. The hard truth is that we can't do anything to change our feelings directly. Feelings follow behavior. We can do something different, and then our feelings will probably change. We can't afford to wait for motivation; <u>that</u> fairy godmother doesn't visit those who won't get up on their feet.

the inner critic

Think back to your list of everything that's wrong with you. Remember the voice in your head that was doing all the talking? That's the Inner Critic. Most of us, when we're unhappy, are bouncing around between two parts of ourselves. The Inner Critic is the voice that's constantly judging you and finding you wanting. It's the voice that gives you a disproportionate share of the blame when things go wrong. It's the voice that makes mountains out of molehills. *What's wrong with you? There's nothing to be scared of, don't be such a baby! Why haven't you started exercising yet? You can't stick to anything!* Sound familiar? It's something most of us hear whenever we're feeling stressed.

The other part of the self is busy defending against the attacks of the Inner Critic. Call it the Timid Defender. It wants to silence the Critic, but it can't, because it uses the usual habits of the mind—denial, rationalization, dissociation. Alcohol and drugs. Shopping and overeating. It has us trying to escape or forget about the Critic, but that works for only a little while, because while we're escaping or forgetting, we're giving the Critic more ammunition. *You idiot, pretending to be something you're not. Trying to drown your sorrows. You can't get rid of me that easily!*

And that is how unhappiness persists. We blame ourselves far too much, and make ourselves more miserable. Then we defend ourselves ineffectively, and perpetuate a vicious circle. We have to try something radically different. That's what therapy does. I don't turn off the Inner Critic and I don't strengthen that Defender; instead, I help people detach from this struggle. When people are beating themselves up, I suggest they're being too hard on themselves. When they're in defensive mode, I help them face what they're afraid of.

A good friend of mine uses the phrase <u>compassionate curiosity</u> to describe the ideal therapist's attitude toward the patient. We begin therapy with a much more compassionate, kind, understanding stance toward the patient and his problems than the patient has himself. And we are curious, in a calm, unafraid way—we want to understand how things got to be so bad, and we assume that by fearlessly facing reality we will help the patient find relief from his distress. Compassionate curiosity is the attitude most of us need to apply to ourselves as well. What a change that would be for almost everyone I know! That battle between the Inner Critic and the Timid Defender is much like the way inconsistent parents treat their children. When the Defender is in charge, we indulge and spoil ourselves, we let ourselves off the moral hook, we make promises to ourselves we know we won't keep. But that Inner Critic is still there, waiting for our defenses to slip—as they almost always do—always judging us, finding that we don't measure up. We vacillate between spoiling ourselves and punishing ourselves. And, as with children who are raised that way, we end up frightened and confused, with no self-esteem and a lot of self-hate. Compassion replaces all that with patience, gentleness, love, grace, mercy, concern. It suggests giving up judging and replacing that with empathy, a willingness to feel everything that the self feels, without fear but with confident strength.

IT'S TIME TO LEAVE BEHIND THE INNER CRITIC AND THE TIMID DEFENDER.

Curiosity suggests a little cool detachment from the emotional heat, a desire to understand objectively why we feel what we feel, why we do what we do—especially when it's troublesome or self-defeating. *Why did I get angry just then? What's making me so blue today?* We look at ourselves, not to torture ourselves, not to give ammunition to the Critic, not with desperation for a quick fix, but with compassion, sincere interest, and the belief that there are answers that make sense. <u>No matter how nonsensical our behavior, no matter how odd our feelings, there are always reasons—and knowing the truth will help set us free.</u> We look a little deeper than usual, with more objectivity, and we don't just slap ourselves on the wrist and make an empty promise to do better next time. *Why? What's bothering me? Why am I afraid to look?* We understand that our feelings are just human; they won't destroy us or drive us crazy. Most likely, they are tapping on our shoulder, trying to tell us something important.

The Inner Moe

When we're bouncing around between the Inner Critic and the Timid Defender, who's at the controls? Who's running our lives, making our decisions? We have the Three Stooges up there in our heads, Moe slapping us around, Larry whining excuses. Curly, the id in this metaphor, is the one who <u>feels,</u> who lusts and craves things and gets us in trouble in the first place. Nobody's in charge, and the plane is yawing and swooping all over the sky, never getting anywhere and always in danger of crashing. We need a wise, calm, resourceful pilot to step in and get rid of these characters—a Lincoln, a King, a Churchill. Atticus Finch, Ma Joad. Yet we need to find this person within ourselves. That's where mindfulness comes in.

mindfulness

Mindfulness is not by any means a new idea with me, but now it's all the rage in psychotherapy, meditation, and alternative medicine circles. A recent survey of clinicians found that they ranked mindfulness the third-most common psychotherapy approach—a remarkable growth, considering that it was just barely on the scene a few years ago. Indeed, it runs the risk of becoming a great idea robbed of its value by overuse. So let me try to be very clear about how I'm using the term. First of all, there is *mindful living*, which means deliberately cultivating a new attitude toward your thoughts, feelings, and experience—an attitude of openness, compassion, and objectivity; a deliberate effort not to be guided by old habits of thinking and behaving but to see each experience in its uniqueness. Then there is _mindfulness meditation_, which is a specific kind of meditation practice, used both as a means of achieving mindful living and for other benefits. We'll get to meditation in a little while; for now, let's focus on mindful living.

If you don't know what mindfulness is, you surely know its evil twin, mindlessness. It's that frantic, hypervigilant frame of mind that has us always rushing to cross to-dos off our lists, in a hurry, not listening, not concentrating, distracted, not fully present. Mindfulness is being present, but also detached. It means fully experiencing your thoughts, feelings, and experiences without being distracted by irrational worries and fears. It means looking at yourself with compassionate curiosity, an attitude of trust and love that still acknowledges you can be a mystery to yourself.

Mindfulness, to me, means using your mind in a new way, consciously and deliberately. It's turning the observational powers of the mind on itself, looking with compassion and curiosity at what's going on inside the head, and then turning the same skills on the world. It means becoming more observant and deliberate; more thoughtful about reacting to emotions and impulses; more curious, more ready to look beneath the surface, not so hasty about jumping to conclusions; kinder, more patient, more tolerant of ourselves and others. Ellen Langer, who has written about and researched mindfulness for years, calls it noncategorical, creative thinking: escaping from our paradigms into a heightened state of involvement.

In one of her experiments, Langer gave a group of nursing home residents a plant for their rooms. Half of them were told to take total responsibility for the plant: its feeding, watering, pruning. They were also encouraged, by the way, to participate actively in decision-making regarding their care, their medication, and the setup of their rooms. The other half of the group were told that they could rely on the staff to take care of the plant, just as they could rely on the staff to take care of them. Eighteen months later, twice as many of the second group, who ceded responsibility to the staff, had died. And among the living, those who were taking care of their own plants were more active, vigorous, and social. Their physical health had actually improved in the interval, while the other group's had deteriorated. Langer has written extensively, more than I can go into here, on how to modify our environment to stimulate mindfulness, creativity, and curiosity; I highly recommend her books.

do: WATER YOUR OWN PLANT—BE AS RESPONSIBLE FOR YOUR OWN LIFE AS POSSIBLE.

One of the key ingredients of mindfulness is sometimes called "metacognitive awareness"—the ability to see that all the thoughts and feelings in your mind are to some extent just a passing parade, which you can observe from a little distance, without getting caught up in it. You develop a part of your mind that doesn't get swept away by the urgency, that hangs back and keeps the larger picture of yourself, your goals and values, in mind. I have suggested to patients that they think of distressing thoughts or impulses as an old-fashioned steam locomotive. You're standing on the platform as it comes roaring into the station, huge, loud, whistles blowing and steam escaping. It's an overwhelming experience <u>but you're standing on the platform and you have some choice about whether you get on the train or not.</u> It may be that all your life you have just gotten on the train without thinking about it, but practicing mindfulness skills makes it easier and easier for you to deliberately decide whether or not to let your thoughts and feelings run away with you.

It must be said that many unhappy people are excruciatingly "mindful" about their thoughts, feelings, and so forth, but in a negative way. I'm talking about people who ruminate excessively about their experiences, digging as if for lice at every remembered incident, raking themselves over the coals: *How could I have said such a stupid thing? Was the dress I wore appropriate? Did I eat too much? Did I drink too much? Did people notice?* That kind of obsessive self-consciousness is a hallmark of depression and hangovers, and is not mindful at all. It is not deliberate, but automatic—in fact, almost uncontrollable. Mindfulness is both deliberate and gentle; it assumes compassion and avoids judgment.

Mindfulness has a paradoxical quality. It means being deeply in touch with your experience, both external events and what's going on in your mind, but at the same time, it means being a little detached from your experience;

slow to be swept away by it. It means seeing things clearly, as they are, with no defenses, illusions, wishes, or pretensions. But it also means viewing yourself and your experience with compassion and kindness. It means suspending judging. It means learning that judging is a destructive mental habit, a quick way of classifying experiences into blacks and whites that robs life of its richness and subtlety.

LOOK AT YOUR
THOUGHTS,
NOT FROM YOUR
THOUGHTS.

Regular meditation practice is extremely helpful at developing a mindful attitude, but it's not the only way. Spiritual experiences, feeling awe at beauty or nature, take us out of ourselves and make us see the world differently. Deep, intimate conversation where we get to see things from another's perspective—and learn new things about our own—is a mindful experience. Regular writing, whether in one's own journal or writing creatively, requires you to examine your experience in a deeply mindful way. Play can be mindful as well, and participatory experiences like music and dancing have the ability to shake us out of our moods. Learning to stretch your perception, as you do when you learn to paint or draw. Psychotherapy, done right, helps us develop a more mindful attitude. Just learning about the principles of mindfulness will help. A problem, though, is that experiences like these tend to be only occasional, and mindfulness requires practice. If we truly want to rewire our brains, we have to keep going back to the psychic gym and do a lot of reps in order for new circuits to form and replace the old destructive habits that keep us miserable. Meditation is the gym.

EXERCISE 6:
A TASTE OF MINDFULNESS

Try this. It only takes a minute. Get into a comfortable seated position, put your hands in your lap, close your eyes, and take a few deep breaths. Now extend your left forefinger and touch it with your right forefinger. Explore the surface of the left forefinger using the right. You will notice the ridges and whorls on its surface, and you will get a mental image of its location in space. You may "see" your left finger in your mind's eye.

Now stop and reverse the process. Explore your right forefinger with your left. You will notice the same things about your right forefinger, and get the same mental image of it.

Before you read on and start thinking, take a few moments to let this experience settle in.

Now consider this: Why can't you notice the ridges of the right forefinger when you are using it to explore the left? Why don't you develop the same mental image of the right that you do with the left? And then, when you switch fingers, why does your focus stay on the finger that is being felt, rather than the one doing the feeling?

How in the world did you do that? Somehow you "decided" that one finger was to be the active agent of feeling, and the other was to be the passive object of being felt. You can reverse their roles, but you can't do both at once. Your "decision" affects what you perceive, very definitively and dramatically.

Now, explore your mind with your mind. Let your attention wander over the surface content of your thoughts and feelings. In the same way you decided that one finger was to be the object of exploration, make your mind the subject of mental exploration. Pay attention to what it's doing. What is it thinking about? What is it aware of? What is its mood? How alert is it?

The heart beats, the stomach digests, the brain thinks; don't think about what it's thinking, rather hold it in your mind's eye as it thinks.

This is a form of mindfulness, of seeing our own mental processes with a little bit of distance, objectivity, and curiosity without getting swept away by those processes.

(Adapted with permission from *Undoing Perpetual Stress* by Richard O'Connor. © Berkley Press, 2005)

At this point, you may be thinking to yourself, *Mindfulness seems pretty simple; I just need to adjust my thinking a little.* Or you may think it sounds so simple that it's hard to believe it will have any real effect on your stress and confusion. Maybe not taking it seriously is one of the reasons so few people can do it. Because the truth is, mindfulness is a difficult art that requires us to develop a high degree of skill in mental balance and coordination. But so does juggling, and that can be learned in three months. There's an AA saying: *Just because it's simple doesn't mean it's easy.* You're going to run right into what therapists call <u>resistance,</u> the stubborn tendency we have to cling to our problems despite all evidence that we'd better change our ways. Resistance comes from fear, but it gets manifested as a thousand different distractions, obstacles, and arguments against doing what is good for you. If you seriously sit down and try to meditate for a few days, or if you simply keep reminding yourself to be mindful, you will find that it's not as easy as it looks. You will want to stop. You'll keep forgetting to practice. Your brain will always be trying to lead you down a different path. Mindfulness brings us smack up against a lifetime of bad habits and makes us face fears and other feelings that are extremely powerful despite the fact that we're unconscious of them. Practice is essential. You're going to be challenging years of what life has taught you about how to deal with your emotions.

EXERCISE 7: MINDFULNESS IN DAILY LIFE, OR GETTING UNDER YOUR OWN DEFENSES

Be sure you get some contemplative time every day—in deliberate meditation, in walking, in a hot bath—somewhere there are no distractions. As you practice the following steps, cultivate an attitude of compassionate curiosity toward yourself.

- Monitor your associations. Learn to develop an observing eye that notices where your thoughts go when you're not paying attention. When you're driving, or walking, or falling asleep, does your mind dwell on successes or failures? Do you keep returning to instances of shame or humiliation? Do you constantly worry about whatever is the next item on your mental list? Are you afraid to think too deeply about the future? Those are good clues to what is frightening you.

- Pay attention to your dreams. Keep a pad of paper by your bedside and write down whatever you can remember when you first wake up. Look for themes. Are you lost, or trapped? Fighting or fleeing? Is there a childhood scene that keeps reappearing? Dreams like these often represent your attempts to solve a problem that's been pushed into your unconscious.

- Look for patterns in your life. Do you always feel exploited? Disappointed? Rejected? Do your relationships always end badly? Do you keep finding overly critical bosses? Maybe some of this is baggage you carry with you.

- Where does it hurt? Sometimes there is a symbolic meaning to physical symptoms. Digestive problems may mean you're trying to swallow something you shouldn't. A backache can mean you're carrying too heavy a load. Chronic fatigue can be a way of saying you're scared and overwhelmed. Breathing problems may mean someone is cutting off your air supply.

- Talk to your intimates. Are there things your best friend would tell you if you gave permission? Are there ways you keep shooting yourself in the foot, which others can see but you can't?

- Look back at your autobiography. At what point did things start to go wrong? When did you begin to be afraid, or feel that you were different or defective? What was going on around you at that time? Were your parents having trouble, or was there trouble in school? Were you ill? Did something harm you or scare you and then you got no help for it?

- If you were a character in a novel or a movie, what would be your role? Who would play you? Would it be a comedy, a tragedy, a romance, an adventure? Would you be the best friend, the victim, the comic relief? What's in the way of you being the hero or heroine in your own story?

- If you notice patterns or issues that may be causing you unnecessary misery, talk about them with a trusted friend. The act of putting problems like this into words helps you focus on them in a more organized way than simply remembering. Ask your friend to listen, to ask smart questions, to give you feedback as appropriate, but refrain from giving advice. (A good therapist would be even better than a friend in this role.)

mindfulness meditation

For those who can take mindfulness a step further and practice regular meditation, the news about mindfulness potentially goes far beyond the obvious benefits of clear thinking, wise decision-making, and emotional centeredness. New research is showing that mindfulness meditation practice actually rewires our brains and builds new neural pathways. It promises to heal the damage of stress so that we are able to experience a greater degree of pleasure. Mindful meditation practice affects how the brain deals with emotions, especially in the prefrontal cortex (PFC), which many brain scientists consider the actual physical location of our self-awareness. Meditation practice results in an increase in activity in that prefrontal area, where the brain processes positive feelings and controls negative feelings, an increase that lasts even when we're not meditating. This area of the brain contains a set of neurons that control messages of fear and anger from the amygdala. It seems that the more we practice this effect, the easier it gets. We learn to control disturbing emotions like we learn to ride a bike: After a while, we don't have to think about it; it just happens.

The Benefits of Meditation

Jon Kabat-Zinn's Mindfulness-Based Stress Reduction Program, a program combining education and discussion with daily meditation, has been shown to have some remarkable benefits both for the mind and body after only eight weeks. (Readers can find a program in their area through the University of Massachusetts Web site, http://www.umassmed.edu/cfm/mbsr.) It helps significantly with many stress-related disorders, including major depression, anxiety disorders, chronic pain, bulimia, psoriasis, mixed neurosis, and fibromyalgia. Even among people who seem "normal," an eight-week MBSR program has produced the kinds of shift in balance between brain hemispheres that are reliably associated with more positive mood. (See page 120, "The Left/Right Ratio.") It boosts the immune response both among healthy volunteers and cancer patients. Its practice improves interpersonal relationships and an overall sense of well-being. A mindfulness-based program of treatment for depression has been proved to be much more effective at preventing relapse than conventional treatment.

All those benefits don't happen without changes in consciousness. The goal of practicing mindfulness meditation and developing those skills is to achieve the state that Buddhists call "wise mind"—an integration of the logical, emotional, and intuitive minds—a detachment from endless striving. With problems as diverse as chronic pain, anxiety, and depression, mindfulness teaches the patient to sit with, observe, and experience the feelings while resisting the urge to seek immediate relief. This is similar to the process psychologists call <u>extinction,</u> which means breaking the connection between a stimulus (distress) and a response (seeking relief). It's not simply that the circuits linking the sight of a Dairy Queen and the feeling of hunger have fallen into disuse; instead, a new circuit pairing the Dairy Queen with self-control has been formed.

In meditation, a new brain circuit is developed that takes what Daniel Goleman calls the "high road" through the logical brain and overrides the "low road" connection from the amygdala directly to mindless relief seeking. We've gotten off one footpath and shifted to another, and the more often we use the new one, the easier it becomes. Attention is the key. Focusing on bodily sensations (the breath, posture, the belly, and so on) shifts

do: GIVE MEDITATION A GOOD TRY.

attention away from the verbal chatter that usually fills our minds. That apparently leads to greater integration of the left and right hemispheres, the "logical" brain and the "creative" brain, as shown by actual structural changes in the connecting areas of meditators' brains. Let me repeat that: <u>Mindfulness practice changes the brain.</u>

If you're ready to try meditation, here is my stripped-down technique. If you want to try it, see if you can do it every day for a week. You need to give it at least that much time to see if you might consider doing it regularly. Then keep trying. If you can get up to a half hour, five days a week, you're doing enough to start experiencing the benefits.

EXERCISE 8:
A SIMPLE MINDFULNESS MEDITATION

Find a quiet place where you will not be interrupted for a half hour or more. Turn off the phones, the TV, the stereo. If you have pets, make sure they won't distract you. I find it helpful to turn on a fan, both for the cooling effect and for the quiet noise.

Sit in a comfortable position. If you want to sit on the floor, it helps to have a thin pillow under your butt. Tuck your feet under your knees, but don't strain. Sit upright, with your back straight. Let the weight of your head fall directly on your spinal column. If you want to sit in a chair, try to put your feet flat on the floor, hands in your lap or at your sides. Again, sit upright, with your back straight. Posture is important, because it helps keep you from falling asleep.

Close your eyes, and start to breathe slowly and deeply. Not so deeply that you strain yourself, just comfortable. As you breathe, you may find it helpful to focus on a word or phrase, timing it to your breathing. "In . . . Out." You can change this to suit your mood. When I'm fighting craving, I think "Wave . . . Rock." The waves are very powerful but the rock remains. Other times I like, "I am here . . . I am home." You will find phrases that are good for you.

Focus on your breathing. As other thoughts or feelings come to mind, let them pass, and return your attention to your breathing. Visualize these distracting thoughts and feelings as bubbles rising to the surface of a calm pool of water. They rise and burst, the ripples spread out and disappear. The pool remains calm. Return your attention to your breathing.

Don't judge. Don't try to do it right; just try to do it every day. Remember that the distracting thoughts and feelings are the normal noise in your brain. It takes practice and skill to get in touch with the quietness underneath.

When I'm preparing for meditation, and when I feel restless, I like to remember the perspective of Anh-Huong Nguyen, a Vietnamese follower of Thich Nhat Hanh: "If you have a fussy baby, do you shout at the baby? Do you get angry at it? Do you shake it? No—you build a cradle for the baby." That's what we have to deliberately allow ourselves to practice: to treat ourselves with care and concern. That's also what meditation does for our restless, anxious minds; it builds a structure we can feel safe in.

You will find yourself frequently distracted by intrusive thoughts—sometimes nagging thoughts about chores you have to do, sometimes memories that may be pleasant or unpleasant. You may also be distracted by emotions—primarily impatience and anxiety. Remember that these intrusive thoughts and emotions are the normal noise your brain makes because it's so used to functioning under stress. Even the most adept meditators can still get hijacked this way. It may help to visualize, for instance, putting those thoughts into a box or on a list that you can look at later. Or simply say to yourself, "No thank you." Don't get upset with yourself because you do get distracted; don't tell yourself you're not doing it right, simply return to the focus on your breath. Judging yourself is another habit, one you can put aside while you're meditating.

If you get distracted, or get upset, try to cultivate the attitude of compassionate curiosity. Approach your frustration with an attitude of openness, of understanding, of friendly interest. "I wonder what could be going on here?" rather than "I can't do this right."

Twenty minutes is fine to start with. (Less time doesn't have much effect.) When you are ready to stop, open your eyes. Stay seated for a few moments while you appreciate the calm state you are in.

If you have to use an alarm, make it something quiet, not jarring. You can get a tape or CD with nothing on it but temple bells at regular intervals; it's much nicer than any alarm clock. Or you can program the timer on your cell phone or PDA to alert you with your choice of sounds.

Try to meditate at roughly the same time every day, but don't do it when you're overtired or overstressed or have just eaten a big meal. One of the best ways to achieve lasting health and happiness is to give yourself an hour every day devoted to exercise and meditation. I very much enjoy meditation while I am cooling down from exercise.

(Adapted with permission from *Undoing Perpetual Stress* by Richard O'Connor. © Berkley Press, 2005.)

There are many other forms of meditation. Many people, especially those with anxiety or muscular tension, like the "body scan" method. There is a "mindfulness of pain" meditation, and a walking meditation. A favorite for many is the "loving-kindness" meditation, in which you first focus on the feeling you had as a child when someone deeply loved you, then focus on returning that feeling to the other person, then imagine directing that feeling to the whole world. Buddhanet.net will direct you to many ways of meditation from the Buddhist tradition. Christian Centering or Contemplative Prayer follows much the same method, though instead of the breath you are advised to contemplate a sacred word. Whether meditation brings you closer to God or closer to your true self doesn't matter, from my point of view; either way, it works to make you happier, wiser, and in better control.

don't: JUDGE.

Meditation practice isn't necessarily fun. One of the first things you'll notice is how much you're judging your experience and yourself. *This is boring. My back hurts. I must not be doing this right. Meditation isn't for me.* Instead of acting on those judgments, just notice how your brain is always judging. Judging is your frontal lobe, the "higher" mental center, trying desperately to hold on to control, while your focus on the breath is uncoupling it. One of the chief principles of mindfulness is to learn to suspend judging. When we judge, we're putting simplistic, black-and-white labels on our experience—*this is good, that's bad; he's a jerk, she's fantastic.* Judging leads to categorical, rigid, mindless thinking. But don't judge yourself for judging; it's a hard habit to break. Just notice it, and try to let it go. Try to be amused by it. *There I go again, like a doorman at a fancy club: You're in; you're out. My poor frontal lobe must be really scared at the idea of losing control.*

Sometimes when I meditate, I think of the little pond in my backyard. It's a very peaceful scene, with a small fountain, water lilies and frogs, and lots of sunlight. When I start thinking about ways to improve the pond, I know I'm having trouble focusing. *Get a better filtration system, fix the stones around the edge so they stop falling in, change the plantings.* That's the problem-solving mode our minds have been trained to be in—even to the extent of creating problems when there are none. My pond is fine as it is, but my caveman mind is always striving. My insecure mind is always trying to make things better. My consumer mind is always looking for something new. Sometimes just being still is a very difficult thing.

Meditation isn't easy, either. Paul Fleishman, a very experienced meditator, says, "Trying to focus on the breath is like trying to balance on a beach ball." You may never feel you are "good" at meditation, and that doesn't matter at all. After a couple of years of practice, I still usually spend the first ten minutes of

don't: FIX IT.

a session thinking about what I'm going to do as soon as I'm through. It takes that long for the breathing practice and focus to penetrate beyond the busyness of my brain. Sometimes I still have sessions when I feel unable to focus. I just try to keep in mind that my brain is growing new connections even if I'm not aware of it.

Meditation may achieve most of its effect because it is primarily practice in learning how to pay attention. As we'll see in Chapter 7, it's what we pay attention to that determines how the brain grows. Meditation makes us more adept at focusing the spotlight of our attention, so that it becomes easier for us to concentrate on joys and distract ourselves from needless worry. We develop the ability to recognize that the contents of our thoughts are not our selves—and so it becomes easier for us to disengage from distressing thoughts. Without realizing it, we become better masters of our own brains.

Don't expect miracles. Don't expect brilliant flashes of insight; don't expect that your mood will be suddenly brighter; don't expect that all your bad habits will just drop away, or that you can now solve all of life's problems. You can expect that you will make progress on these things slowly and gradually. Remember that it takes three months of daily practice for juggling skills to be etched into your brain; give meditation practice the same amount of time.*

A note of caution: It's not unusual to experience an "altered state" sometimes when meditating. You may feel time stopping, or temporarily lose your sense of identity, or feel intense emotions, perceptions, or insights that seem completely new to you. Try not to be alarmed; most people find that the calmness that comes with mindfulness helps them merely be welcoming and curious about those experiences. But some people, especially PTSD sufferers, may not easily be able to calm themselves after something like this. If that is you, then it would be very helpful for you to find a therapist experienced in meditation techniques to help you past that barrier.

On the other hand, most people practice meditation without ever experiencing an altered state; don't feel shortchanged if you don't.

Two excellent resources to help learn mindfulness meditation at home are:

- Jon Kabat-Zinn's *Wherever You Go, There You Are,* along with his *Guided Mindfulness Meditation* CD.
- *Insight Meditation,* a kit of CDs, workbook, and study cards, by Sharon Salzberg and Joseph Goldstein.

---

* By the way, I keep saying that experience changes the brain, so I believe it's possible that training oneself to be mindful, without practicing meditation, can result in the same kinds of brain changes that meditation practice does. But there's no direct research evidence for that, and meditation is the kind of disciplined, repetitive practice that we know can rewire us. So take a positive attitude about developing mindful awareness without meditation, but remember you may be missing out on the most effective way to get there.

If you have the opportunity to go on a weekend retreat, or take a course with an experienced practitioner, go for it. Participating as part of a group, with a real-life guide, adds a whole other dimension to the experience.

mindfulness and Buddhism

We tend to associate mindfulness with Buddhism, and indeed, current mindful meditation methods are derived from the 2,500-year-old Vipassana tradition. But a contemplative, meditative practice can be found in almost any religion.

However, the closer you look at Buddhism, the less it seems like a religion in the Western sense, and the more it seems like a psychology or philosophy. Buddhism is interested in finding the truth, and in doing so empirically, which makes it very congenial to science. There is no belief in divine revelation; there is no divinity. There is very little telling us how we ought to behave. Sin is not in the vocabulary; rather, ignorance is seen as the chief source of misery.

Buddhism teaches that suffering comes from the illusion that things are permanent and can be relied on for happiness. Suffering comes from trying to hold on to things as they are or as we want them to be, not accepting that we are in a continual state of change. Buddhism focuses on living in the present "skillfully"—free from desire and other negative mind states. There is little talk about a next life, or divine beings. Instead, you'll find lots of practical advice, along with the familiar Zen *ko'ans*, or paradoxes, designed to make you think mindfully.

Karma is a Buddhist doctrine popularly understood as a vicious circle. Your present good or bad luck is at least partly a result of good or bad acts that you did in the past. The concept of <u>skillful action</u> gives you a way out of the vicious circle, because you have the power in the present to change how you respond to your bad luck. Karma really means that skillful action in the present can change what happens to you in the future; it is more like a spiral of growth than a vicious circle. "Skillful" in this sense means ethical and compassionate: It's skillful to speak the truth, to respect the rights of others, to rise above envy and competition, to wish well for others, to be mindful. If you can do those things, it's quite likely your future will be happier than that of someone who lies, cheats, and gives in to jealousy. Calling those qualities skills emphasizes that they are not inborn traits, but rather habits that we have to learn and practice. Although practice may be difficult right now, it makes life easier in the future. That's good karma.

There is a fundamental difference between Buddhism and the Western view of man. Westerners tend to think of man as perfectible. *If I'm good enough, I'll go to heaven. If I'm rich enough, I'll be happy.* Even in psychotherapy, we tend to believe that if we heal the trauma, or see the insight, we can end misery. In Buddhism, the fundamental problem is just that yearning for perfection, and the refusal to see that yearning itself is the source of misery. If we accept that our struggle is not to get more, but to want less, we can reduce misery. Buddhism doesn't suggest that there is any other life than this one or that there are forces more powerful than humans. Instead, we are here alone and this is our one chance. Buddhism suggests a method for living in a world of fear and pain, nothing more than a method, but one that has had some success for more than 2,500 years.

the left/right ratio

Richard Davidson, a leading brain researcher, has created a lot of interest with his observation that Tibetan monks, skilled in meditation, are the happiest people on earth. That's because they have the highest left–right ratio of anyone he's studied, and that ratio goes up further when they're meditating. What's that ratio? There is good evidence that certain little areas in the right and left hemispheres in the brain, known as the prefrontal cortex (PFC), are responsible for a great deal of our relative happiness and misery. More activity in the left PFC?—happy! More in the right?—sad! People who smile when watching an amusing film clip have more brain activity in the left prefrontal cortex. When we're asked to think of sad events, the corresponding area on the right lights up. If you're afraid of public speaking, and made to give a speech, the right PFC lights up like the Fourth of July. This left–right difference is true even for babies. A sweet taste lights up the left side of the brain, a bit of lemon juice the right. At ten months, babies already have some temperamental differences. Those who tend to have more activity on the right side of the brain are more likely to cry when Mother leaves than those who are more active on the left. In the left hemisphere, this area seems to be a central processing point for good feelings, and when activity there is suppressed, people feel depressed. The corresponding area on the right is a center for bad feelings, and when it's suppressed, people feel good. People have their individual left–right ratios that are pretty stable over time, and a high left–right ratio corresponds to many different measures of positive emotion and happiness.

It's not only happiness, but also health that seem to be affected by this left–right ratio. Apparently, the more activity in the left PFC, the better your immune response. At least, that's what Melissa Rosenkranz found when she injected healthy volunteers with flu vaccine. Those who were more right-brained produced less flu antibody in response to the injection; their immune responses weren't as effective as their left-brain cohorts.

Davidson and some colleagues developed an eight-week mindfulness training program for Westerners and found that, at the end, graduates have a higher left–right ratio that stays with them months later. The meditators reported less anxiety and fewer mental and physical symptoms of stress. Their immune responses also improved.

So meditation practice leading to a mindful attitude may change that left–right ratio in the brain. We don't know yet if other ways of cultivating a mindful attitude may have the same effect. But this seems to be a vital key to greater happiness. We've referred several times to the idea of a happiness set point—that each of us has a kind of thermostat for happiness that always returns us to our own particular setting. There are literally hundreds of studies of thousands of people showing that, whatever happens to you, the best predictor of how happy you are at the end of the study is how happy you were at the beginning of the study—whether the study took a few weeks or years and years, whether you got rich or got poor, whether you got sick or stayed healthy, whether you had bad luck or good. Changing that left–right ratio may reset the thermostat, making us a little warmer if we're too cold—permanently, or at least as long as you keep practicing mindfulness. No drugs, no magic, no mysterious machines: just focused attention.

that pilot again

Because we're fighting that Inner Critic, because so many of us can't get over the deep belief that there's something wrong with us as we are, most of us go through our lives craving validation—from our parents, from our spouse, from the boss. We have an innate need to have our feelings recognized and understood. It's not the same as approval; it's more subtle and basic than saying, *You're right!* It's saying, *I understand how you feel that way. I might feel the same in your shoes.* When we feel a lack of validation in the world, we feel alien, inadequate, depressed. Validation is one of the basic healing elements that therapy provides. The therapist is saying, *Your feelings make sense to me.* Often the patient is not getting that message from anyone else in the world—including himself. The secret fear that drives many people to therapy is the feeling that you're losing your mind, because the way you feel isn't making sense to your loved ones or yourself. You don't realize it, but you're caught in the trap of judgment—you are continually evaluating yourself negatively.

Mindfulness suspends that, and it provides a kind of validation for the self. We hold ourselves in our own mind's eye, without judgment, but with focus and compassion. We provide what therapists call a "holding environment" for ourselves, and just as what happens when a parent provides that holding environment for a child, we're allowed to explore our interior world, our deepest selves, in safety—and the neural network in the brain that represents our self is thereby strengthened and repaired. Both neurologically and emotionally, we become more coherent, accepting, solid. Dan Siegel points out that research shows that both secure attachment and mindful meditation practice are associated with better regulation of body systems, balancing emotions, attuning to others, modulating

MINDFULNESS REMOVES THE NEED FOR OUR DEFENSES.

fear, responding flexibly, and exhibiting insight and empathy. And mindfulness practice, just like good parenting, changes the brain by promoting integration of the prefrontal area. When we feel safe and unafraid, whether we're a child secure in a parent's love or an adult in a mindful state, we're healthier, happier, more curious, more open-minded, better able to think and feel; and the more we feel that way, the more our brain adapts to make this the normal state.

Defenses distort reality and twist our character; paradigms are the rigid expectations that determine how our lives will go like cars on the interstate. Mindfulness is a way to get underneath defenses and relax paradigms. It leads us off the interstate and down some new pathways in the brain. Defenses protect us from unwanted feelings, but mindfulness teaches that feelings are not to be feared. When we can experience our feelings fully without mindlessly reacting to them, we don't have to pretend that we don't feel. Mindfulness emphasizes nonjudgmental acceptance. Whatever enters our mind during mindful meditation practice—memories, thoughts, feelings, physical sensations—is to be observed as a unique event and not put into categories like good/bad, healthy/sick, wise/foolish. Learning to stop judging like this takes a lot of practice, because contemporary life makes us feel it's urgent to react instantly to our experiences so that we can be prepared for whatever comes next. Reacting defensively—denying, projecting, dissociating—is perhaps our most common instant reaction. But ironically, defending against negative emotions, like anger, fear, shame, or guilt, leads only to depression, anxiety, and pain. The emotional energy is always there, just blocked, and it takes a different course to come round and hurt us. Mindfulness teaches us that no emotion, no reality, is negative; it just is, and it's wise to accept it. When we can accept ourselves like this, we have no need for defenses. Instead of having your scared, mindless, defensive mind making the decisions in your life, you can make them with your full, responsible consciousness. Our rigid paradigms melt away, too, and instead of being guided by prejudice and fear, we can see reality, including the reality of other people, in all its beautiful complexity. The new pilot in our mind sees things as they are and makes decisions that are not guided by fear, anger, or desire.

When people practice mindfulness and experience the guidance of the new pilot for the first time, it's a revelation. They are able to see themselves and their daily battles with unnecessary misery in a new way, from a different perspective, as we would view a friend we care deeply about who seems to be flailing around in a panic. The Inner Critic seems just horribly mistaken. Many people believe this is a life-changing event; that they'll never see themselves the same way again. Unfortunately, that's underestimating the power of stress to drag us down into mindlessness again. But people do re-member the new perspective, the new pilot, in a very gut-based way, and it becomes easier and easier to reconnect with that calmness and security each time. The new pathway remains there in the brain, even if we get lost for a while.

So besides recalibrating the happiness dial, a mindful attitude has other benefits that may be more important in the long run. It teaches us patience and perspective. It helps us stop kidding ourselves by enabling us to see how we really feel. It gets under our own defenses. It teaches us that thoughts, feelings, and impulses that seem so compelling are, in fact, transient—and that knowledge enables us to focus more on what's truly important. It gets us experiencing life more deeply. By helping us see reality more clearly, it helps us make better decisions. We become more thoughtful and reflective, at the same time as we are more deeply engaged emotionally and spiritually. We develop mental muscles of concentration and focus that come to help us out in every aspect of our lives. In other words, learning mindfulness seems to improve all three components of happiness:

1. It leads to more experiences of joy, connection, spirituality, and the other immediate experiences of happiness.
2. It leads to greater life satisfaction, since we make better decisions and evaluate ourselves more objectively.
3. It helps us control or let go of negative emotional states.

less misery

Cultivating an attitude of acceptance and mindfulness will go a long way toward helping you find greater happiness. That in itself may be the answer many readers need, but getting there is a lifelong process, and not immediately possible for everyone. Some people are going to find it very difficult to practice meditation regularly. Others are going to be too over-whelmed with current stress or their own bad habits to achieve a mindful state without help. Still others may need specific help with aspects of them-selves, or certain areas of their lives, that won't let them get to a happier place without specific, focused attention.

You may remember that psychologists define happiness as the relative absence of negative feelings (misery), an abundance of positive feelings (joy and others), and a feeling of satisfaction with their lives. I added that a sense of meaning or purpose also seemed an important part of happiness. The next four chapters will help you to reduce unnecessary misery, gain the ability to feel more joy, find greater satisfaction, and look at the larger purpose of existence.

Psychology has learned a great deal over the past couple of decades about how our own thinking habits can make it almost impossible to feel good, happy, or proud of ourselves. We also understand a great deal about how and why we can be so skillful at sabotaging ourselves.

For example, many of us have the feeling that we know exactly what to do to make ourselves happier, but that we lack the will power to do it. Some call it motivation, drive, or self-control. We might say we're too tired, too depressed, or too overwhelmed to break out of our ruts. We believe we lack something, will power being the most common label. People generally believe that will power (or self-control or drive or motivation) is a relatively fixed trait—you either have it or you don't. Indeed, it's easy to see the world as divided between the people who jump out of bed at 5:30 A.M. to run for six miles before a breakfast of oatmeal and prune juice, who get to work early and are never distracted or bored, whose cars and kids are always polished and gleaming—and the rest of us, who tend to envy and resent those self-disciplined freaks. We're missing the point—will power is built by practice. Science knows now that "will power" is a set of habits and beliefs about self-control and change. Will power is a skill like tennis or typing, something that you learn through repeated practice. You don't have to become a self-disciplined freak to build your will-power skills to the point where you can reduce a great deal of unnecessary misery in your life.

That brings up an ancient question: To what extent do we have free will, the freedom to choose our own actions, and to what extent are we compelled by forces outside our control: original sin, our genetic heritage, or our lousy childhood? There is no simple answer to this, but here is my guideline: When we believe something is outside our control, we'd better check ourselves for rationalizing. *I can't help it. I can't lose weight, it's in my genes. I can't help being depressed—it's a mental illness. I didn't want to hit her, but I lost control. I'm a loser, an alien, a reject—misunderstood, victimized, helpless. I'm special, gifted, entitled to break the rules.* When things are too ambiguous, when we can't explain why we don't act as we should, we rely on stories like these to get us off the moral hook and justify taking the easy way out. The bottom line is that it's a mistake to view free will and self-discipline as an either/or. Much of the time it's true that what we do, feel, think, and see is determined by forces we're not aware of, but in the present moment, we always have a choice. A worthwhile goal is to free ourselves as much as possible from those unseen forces, including our own character armor, and strengthen and broaden our capacity for self-control.

I'm not saying that self-discipline is the key to happiness. The guy who's out jogging at five thirty isn't necessarily any happier than me sleeping till nine. Good for you if you're happy with your weight despite a few extra pounds; more of us should be. But self-discipline is the key to getting out from under many of the nasty little mental habits that keep us miserable. It's a very simple fact of life that the more you practice anything, the easier it gets. If you practice sleeping through your alarm, it gets easier. If you practice getting up, that gets easier, too. Your brain learns whether you're trying to teach it or not. Although there is lots of confusion in life, in most little decisions, you know the right thing to do. (You may hate it, but you know it.) In the present moment, you can choose. The more often you choose the right thing, the easier it will be to do next time. The brain makes new connections as we practice. The more you practice will power, the more will power you have. The more you believe in your own power to make decisions and influence the course of your life, the happier you'll be.

LEARN WILL POWER LIKE JUGGLING

Remember the jugglers? It took three months of daily practice until the researchers could see changes in their brains. Will power, like juggling, is a skill you can learn, not something you're born with or without. But if you want to get it written into your brain circuitry, you'll have to practice every day for a while. Meanwhile, here are some tips to make it easier.

Avoid triggers and distractions. If you're an alcoholic, stay out of bars.

If you eat too much, avoid food shopping. When you have to shop, go in with a list, rush in, and rush out. If you watch too much television, don't sit in your favorite chair. In fact, move it (or the TV) to another room. If you're trying to work at your computer, turn off your Web browser and e-mail. (I actually go to the extent of unplugging my wireless connection, so I have to get up and go to another room before I can waste time.)

Avoid enablers. These are people who make it easy for you to perform your self-defeating behavior. People you go on a smoking break with. People who encourage you to take unnecessary risks. Explain to these people that you have to put some distance between you while you overcome your bad habit. Your spouse may be an enabler, if he or she encourages you to be lazy or feeds you too much food. Try to explain and enlist his or her help.

It's usually worse than you expect. Remember it took three months of daily practice for the jugglers. We psych ourselves up to go on a diet, for instance, by telling ourselves we can lose five pounds the first week. When we don't, we give up. Instead, prepare yourself for the long haul.

But it's not so bad as you fear. Nobody died from starvation on a diet, and most people don't really experience a lot of discomfort. Same goes for giving up any bad habit. You may have a couple of rough days, but they don't last. And pretty soon, you start to get some good feelings— pride, self-respect—from sticking with your regimen.

Don't try unless you're ready. All the times you've made a half-hearted attempt and given up have eroded your confidence and will power. Don't try again unless you've really thought this through and are ready to go to the mat with your problem.

Ask for help. Make a public commitment—that in itself will help keep you honest—by asking everyone close to you for their help. They might, for instance, avoid talking about food or wild parties while you're around. They might be especially attentive, giving you some recognition for progress or sympathy when you're having a tough time. Or join a group, if there is one for your problems: AA and Weight Watchers are very effective, and the group support helps a great deal with your own will power.

Stimulus control. If you have trouble getting down to work, for instance, try this: Work only at your desk, and only work at your desk. When you find yourself distracted or anxious or unable to decide what to do next, get up from your desk and give yourself a short break. Take your misery elsewhere. Don't try to work when you're not at your desk. Eventually the desk (computer terminal, kitchen, easel) becomes a less dreaded stimulus because it is associated only with productive activity.

Reward yourself. You're doing something that will change your life, and you need to give yourself recognition. You might want to give yourself a gift or a trip when you've conquered the problem. Or give yourself smaller daily indulgences as tokens for progress.

Baby steps. Unfortunately for real therapists, Dr. Leo Marvin (*What About Bob?*) was right. You have to learn to walk before you can run. This will power business is tough. Measure your success in inches. You'll get discouraged, and you may even slip up sometimes. Be sure to give yourself a lot of credit for every good day you have.

Don't obsess—distract. Our brains are constructed so that we can't force ourselves not to think about something, especially a worry or a temptation. You can't make a self-destructive impulse disappear by wishing it away, but you can think about something else. Make a list of good memories that you can refer to when you need it, or a list of pleasant activities you can use as distractions—talking with a friend, a walk, a cup of tea, turning the music up loud and dancing by yourself.

Don't let a slip kill your resolve. Don't slip, but if you do, don't beat yourself up too much. Too many people leap to the conclusion that if you fall off your diet once, you've ruined your chances for success. That's a rationalization for quitting. Instead, remember that you're attempting a very difficult thing. If you can't be totally perfect, it doesn't mean you're hopeless. Nor does it give you an excuse for giving up. Remember, you're committed to this for three months.

Savor the positive results. Pay attention to your feelings as you get out from under that burden you've been carrying around. You may feel

> freer, stronger, proud of yourself. You may look better, have more time, and get more done. Let yourself savor those feelings mindfully, with focus and pleasure.

relying on habits

Chances are that you brush your teeth at set times, without thinking about it: just after breakfast and right before bed. Imagine if you couldn't remember those habits, if you had to deliberately think, twice each day, about when to brush your teeth. That would be a total waste of brain space. You've built up a nice little habit that saves you several minutes and some decision-making each day. That's a very important shortcut to less misery: building good habits so you don't have to make too many decisions.

You can do exactly the same thing with behavioral routines that are a little more complex. You can make a habit of going to the gym or working out on the same days, at the same times. You keep your equipment ready, always in the same place, so you can get out before you have time to think about it. Once it becomes a habit, you make it much more likely that you will get your exercise, and you save yourself all the mental torture of deciding whether to go or not, the time of finding your stuff, the guilt if you don't go. You just go.

Another area is working productively. If you're like me, you probably have spells when you can work in a pretty well-focused fashion for an hour or so. Then you start to lose focus and the time-wasters creep in. Checking e-mail. Checking the headlines, the weather. Googling a phrase you can't get out of your head. Which leads you to another interesting link, and soon you're Web-surfing. Then you start to feel guilty, you try to get back to work, but you realize you're hungry, and that makes you remember there's a tooth that's bothering you and you have to call the dentist, and while you're on hold with the dentist, you get distracted by shopping in an online catalog, and then you really feel guilty, but you really are hungry, so you go get something to eat, and pretty soon it's 2 p.m. and you've had exactly one productive hour.

There used to be jobs in America where you could get paid for working like that (maybe there still are some, probably in the government), but in the new economy, or if you're working for yourself, you won't last long.

It is really much more effective, and less misery-producing, to give yourself authentic breaks without feeling guilty. The trick is to make a clear distinction in your mind between working time and goofing-off time. After you've worked for a respectable amount of time, when your mind wanders, give yourself some time to goof off—a set amount of time—and let yourself play without feeling guilty for a while. When your time is up, get back to work. Chances are that your brain will still want to goof off; if so, just make a list of all the little distracting ideas that pop into your mind. Write them down so you can get to them later, if necessary; for now, really try to get back to work. If you can't after fifteen minutes, you obviously need another break, so take it. But chances are very good that if you can stay in your chair for fifteen minutes, you'll end up doing something productive, and can keep it up for another hour or so.

There are two things about this effort that are really important:

- Motivation follows action instead of the other way around. When we make ourselves face the task we're putting off, it's usually not as bad as we think. We start to have some ideas, and then we begin to feel good about the progress we're making. It's a mistake to wait for motivation to hit us; we usually can find it if we don't permit ourselves to be too distracted.

- We're training our brains to work effectively. We're activating a set of neurons that will form a network that will be activated next time we try to work, and that network will make it easier for us to focus next time. Likewise, we're teaching the neurons of distraction that they have to take turns. If we worked this way every day for three months, like the jugglers practiced, some brain researcher could identify growth in the areas of our brain devoted to whatever kinds of skill our work entails.

Practice makes everything easier next time. Learning takes place whether we know it or not. If we practice being inefficient, we get better at being inefficient. It we practice being productive, it gets easier to be productive.

So here are the principles for making a change in your life or behavior:

- Make a decision once, and stick to it.
- Make the daily practice of your decision automatic.
- Don't waste time thinking about things you've already decided on.

Those principles can be applied to many other areas of life that will greatly reduce unnecessary misery:

- Putting money aside
- Eating healthy, sticking to a diet
- Paying the weekly bills
- Grocery shopping
- Cooking versus eating out
- Throwing out catalogs
- Walking instead of driving
- Reading versus television
- Practicing a new skill or hobby
- Disarming your Inner Critic

If you practice these ideas, before you know it you'll have self-discipline. That feels <u>good.</u> You'll be proud of yourself. There's a real sense of satisfaction that comes from going shopping and realizing that you aren't tempted, or from putting in a focused and productive day at work, or from eating healthy and not experiencing cravings. This sense of satisfaction gives you a head start toward our next step in reducing unnecessary misery: silencing the Inner Critic.

disarm the inner critic

> Nothing in life is quite as important as you think it is
> when you are thinking about it.

I hope you saw from the exercise in Chapter 5 that had you write down everything that's wrong with you, just how absurd that list is—full of trivia that are merely human, things that no one else holds against you (or even knows about). But chances are that seeing the absurdity of it didn't make that Inner Critic go away. Our brains are programmed to be anxious, watchful, never satisfied, and we take that attitude and turn it on ourselves. Genetically, we can't let well enough alone, including ourselves; there's always a fault to find.

Jeffrey Schwartz, a psychiatrist at UCLA, spent some time recruiting people with the most severe cases of obsessive-compulsive disorder (OCD) in the Los Angeles area for his research, and in the process he showed how psychotherapy can rewire the brain. With all the resources of the UCLA labs behind him, he takes scans of his patients' brains when they are actively experiencing their symptoms, and is able to show them the part of the brain that is malfunctioning. (His theory is that there is a "worry" circuit in the brain that focuses our attention on anything that's out of place in a familiar scene, and that with OCD patients, this circuit fails to get turned off when it should. Therefore your brain doesn't register that your hands are clean, the doors are locked, the stove is off—and you're compelled to go back and keep checking.) Schwartz teaches his patients to reframe their symptoms: *It's not really that I need to wash my hands; it's just a brain-wiring problem telling me to wash my hands.* With continued education, therapy, and group support, patients are able to stop themselves from engaging in their compulsive symptoms. At first, that is very difficult for most, but soon they reach a moment of enlightenment: "The week after patients started relabeling their symptoms as manifestations of pathological brain processes, they reported the disease was no longer controlling them." With continued practice, Schwartz is able to show the progress in their brain scans: the worry circuit is weaker and weaker.

You can apply the same principles to silencing the Inner Critic. While it's probably more complex than a single brain center, it still is true that the Inner Critic is a well-worn path in your brain (if not a superhighway), a very familiar circuit that is easily stimulated by certain events or thoughts. Once the Critic is turned on, it just keeps on doing its thing, telling you what an incompetent, reprehensible ignoramus you are. When you hear that voice, try to picture it as simply faulty brain wiring. Just like the smell of good cooking turns on the hunger circuits in your brain, disappointments, injuries, and painful experiences turn on the Critic circuit. Your brain associates the current pain with sources of similar pain in the past. Just yesterday I saw a patient who had a horrible experience in a setting where everyone ignored him—for a week! (He took a vacation by himself, something good for some people but awful for others.) He felt terribly lonely, completely rejected, and humiliated. When he got home and started letting himself feel his feelings, he turned that loneliness into self-hate. His thoughts became *I'm loathsome, hideous, there's something terribly wrong with me, it's my fault, I'm hopeless, things will never be better.* It was bad enough he was made to feel so awful, five times worse that his Inner Critic uses that as fuel to turn up the heat.

It's very difficult at first to make the discrimination you need to make: *I'm hurt, not defective; I feel terrible, but who says it's my fault?* Each time you practice, it will get easier. It may help to give the Inner Critic a name. I had a patient who identified it as his mother's voice, and he learned to respond politely but not get hooked: *I hear you, Mom, but right now I have to go do my laundry.* <u>Fighting the Inner Critic just gives it strength; we have to learn to disengage.</u>

The Inner Critic is a manifestation of what dynamic therapists call a punitive superego, which many of us have integrated from parents who were overly critical or never satisfied or both. You bring home a report card with four A's and one B—they focus on the B. You're five pounds overweight—and that's a big deal. The Inner Critic is usually your parent of the same sex as you—father for boys, mother for girls. Try to picture this parent as a little ridiculous, getting old now and a little frail, a little disheveled, unshaven, morning breath, probably not very happy with his or her life. You just happened to be the unfortunate target of a parent who didn't know any better. *Yeah, Mom, I know I should lose five pounds, but it's not really the most important thing in the world.* Give the Inner Critic a name, a personality; something to remind you it's just a voice in your head, not The Truth. It's the Inner Moe again; slap him right back. Anne Lamott, who has chronicled her battles with life in a hilarious series of essays and memoirs, says in reference to her conflicting feelings at her mother's death: "My mind kept thinking its harsh thinky thoughts, but I'd distract myself from them gently, and say, 'Those are not the truth, those are not trustworthy; those are for entertainment purposes only.' "

Another way of developing a punitive superego comes from having unrealistically high standards for yourself. Sometimes we just want to be the star, and are never satisfied if we're not. Some people focus on every blemish, every tiny little defect, and are never able to step back and see that on the whole, they're a pretty attractive/competent/successful/loved person. That is a tragedy. Being stuck with a punitive superego is a sure route to unnecessary misery, because it makes you live your life to avoid punishment, not to gain joy or satisfaction. The best you hope for is not feeling bad. A nurturing superego is what you get from parents (grandparents, teachers, and the like) who teach you that it's good to be happy about your accomplishments, even when they're not perfect. Instead of trying merely to silence the Inner Critic and avoid its determined assaults on your self-esteem, you live your life knowing that doing well leads to feeling well. Instead of never being satisfied unless you hit the ball out of the park every time at bat, you feel pretty good about a .275 batting average.

EXERCISE 9:
BUILDING A NURTURING SUPEREGO

If you have a persistent Inner Critic, it will help you to be ready with some positive rejoinders when he next drops in for a visit. Remember that you have an Inner Moe who expects to be able to slap the hapless Inner Larry around without challenge. Instead of responding like Larry (making excuses, whining), respond like a grown-up.

IF THE CRITIC SAYS	YOU MIGHT SAY
What a dump! Can't you ever get organized?	Attacking me isn't going to help. Let's spend ten minutes on it.
Look at you! When will you ever lose that weight?	You're in the same body with me; what gives you the right to talk?
Don't even think of going to that party; you know you'll just feel awkward and rejected.	I will go, but keep my expectations in check. I'll try to talk to one new person. I'll try to smile at people.

(continued)

That was a terrible presentation! Did you notice that woman in the fifth row who just read her book? Everyone was bored with you.	She might have had a deadline to read that book, or maybe she was just rude. There were lots of other people who seemed to be paying attention.

Try this yourself: What does your very own Inner Critic have to say about you? And what might be an appropriate, adult response?

These approaches to dealing with your Inner Critic do not come naturally. They require mindful awareness. The natural response, and our automatic response to criticism, is to get defensive—to use our defenses to deny or distort reality. So we take it out on the dog, or our spouse, or we get drunk and try to forget, or we rationalize or bargain with ourselves. *I'll do better tomorrow.* That may temporarily buy us some time, but in reality, it just gives more ammunition to the Inner Critic. *You thought you could forget about me? Think again!* We have to learn to interrupt the default circuits in the brain, the ones that we've been using all our lives that never really do us any good. That's why it's important to recognize the Inner Critic as not you—it's just a voice in your head, merely the product of your thinking. Once you master that step, it's easier to respond in a nonhabitual, mindful, creative way. Think of the new pilot in your mind, the Wise Mind who can listen skillfully and tune out the noise in the brain.

less negative thinking

Our brains are great at problem solving. It's really what separates us from animals. Every one of us faces thousands of puzzles every day, and gets them almost all right: change for a dollar, what we need from the store, enough gas in the car, how much time to get there—we do those things automatically, in the background, and take them for granted. Being so good at navigating through daily life, it's only natural that we turn the same skills on ourselves, and make ourselves miserable in the process. When we're unhappy, when things aren't going our way, we tend to look at ourselves for the solution. <u>We tend to look at</u> <u>life, and at ourselves, as problems to be solved, and that's a big mistake.</u>

Try a thought experiment: Say you're feeling sad. <u>Try not to feel that</u> <u>way. Try as hard as you can. Make yourself happy instead.</u> As soon as you read that, you know it's nonsensical; you can't control your emotions that way. Chances are you try it all the time, somewhere under the level of total awareness. After all, it seems logical enough; we have such magnificent brains, we ought to be able to control a simple thing like a sad mood. But it's like the "don't think of a pink elephant" command. Ironically, whatever we try not to think of is going to keep popping up in our minds as long as we keep trying to suppress it. So you'll be constantly reminded of your sad feelings, and that will make you sadder. It will also make you feel inadequate and incompetent, because you can't do a simple thing like get out of your sad mood. (In case you were wondering, by the way, it doesn't do your happiness quotient any good to be smarter; the correlation between subjective well-being and IQ is .06—almost nothing at all.)

Remember when you were learning to ride your bike, and there was a telephone pole fifty feet away, and no other dangers around? In theory, you can go in any direction you want—but you find yourself drawn to that telephone pole like a magnet. You try desperately to steer away, but the harder you try, the closer you get to the pole. You knew the moment you saw it that you were going to hit it, and you do. That seems to be the way it is with certain thoughts, feelings, or memories that we want to avoid. They have a "sticky" quality, like the little seals on the top of CD cases that you can't get off your fingers. The more you struggle, the more stuck you get.

Getting Unstuck

The story is told that Tolstoy's older brother once said he had to stand in a corner until he could not think of a white bear. We know you just can't do it that way. However, if we can't make ourselves not think of white bears, we can make ourselves think of hyacinth macaws instead. Distraction is a pretty good strategy for sticky thoughts. If we could focus our thoughts on some other object—like the finish line—we just might avoid that telephone pole.

One trouble with being human is that it seems like we can't suppress our unpleasant feelings without suppressing the positive ones as well. We have only a volume switch, no tuner. It seems like we're not given a choice: either feel everything, the good with the bad, or feel nothing at all. The purpose of practicing mindfulness is not to disengage from our feelings like a hermit retreating from the world into 24-7 meditation, but to experience our feelings even more deeply, in a new way: from a calm center, with the confidence that even the most distressing feelings will pass. We learn to recognize that our thoughts, feelings, and sensations are always fluid and changing and hence, not to get too worked up about. Daniel Siegel calls it discernment: "You come to see these activities of the mind as waves at the surface of the mental sea. From this deeper place within your mind, this internal space of mindful awareness, you can just notice the brain waves at the surface as they come and go." So when you bitch about the price of gas, you remember that guy in Shanghai who wants gas, too, and realize that we have to share.

One of the few effective strategies for getting out of sad feelings and sticky thoughts is to get up and do something. <u>Feelings follow actions; our bodies lead the way.</u> Sometimes, when I'm working with someone who's pretty depressed, who's contemplating the nature of existence, the emptiness of the universe, and the futility of his life (but has some sense of humor), I'll say something like, *You know, if you just got up and went for a walk, you might feel better.* (This won't work with someone who's severely depressed; they'll feel that I'm not taking them seriously.) I'm being deliberately provocative. Most depressed people know that, and <u>hate</u> it. Their depression seems so important,

FEELINGS FOLLOW
ACTIONS.

so real and full of meaning that they don't want to be told that doing something rather mundane can put an entirely different perspective on those thoughts. But it's true. By being provocative, I'm teaching them mindfulness, because even if they don't go for a walk, they will be more aware that their depression is not quite as powerful as it seems.

Here's another way: Subjects in a series of studies were assigned to three conditions. In one, they were to write a few lines each night about recent events they were grateful for; in the next, they were to report on hassles they'd experienced recently. A control group was asked merely to report on the events of the day. The gratitude group experienced several benefits: an increase in positive feelings, better mood, more exercise, and better mood as reported by loved ones. This would be a good habit to build.

How about this as another revolutionary idea for reducing unnecessary misery: <u>When something makes you feel bad, don't do it.</u> But that is much more difficult than it sounds because we're not very good at drawing the connections between our inner states and outside events. We know that women who are exposed to repeated images of other women who are unusually attractive—for instance, when they read a lot of women's magazines—feel less attractive themselves, and their self-esteem is diminished. But are women aware of this? The same thing happens to men when they read descriptions of other men who are more dominant or successful. Do men draw the connection, that they feel less of themselves when they read about Masters of the Universe? Unfortunately, we just don't seem to be wired to pick up those connections. It's much the same as our blindness to the hedonic treadmill. It's a little miracle that therapists perform every day, very impressive to our clients, pointing out that *maybe the reason you feel so depressed today is that you had a fight with your husband last night.* But it's a cheap trick, because anyone who took the trouble to listen would see the connection—that is, anyone but ourselves, because our defenses blind us to those connections. We can do it only if we learn mindfulness.

The Hockey Buzzer of the Mind

You know that extremely annoying buzzer that sounds in hockey and basketball to mark period changes: <u>BRRAAAAP!</u> You can use that as an aversive stimulus when you find your mind going down paths you don't want it to take. Just imagine that sound in your head: Self-blame? <u>BRRAAAAP!</u> Excessive worry? <u>BRRAAAAP!</u> The behaviorists who followed Skinner were able to show that giving yourself a mild unpleasant experience helped to break some bad habits. For instance, wearing a rubber band on your wrist and snapping it when you think of smoking. The hockey buzzer is a little shock to the system, a little joke you play on yourself, that can quickly get your mind off the track you want to avoid. Of course, you have to follow the thought you are buzzing out with a more healthy thought.

thinking badly

If there's one thing that psychologists can be said to have investigated six ways from Sunday, it's the link between thinking and unnecessary misery. There is a very strong relationship between certain ways of thinking and depression/anxiety/stress. There's lots of evidence that changing those thinking patterns can alleviate much of that suffering.

Though excessive rationality is overrated, and our best decisions are made with our whole minds—logical, emotional, and intuitive—still: if we are trying to be rational, we should be as rational as we can be. If we expect our magnificent cerebrums to help save us from unnecessary misery, then it behooves us to use them right. You can't think well if your thinking is based on faulty assumptions. Neither can you think well if you don't follow the rules of logic. Let's review:

False Assumptions

These erroneous assumptions about the world and ourselves were first identified as cognitive behavioral therapy was developed to help depression sufferers. You don't have to be depressed to be operating under these assumptions, though if you do, you'll make yourself pretty unhappy. Although these assumptions operate unconsciously, most people will admit ruefully that they recognize themselves in some categories. When we're under stress, or in the grip of powerful emotions, these cognitive errors become all the more likely:

- Catastrophizing: If (blank) happens, it'll be a disaster. Of course, there are real catastrophes. But some people are unable to refrain from assuming the worst possible outcome. *The funny-looking mole is cancer. The flight delay means a crash. If Johnny doesn't get into the right kindergarten, he won't get into the right college.*

- Everything has to be perfect, or else . . . *(people won't like me, I'll be a failure, I'll be rejected, I'll be worthless, I'll be humiliated).* Perfectionism is simply devastating. Those depressed people who are the most perfectionistic generally have the worst outcomes in treatment. When we set impossible goals for ourselves, we guarantee we'll never achieve them, a sure route to misery. Perfectionism also means focusing on the details, not the meaning, and never getting the real substance right.

- <u>I have to be liked by everyone.</u> In adolescence, we all experienced the powerful wish to fit in and be accepted, and most of us also experienced some of the pain of being rejected. Hopefully we also began to learn that fitting in requires compromising on important values. Being a people-pleaser is a thin substitute for the kind of self-respect that comes from trusting your own values, and speaking your own mind.

- <u>I can't live without you.</u> If we give someone this power over ourselves, we're saying there's nothing we wouldn't do to preserve the relationship. Do we really mean that? Would we steal, lie, commit murder in order to please the other person? Hopefully not—and if not, then it <u>is</u> possible to live without them. People who take this position are mindlessly controlled by the fear of abandonment.

- <u>I'm defective/damaged/inadequate.</u> All of us are defective in some ways; all of us have suffered some damage. But some families need a scapegoat, and there are people who have had this belief drilled into them by parents or family members so deeply that it has become an important, devastating part of their identity. Others have adopted this role because they've become demoralized and given up on change. Naturally it leads to hopelessness and lethargy.

- <u>I have to look like everyone else.</u> If you're chubby or skinny, short or tall, have weird hair or big feet, chances are that people in your life have made a big deal out of that, and in the process made you very self-conscious. Those feelings can go very deep, and be the source of tremendous pain. Television, where everyone is beautiful, doesn't help, and Internet spam plays on some deep insecurities. But with maturity, we begin to realize that *(a)* we're not responsible for our looks, *(b)* outward appearances are a very shallow value, and *(c)* there are many amazing, wonderful people who don't seem to mind at all that they look a little different.

- <u>Everyone does it.</u> This is an all-purpose rationalization that permits the individual to behave in ways he knows are wrong. It shifts the blame from the individual to society: *If everyone else does it, I'd be a fool not to.* But like all defenses, it's not totally effective; it doesn't entirely protect us from guilt. Thus it adds another piece to our character armor, because you have to keep on justifying why you're doing something that you know to be wrong.

I hope it's obvious how beliefs like these contribute to misery, but there is one subtlety to point out: They all set up vicious circles that create the very conditions we're trying to avoid. If you try too hard to be liked, you come across as needy and desperate. If you believe you're unlovable, you're not going to try very hard to make yourself lovable. Cognitive behavioral therapy works by helping people identify unconscious beliefs like these and shine a bright light on them so their assumptions can be questioned and their effects identified.

Logical Errors

In addition to faulty assumptions, the cognitive therapists studying depression identified a number of logical errors that they found to be quite common among their patients. Later research—and a little introspection—demonstrated that these logical errors are by no means unique to depression; anyone can, and frequently does, make them every day in trying to solve problems and make decisions. If we want to believe that we've reached our decisions logically, we should be sure that we've followed logical rules.

Here are some of the standard errors in logic characteristic of depressed, and nondepressed but counterproductive, thinking. Some of these may seem far beyond the bounds of rationality to you, but if you look at yourself honestly, you'll probably see some of them at work:

- <u>Overgeneralization.</u> The assumption that if something is true under these circumstances, it's likely to be true in all circumstances. *My wife doesn't understand me; women can't understand men.*
- <u>Selective attention/Disqualifying the positive (or negative).</u> The process of attending only to information that fits our

preconceptions. Depressed people selectively ignore good news; manic people selectively ignore warning signals. *Everyone laughed at my jokes except George; they must just be trying to butter me up. George is the only honest one in the bunch.*

- <u>Selective responsibility.</u> Depressed people take responsibility for bad events but not for good events. *Good things are pure luck, bad things are my fault.* But there are plenty of people who go too far the other way. *I won five hundred dollars in the lottery! I <u>knew</u> I would win!*

- <u>Assuming temporal causality.</u> Assuming that since event B followed event A, then A was the cause of B. This is the source of much superstition. Ask any baseball player: *I wore these socks the last two times I hit it out of the park. I'm going to keep on wearing these socks.*

- <u>Excessive self-reference.</u> This is the fundamental attribution error again, the distortion that would have us believe that it really *is* all about me. In a negative frame of mind, it can lead to the belief that everyone is watching you all the time, especially when you make a mistake; and the belief that whenever things go wrong, it's because of something you did.

- <u>Black-and-white thinking.</u> This happens when we simply divide our experiences up into categories of good or bad, right or wrong, without any shades of gray. *Jerry's a good friend; Jerry can do no wrong.*

- <u>Emotional reasoning.</u> Simply believing that feelings make it so. You see this happen in arguments: In the heat of battle, you are absolutely convinced of your point of view. Later, you might admit you forgot some important facts.

Logical errors like these are what make it possible for us to maintain our distorted paradigms and false assumptions about the world. They're more examples of faulty wiring in the brain, default circuits that have built up over time to the point where we simply can't see how wrong they are. They reinforce their own existence because they keep having us come out with the same conclusions.

Cognitive behavioral psychotherapy (CBT), focused on correcting faulty thinking patterns like this, has been around for thirty years and is generally accepted as the treatment of choice for depression and anxiety. But a new wrinkle has come from some experienced cognitive therapists who have been rethinking how their method really works and using more mindfulness-based techniques to improve it. They believe that CBT may be effective not so much because it changes the way you think, but because it changes your attitude about your thoughts. Not that you have to disprove every cognitive error, but that the method inadvertently teaches you some distance from your thinking process, that metacognitive awareness again. Instead of arguing with the Inner Critic, you politely walk away. In revising their methods, they personally have been led into practicing mindfulness meditation, and have developed a treatment method that provides more lasting relief from depression than traditional CBT. *The Mindful Way Through Depression* is useful not only for those with depression, but also for anyone who feels stressed out or less happy than he could be.

less self-defeating behavior

Many of us feel we have been ordered around since we could understand our first words. We've been pressured all our lives to do what's good for us, and <u>we're sick of it!</u> By the time we've become adults, we've internalized all that pressure; it's become the Inner Critic who's never satisfied, who beats up on us just because he can. We've come to associate being good with giving in to arbitrary authority, that Inner Moe. But we have an Inner Curly who will taunt the Inner Moe with Bronx cheers and thumbs to the nose. Unfortunately, when they fight, we lose.

We all recognize the pouty lower lip of the two-year-old who's being told to do something he doesn't want to do. That two-year-old lives on in all of us, to some extent, and it's a good thing. If we always did what the Authorities told us to, we'd have very boring lives, and we'd be a very scary society, rather like Germany under Hitler or China under Mao.

Now we're adults, and we know only too well what's good for us. *Don't drink too much, don't eat too much, don't gamble, don't smoke. Clean up after yourself. Get your work done on time. Exercise regularly. Floss. Save your money. Don't use drugs. Drive defensively, and don't forget to buckle up!* Who is this nag in your head, this square, this tyrant of the conventional? How many adults do you know who manage all that? We can all be a little self-destructive, and one reason is that it can represent independence, adventure, fun. Too often, we feel like we're being good for the Man, for the bosses, for our parents even if they died twenty years ago. <u>Passive aggression</u> is the classic defense against a rigid authority, and that means—unfortunately—we get a sense of independence out of treating ourselves badly. It's a way of expressing your independence from that punitive superego. Rebellion is always an expression of nonconformity, sometimes of creativity, but there are some things, like common sense or good health, we shouldn't rebel against.

Procrastination is one way of being passive aggressive, but it's even more self destructive than usual because you're being passive aggressive with yourself. If you're feeling sorry for yourself and deliberately leave a pile of dirty dishes in the sink, the present you is just leaving a stink bomb for the future you. You're going to be mad at yourself in the future because of your inaction in the present; you'll add a little to your burden of guilt and shame. Procrastination is also a way for us to be satisfied with second-rate results; we can always tell ourselves we'd have done a better job if only we'd had more time. And we can give ourselves a thrill almost like flow (see Chapter 8) by putting things off till the last minute and then getting an adrenaline rush by snatching a small victory from the jaws of defeat. If you're really good at rationalizing you can keep yourself feeling rather satisfied this way, but it's cheap happy. You're whittling your expectations of yourself down lower and lower.

EXERCISE 10:
IDENTIFYING YOUR OWN
SELF-DEFEATING BEHAVIOR

Go back to your list of everything that's wrong with you. This time try to look at it with new eyes, with the benefit of compassionate curiosity. Imagine you're a loving parent who just found this list in your teenage son or daughter's room. You would probably be moved with empathy.

What would you say to help your child? Of course, you would point out how they're being unfairly hard on themselves, how they're expecting too much, how they have to allow themselves to be merely human.

But what if there were some things on that list that bothered <u>you</u> about your child? I don't mean the usual things like rudeness or sloppiness, I mean things that you know will mean a certain amount of unhappiness in their adult lives. Ways they shoot themselves in the foot—shyness, unassertiveness, giving up too easily, getting angry too fast, being overly sensitive to rejection.

If you were your own loving parent, what advice would you give yourself about your list? What would you tell yourself to accept, and what would you try to change? What do you have some control over? What are your self-destructive habits? Or maybe it's a deficit—not knowing how to do something that would really be helpful—social or organizational skills, for instance? What could you change if you really tried? Think about what we said about how will power grows with practice. Would you like to try to change?

Pick out one of the items on your list and give some mindful attention to how you might change. Think about this, and we'll return to this project in Exercise 14, Chapter 10.

Another key element that helps keep us unnecessarily miserable doing things that don't make us happy is what psychologists call secondary gain—the hidden payoff we get for being miserable. Secondary gain is basically what the child who gets a tummy ache in order to stay home from school is after—a little TLC from Mom, the chance to watch TV all day. The adolescent fantasy of the tragic romantic misunderstood artist, to compensate for feelings of rejection and alienation. This is a key element of much adult illness, too, and many people who have been sick for a long time have become used to getting attention through their illness. They've let other parts of their personalities wither, and so they're scared that no one will give them attention if they recover. Secondary gain can also be a part of why people martyr themselves for others (they get to feel holy), why they stay in jobs that they constantly complain about (they're afraid of change), and a host of other unhappy habits. One of my patients spoke of her depression as a big soft comforter. It wasn't really comforting, but it was safe and familiar. Sometimes she felt as if she was entitled to be depressed, to quit struggling, to snuggle down and watch old movies and feel sorry for herself.

don't: GET TO LIKE YOUR MISERY.

If you identify secondary gain working in yourself, think about it this way: It automatically handicaps you; it puts you in a one-down position relative to others. They have the power to give you what you crave: attention and love, while you can only ask for it, not earn it. Use your autobiography (Exercise 4) to think back to the time when you first thought this might be an effective way of getting your needs met. Chances are you were pretty young, scared, or traumatized then. Think about getting attention and love in other ways. You'll develop a lot more self-respect.

regaining self-control

One good way of avoiding unnecessary misery is not getting into trouble. This isn't always easy: There are going to be times when you feel you're losing it. Something very upsetting has happened, and your head is spinning. It may be something that would throw anyone for a loop, or it may be intensely personal to you. You feel your heart pounding. Your brain is going 90 mph, full of too many thoughts, feelings, questions. You wouldn't be human if this didn't happen to you sometimes. (But if it happens more often than once a month, you're under too much stress and ought to change your situation.) You want to minimize the damage; you want to avoid mistakes that would make matters worse. Here are some guidelines:

Learning to Control Emotions
- Take a few deep breaths and detach. Take a mental step back and go into observer mode. Focus on calmness and objectivity.
- Make sure you're not hungry, angry, lonely, or tired (HALT—an acronym from AA).

- Don't use any drugs, including caffeine and alcohol, that will change your mood or lower your inhibitions.
- Make sure you have your facts straight. Don't make snap judgments. Ask a lot of questions.
- Use mindfulness to observe your thoughts and feelings. Your first reaction may be a defense, a distraction. Anger may be a disguise for fear. Jealousy may mask the insecurity that comes from knowing we haven't been attentive enough. Some emotions have more than one layer; something different might be seen underneath if you observe carefully.
- Talk to friends and loved ones whom you can trust to be objective and supportive.
- Remember your basic values, and act accordingly. Don't go off half-cocked and do something you'll regret later. Don't hurt people you care about. If you're sure you've been wronged, don't go after revenge, but think carefully about the wisest, most productive response. Make up your mind to do something about it when you're calmer, and then wait.
- Don't give in to emotional impulses. Many of our regrettable emotional decisions stem from seeking relief from what seems like an unbearable emotional state, not solving a problem. Don't quit your job, tell off your boss, break up with your girlfriend, move, or give things away unless you're in a calm state. Doing nothing for a time is better than doing something stupid.
- Pay attention to what your body is doing. If you're overly excited, angry, or scared, do some relaxation exercises to help calm down. If that seems impossible, do some aerobic exercise first to help work off some of the stress.
- If you're stuck obsessing pointlessly, remember another AA maxim: *Move a muscle, change a thought.* Get out of the situation and do something physically different. A long, vigorous walk is great therapy. A tennis or golf game can work wonders if you have an understanding partner. Try a hot bath or a good movie.
- Make yourself do something useful, something else that isn't related to the present situation.

- Remember that each time you manage to weather a storm like this, you've made it easier to do next time. Your brain has made some new connections that will make emotional control easier in the future.

One more thing: Talk about it. "Critical incident stress debriefing" is now an accepted procedure for preventing PTSD among emergency workers. There is a lot of research showing that when people are helped to process and confront traumatic experiences, their health improves greatly—despite the fact that they may still be in emotional distress as they're talking about it. It's not just "getting the feelings out"—there's also evidence that the more you regain self-control and mastery from putting the trauma in context, the better the improvement in your immune system.

controlling consumerism

One area that leads to a great deal of unnecessary misery for us is consumerism. Much of that misery is not only unnecessary, but it's invisible as well. We take it for granted, because it seems normal, but it's normal only at this unique time in human history. The basic message is that happiness is easy; you just have to buy the right products. That sets you up for a big letdown, but the hidden implication is that it's your own fault if you're not happy—just look at how happy everyone on television is.

The social psychologist John Bargh had his experimental subjects take what they thought was a language test. In one experiment, half the group read about elderly people while half read about something else. Those who read about elderly people walked down the hall more slowly after they thought the experiment was over, but actually that was the point: Bargh was timing their reactions. A second experiment had half the group read about rudeness, half not. Those who read about rudeness were quicker to interrupt the experimenter—who was engaged in a discussion with a colleague—when they were done. So—do you really think you're immune from commercials on television? Do you really think that depictions of violence in films and in music have no influence on violence in our society? Bargh has gone on to document what he calls the "chameleon effect"—the unconscious tendency we all have to mimic the people around us—actions, feeling, attitudes. When the people we're mimicking have higher status, the chameleon effect is stronger. Of course, almost everyone on television is presented as having higher status than us.

Depressed shopping is a new phenomenon. I see a lot of it with my patients. They get bored, or lonely, or scared, and go shopping. What they're really buying are consolation prizes, stuff to console themselves with because life isn't bringing them real satisfaction. Of course, they end up spending money that would have been better spent on another purpose—because they don't really need these things—and so they add to their sense of being out of control. Now that everyone's on the Internet, you can't escape triggers, and you can go shopping for consolation prizes without getting out of your pajamas.

don't: GO SHOPPING IN YOUR PAJAMAS.

Consumerism is very powerful, and can be very subtle. It doesn't help that there are things we have to buy—cars break down, computers go out of date, and the new models are very sexy. Then there are acquisitions that are instrumental toward greater happiness: an exercise machine, hobby supplies, a new guitar, a sailboat, a Jet Ski, a cabin at Vail—it's a slippery slope, greased by rationalization. We're wired to compare ourselves to others, to compete for the trappings of status.

My best advice about using money wisely is to read *Your Money or Your Life,* and live by it. If you value and make a habit of frugal living, you will find yourself much less tempted by consumerism. It's like we said about making a decision once, and automatically following it. But instead of automatically brushing your teeth, you automatically save money. Remember that while money doesn't buy happiness, the lack of it certainly breeds misery. Nobody ever said it better than Mr. Micawber (from Dickens's *David Copperfield*): "Annual income twenty pounds, annual expenditure nineteen nineteen six, result happiness. Annual income twenty pounds, annual expenditure twenty pounds ought and six, result misery." The real value of money lies in its power to buy you freedom and security, which consumer spending will deprive you of.

Teach your children the tricks of advertising (and remember them yourself):

- Products are associated with beauty, popularity, virility, power, youth. Everybody is pretty or handsome.
- The background music is meant to affect us emotionally—to lull us or stimulate us.
- Possessing the product is supposed to make us better than others.
- There's a big sale <u>right now,</u> and if we don't take advantage of it, we'll regret it.
- Some messages are about fear—without the product, we'll be at some disadvantage; we might get sick or lose money.
- Some ads are very clever; the message is that only discerning people will get the joke and buy the product.
- Most advertising has a subtext of competition. Remember that keeping up with the Joneses is just stepping on the hedonic treadmill.
- Remember that getting what you want doesn't make you happy. Learn to develop pride in mastering your wants.

Another way consumer culture adds to our stress and reduces our overall satisfaction is by giving us too many choices. Barry Schwartz argues that when we make decisions, we fall into one of two groups, "maximizers" and "satisficers." Maximizers place a very high value on getting the very highest value; they do their homework, they read *Consumer Reports,* they comparison-shop. Satisficers, on the other hand, shop with a level of acceptability in mind. If an item meets that level in terms of price, quality, and convenience, they buy it and are through shopping. Unfortunately the proliferation of choices (remember 285 styles of running shoes) means more pressure on all of us to act as maximizers. After all, with so many choices available, we will have only ourselves to blame if we don't get the best bang for our buck. Maximizers are setting themselves up for a lot of dissatisfaction.

In an interesting set of studies, shoppers were found to be more likely to purchase from an assortment of six chocolates or jams than from a choice of twenty-four or thirty. Those who had fewer options reported themselves happier with the choices they'd made. Schwartz and his colleagues point to two factors at work: One is the avoidance of potential buyer's remorse. "The more options there are, the more likely one will make a nonoptimal choice and this prospect may undermine whatever pleasure one gets from one's actual choice." The second factor is that, to make an informed choice from thirty, you need to spend a lot of effort and time researching each option. People may decide that it's just too much trouble, and walk away—or buy on impulse and increase their chances of buyer's remorse.

BE A SATISFICER.
SHOP THOUGHTFULLY,
ENJOY DEEPLY.

Another study asked residents of the United States and five European countries where they'd rather buy an ice cream cone: at a shop with a choice of ten flavors, or at a shop with a choice of more than fifty. Only in America did a majority of people say they preferred the wider choice. Are Americans so beguiled by the concept of choice?

multitasking

The concept of multitasking is a marketing ploy to make the fact that you're too damn busy sound like a good thing. You're supposed to be proud of how in demand you are, and how well you can handle stress. But multitasking just ensures that nothing ever gets done well. Say one of your favorite pieces of music is Pachelbel's Canon. Say another is the Beatles' "Twist and Shout." Okay, play both at the same time. That's multitasking. In order to do anything well, we have to give it our full attention.

A team of researchers set out to study a new method for assessing women's feeling cycles during the day, and they came up with a discouraging result: Taking care of the children was ranked as one of the most frustrating, least enjoyable activities. Yet clearly, in retrospect, many women—35 percent, in a recent poll—think of child-rearing as the most enjoyable, satisfying aspect of their lives. It seems likely that this contradiction comes from the fact that child-rearing is going on all the time, while women are driving,

less misery   153

talking to friends, preparing meals, or watching TV (all of which were rated more enjoyable than time with the children). In other words, child-rearing— most of the time—has to be done while we're doing something else as well, and therefore it's inevitably frustrating. Child-rearing has always had to be done in the background, of course; that's been the traditional woman's role. But you can allow yourself to be distracted by your child's needs when you're doing something like weeding or weaving much more easily than when you're driving in traffic or talking on the cell phone. One of the reasons multitasking is a joke is that the very intensity of, the amount of attention demanded by, the tasks that are common today (driving, cell phone, juggling commitments) is up about 200 percent from generations past.

Multitasking makes you more susceptible to temptation. A group of subjects was asked to memorize a number, then choose between fruit salad or a big piece of chocolate cake. The lower the number they were asked to memorize, the more likely people were to make the healthier choice. Apparently the effort of remembering more digits distracts the thinking brain, allowing the emotional brain to sneak in and hijack our decision. I wonder just how much being overloaded with too much information plays a role in our epidemic of obesity.

You can take your multitasking skills on vacation, too. That's the attraction of the latest resorts. We used to go to the beach and sit for a couple of weeks, sometimes get in the water, often read a book or two. Rent a cottage with your in-laws and drink margaritas in the evening, play Monopoly. Now when you go to the beach, there's scuba lessons and snorkeling and Jet Skiing and parasailing and sand castle contests and fishing and kayaking and beach volleyball and gambling and drinking and dancing and dance contests and spas and massages and hikes up the mountains and excursions to the ruins, and more food than you can imagine. Don't forget that most Americans are so insecure about their jobs (with reason) that they continue to check in with the

don't: GET PROUD OF YOUR MULTITASKING SKILLS.

office while they're away. They <u>need</u> the level of distraction that the new resorts provide in order to stop worrying about their jobs for a minute. But it just puts pressure on us to be maximizers again, to come back from vacation dissatisfied if we didn't get to go parasailing or master the salsa.

Another problem with multitasking is that while we're doing it, we're in reaction mode; we're not setting our own priorities. Rather, we're answering the phone, following our boss's agenda, or the customer's. We're responding to the urgent, not to the important. Keep in mind that no one but you is going to make your happiness a priority. The number of people in the United States who say there is no one with whom they discuss important matters tripled between 1985 and 2004. We're going to see in Chapter 7 that it's what you pay attention to that determines how your brain grows.

do: ONE THING AT A TIME.
DO IT WELL, THEN MOVE ON.

There's no doubt that you can get good at multitasking—carrying on three conversations at once, instant messaging with your thumbs, coordinating, arranging. Do you want to be skillful at multitasking, or do you want to be skillful at actually accomplishing things? Do you want to be constantly reacting to others' demands, or do you want to enjoy your life?

less interpersonal conflict

Our relationships with others are usually the source of most of the joy and pleasure in our lives, but they also can be the source of terrible pain—much of it unnecessary.

Approval and Acceptance

We all crave approval from others, but one of the lessons of maturity is that approval has to be balanced against autonomy. Feeling that we're liked and feeling that we're making our own decisions are sometimes incompatible sources of happiness. We're going to talk more about human relationships as a source of joy in Chapter 7. For now, consider that learning to communicate clearly, directly, and assertively can prevent a great deal of unnecessary misery. Here are my guidelines for mindful communication:

There's a conflict. You want something that someone else doesn't want to give you. Or, you feel you're being disrespected, not listened to, or taken advantage of. You're reading quietly, and your spouse comes in and turns on the TV without asking you. Someone at work has snitched on you to the boss, and the boss has written you up without hearing your side. What to do?

- Clear your head. Your immediate emotional response may be to get angry, to cry, to freeze, to choke up, to storm out. Usually those immediate responses are not the best idea. Get control of your feelings first. Then,
- As coolly and mindfully as possible, evaluate your rights. What's wrong with this situation? Are you being treated respectfully but not getting your way? Or is there disrespect as well as conflict? You always have a right to expect respectful treatment, and that may be more important than the subject of the conflict itself. We all have basic rights we tend to forget about, including the rights to change our minds, to say *I don't know*, to be treated with dignity and respect, and to experience our feelings without being invalidated.
- If possible, arrange a time when you can deal with the situation. For a conflict with a loved one, a coworker, or someone we are in regular contact with, establish a mutually convenient time. But some situations need to be dealt with on the spot, before greater damage is done, and you need to be prepared.
- State the problem in terms of how it affects you. Make it clear exactly how you are hurt or inconvenienced by the other person's behavior. *It hurts my feelings that you never think of calling during the day. When you don't pick up after yourself, it's not fair to me. When you make dirty jokes in the office, I feel offended and uncomfortable.* Just stating the problem in this way may be all you need to do. Sometimes people are not aware of their impact on you. Sometimes people have merely been thoughtless, and will immediately apologize. Sometimes they'll push you to the limit, but then respect the limit you set. So don't make things worse. Use

calm, objective language that avoids personal attacks. Don't speculate about the other's motives.

- State your feelings, making sure your verbal and nonverbal messages agree. This is where the proverbial "I statements" come in. *When you make me do your half of the housework, I can't get my jobs done; I get worried that I can't meet my deadline. When you make dirty jokes in the office, I feel offended and uncomfortable. I shouldn't have to feel this way at the place where I work every day.* The other person is not responsible for the way you feel, but has a right to know about it. If you don't state your feelings, you're assuming that the other person can read your mind.

- If you need to, rehearse assertive nonverbal communication until it comes naturally to you. Don't be embarrassed—lots of people need rehearsal. Enlist a good friend to help coach you. In any conversation, maintain eye contact. Keep your body erect. Speak in a firm tone. If you're afraid you'll choke up, or get tongue-tied, write out what you have to say. You can refer to your notes, or just read it. Or, in these days of e-mail, you can e-mail it to the other person and ask for a time to talk. You're <u>practicing</u> assertiveness here, and you shouldn't worry about doing it perfectly the first time. The next time will be easier.

- Tell the other person what you want. Use simple, direct language. Keep it specific: *I want you to help with the dishes,* <u>not</u> *I want you to show more consideration for me. I want you to stop the dirty jokes,* <u>not</u> *I'd like you to show more respect.* Address the other person's behavior, not his personality or character, to avoid putting him on the defensive.

- Listen carefully to the response. You may be wrong. You may have misinterpreted the other person's behavior or motives. If you're wrong, be prepared to apologize. Then make this a learning experience for yourself. Why did you jump to the wrong conclusion? Assertiveness requires speaking clearly, but also listening carefully.

- If you don't get a clarification or an apology, listen for a defensive response. *You don't understand. . . . Those aren't really dirty jokes. . . . You're just oversensitive.* This means your message is not getting through. If you're not getting through, just repeat. Don't get distracted. Be mindful of what your goals are, and ignore diversions like attempts to change the subject or shift the blame, or personal attacks. Stick to the issue. You may have to repeat yourself several times before the other person sees that their defenses aren't going to work.

- You also should describe the consequences. Clearly spell out what will happen if the other person does or doesn't cooperate. This should not be a threat, but a natural consequence. *If I can get my work done, we can go out later.* When you're dealing with someone you know to be uncooperative, you may point out the natural consequences of his refusal: *If you don't let me get my work done, we won't have enough money to buy the things you want.* Or, *If you don't stop the dirty jokes, I'll have to speak to the manager, or call Human Resources.*

- Be ready to negotiate. Ask the other person if they have alternative solutions to the problem. Be ready to give something up in order to get what you want. Often the other person needs a way out that doesn't feel like complete defeat, and you should consider compromises.

- If you're not getting anywhere, leave the problem in the other person's lap. *I can't change my position. Take some time to think about this, and get back to me.* He may be so surprised or defensive in the moment that he can't think clearly, but will come up with a solution if you let him think about it for a while.

- If you do get through to the other person, as you usually will, be gracious. Express appreciation simply and directly. And it's very important to allow the other person to save face. If he's agreed to change, then you can listen to defensive explanations. Don't allow yourself to get drawn into a long-winded discussion that may undo some of the good you've done, but allow him to salvage his dignity, if necessary.

- Don't feel bad if you get upset and you can't be as calm as you'd like. Your emotional display may get through to the other person more effectively than if you're cool, calm, and collected.

- Remember that each time you practice, you get better at it. As nerve-wracking as it may be to be assertive the first time, you can look forward to it getting easier, as your brain learns to think in an assertive way.

(Adapted with permission from <u>Undoing Perpetual Stress</u> by Richard O'Connor. © Berkley Press, 2005)

Mindful Communication

I've urged a few patients to try an experiment recently, with very positive results. The principle is simple: <u>Say only what you mean,</u> thoughtfully, using clear and exact language. No white lies, no little distortions, no insincere comments designed to get you off the hook or make someone else feel good. Nothing to massage the other's ego, unless you sincerely mean it. While doing this, watch your nonverbal communication and make it in sync with what you're saying. Try to avoid anything automatic or false—a pasted-on grin when you're uncomfortable; trite and empty words—

do: SAY WHAT YOU
REALLY WANT TO SAY.

"great," "wonderful." Look for words and phrases that convey your feelings. You don't have to tell the brutal truth all the time, but what you can say can only be the truth.

At the same time, listen closely to what others are saying. Try to focus. Don't be thinking about what you're going to say in response; your response will come to you without thinking. See if you can feel what the other person is feeling.

What people first notice is that this cuts down on a lot of the verbal noise that used to flow freely from their mouths. Their word count per day goes down dramatically, but they get comfortable being quiet fairly quickly. Then they start to notice how much more at ease they feel. Instead of conversations being a verbal tap dance in which they are straining to make themselves be liked—and feeling further and further out on the limb of their little lies—they can be quiet and attentive. They listen a lot better. They hear what people really want. They may not be able to give it to them, but they have given the gift of honest listening.

The last thing people notice is how much better they feel. More centered, more relaxed. The knot of tension in their stomachs is gone. The shame and guilt that goes with insincerity—which they were not even consciously aware of—starts to lift, and as it does, they feel a sense of freedom and self-respect. They feel more powerful, more in control. It's a great exercise to try for relieving social anxiety. Much of that feeling of discomfort in social settings comes from trying to fill up dead air. Instead, try getting used to saying less. Let others worry about silence.

Here's a different spin on the entire exercise. Try Thumper's mom's advice from *Bambi: If you can't say something nice, don't say anything at all.* Pay attention to how much gratitude and appreciation you express every day. Try to increase it.

the benefits of mindfulness

There are, of course, a thousand other ways our clever little minds can find to heap unnecessary misery on us; I've just hit some of the high points. But there is a theme here: Letting our brains run on automatic pilot not only leads to bad decisions, which in themselves lead to unhappiness—but the process of not thinking, of operating without awareness, feels bad in itself. There is a deep part of our brain that is always honest, that sees through our defenses and distortions; it knows when we're not really in control, when we're kidding ourselves, and it gets worried. It's not the Inner Critic; that's an artificial construct, we don't all have one of them. It's just the part of us that can't help seeing things as they really are, and when it doesn't like what it sees, it sends out stress signals, adrenaline and cortisol, flowing through our bodies and making us anxious and unhappy. Becoming more mindful is a way of getting in touch with that part of ourselves, and that helps us calm down and take control. When we're honest with ourselves, when we operate as a coherent whole, we've taken the biggest single step possible to reducing unnecessary misery. And a step toward joy.

SEVEN

more joy

Remember, happiness isn't normal. The usual resting state of our minds is slightly edgy. The hedonic treadmill is hard-wired into our brains, luring us down the road to More and Then Some, but we can use our brains to counter its effects. This chapter is about focusing on joy, the immediate sensation of positive feelings. Joy requires special attention because there is so much going on in today's world that interferes with our ability to be attentive to how we feel right now—and if you can't do that, you miss a lot of happiness.

do: ALLOW YOURSELF THREE MONTHS OF DAILY PRACTICE TO LEARN A NEW SKILL (LIKE DEVELOPING AWARENESS OF JOY).

Here's a fable from Harlan Ellison, the noted science-fiction writer:

A man lives a drab and boring life, until he just can't stand it any longer, and he kills himself. But he regains consciousness on a dismal distant planet inhabited by ugly crablike beings, of which he is now one. He realizes that he lived on this planet before his life on Earth, and that he was predestined to return here after his death. He asks what crime he had committed to deserve such a miserable life on Earth. No crime at all, they tell him. *In fact your life here was so kind and admirable that you were rewarded with the gift of a lifetime on Earth.* To this world, Earth is the "pleasure planet," where the weather is mild and food is plentiful and water is refreshing, where the sky at night is lit by a million stars and the day is blessed with the warmth of the sun,

> . . . where anguish was so much less known than that known everywhere else.
>
> He remembered the rain, and the sleep, and the feel of beach sand beneath his feet, and ocean rolling in to whisper its eternal song, and on just such nights as those he had despised on Earth he slept and dreamed good dreams . . . of life on the pleasure planet.*

The simplest but most important message about happiness is this: <u>WAKE UP</u>! There is spectacular beauty all around you. Miracles are happening right under your nose. Compared with our ancestors and most of the people in the world today, we live a very comfortable, pleasant existence with great freedom and many opportunities. Don't let it all slip by unnoticed.

I've been using the word *joy* as verbal shorthand to cover the whole range of good feelings, but now it's time to pay closer attention to just what those feelings are. Paul Ekman, probably the greatest living authority on emotions, has a pretty long list of good feelings, with a few I hadn't thought of, and some that English doesn't have words for. But I also found a few I thought Ekman left out. You can probably think of some, too. Here's Ekman's list:

- Sensory pleasures (touch, smell, taste, and so forth.)
- Amusement

---

*I am grateful to Timothy Miller for bringing this story to my attention in his valuable book, *How to Want What You Have.* The original story is called "Strange Wine," and is in a collection of stories by that name.

- Contentment
- Excitement
- Relief
- Wonder (goose bumps)
- Admiration
- Ecstasy
- *Fiero*—the combination of excitement, pride, and relief when winning a difficult challenge
- *Naches*—pride in others' accomplishments—our children, our students (*kvelling* is the immediate experience of *naches*)
- Elevation—feeling motivated to become a better person
- Gratitude
- Schadenfreude—our guilty pleasure in others' misfortune

And I would add to that list:

- Feeling safe and secure
- Playfulness
- Intoxication
- Joy—just plain old delight
- Pride
- Efficacy—feeling in control, that your actions have effects
- Altruism—the pleasure of giving to others, helping out others in distress
- And finally fulfillment, a complex emotional state that has to do with personal growth

It's worth remarking that there's nothing on Ekman's list or mine that has to do with money or possessions.

The fact that I can quickly brainstorm a few items to add to Ekman's list probably means only that there are potentially endless sources of good feelings—a very nice problem to have. Yet, as we've seen, worldwide happiness seems to be dwindling. One of the major reasons why is that we seem to be losing our ability to feel anything at all. We discussed in Chapter 4 all the pressures on us today to control or deny our feelings. The result is that we've learned to fear our own emotions. Ask any therapist, and they'll tell you we're in the midst of an epidemic of <u>alexithymia</u>—the loss of the ability to feel our emotions. This is very dangerous for our whole being, not only for our happiness, because emotions are the very essence of our selves. Their purpose is to focus our attention, and they are supposed to do that by hijacking our thoughts. Good thing, too—to be scared out of our daydream when the bus is bearing down on us, or to be reminded that a sunset is really special.

learning to feel

Emotions give us a self: They tell the infant what she wants, and they give her the problem of getting the world to give it to her, and out of that she builds a whole person. Emotions are the link between mind and body, a complex signaling system of nerves and chemicals that we seem to share with every other animal. We even share most of our feelings—anger, fear, joy, play, lust, a parental instinct, guilt—with higher mammals, except that, as everyone knows, cats have no guilt. Emotions are central to our sense of right and wrong;

do: RESPECT AND VALIDATE YOUR OWN FEELINGS.

they are the value statements by which we evaluate our experience—good or bad, dangerous or safe.

Most important from the standpoint of happiness, we don't seem to be able to stop our negative feelings without choking off our positive feelings, too. So before we talk about feeling more positive feelings, let's talk a little about the ability to feel, period. That's really not so hard to do, but it requires focused attention and practice, and because we're all so time-poor in today's world, those are hard to come by.

We are always learning, whether we want to or not, whether we're trying to or not. That's news that is both wonderful and horrifying. Imagine this: All your life, you've wanted to play the trumpet. Now you're fifty-five, the kids are grown, you've got time in the evenings to do what you'd like. You invest in a decent secondhand trumpet and find a teacher, but you know that practice is the essential thing. You want to practice every evening you can. Trouble is, whenever you practice, the dog starts howling. "It hurts her ears," your wife says helpfully. You don't give a damn about that, you just want the dog to shut up, because it's a horrible distraction. This has been going on for weeks. Even when you just think about playing, your feelings of frustration arise.

This is relevant: A German researcher took single rat brain neurons, stretched them out in a petri dish, ran a tiny electric wire between them, and repeatedly turned on a small current—all on video, using the latest microscopic techniques. Within half an hour, the nerve cells began to grow new dendritic spines—the specialized organelles where neurons receive neurotransmitters. They were learning a new connection. <u>Learning was taking place without a brain.</u>

do: LET YOUR NERVES LEARN JOY.

Learning happens all by itself, whether we're conscious of it or not. Nerve cells will learn whatever they experience.

Back to you and your trumpet and the dog. Sharon Begley has a fascinating book called *Train Your Mind, Change Your Brain,* in which she reviews a lot of neuroplasticity research. Among other things she reports on are some experiments by Mike Merzenich that bear directly on your problem. He took a group of monkeys and put them in an apparatus where they received a tap on their finger a hundred times a day. At the same time, they were listening to music piped in through headphones. Half the monkeys were rewarded with a sip of juice when they indicated that the rhythm of the tapping changed. The other monkeys were rewarded with juice when they indicated that the music changed. Merzenich was teaching the monkeys in the first group to pay attention to the tapping, and the second group to pay attention to the music. After six weeks, in the brains of those in the tapping group, the size of the sensory cortex that corresponds to that particular finger was enlarged. In the brains of the music group, that part of the cortex hadn't changed at all but the part that corresponds to hearing had grown. Remember that the monkeys were treated identically; they all had the music and the tapping going on at the same time. The only difference was what they were trained to pay attention to. Begley says:

> Experience coupled with attention leads to physical changes in the structure and future functioning of the nervous system . . . moment by moment we choose and sculpt how our ever-changing minds will work, we choose who we will be in the next moment in a very real sense, and these choices are left embossed in physical form on our material selves."

<u>What we pay attention to determines how our brain grows.</u>

So here's the solution for your trumpet practice: Put the dog in another room, close the door, and tune her out while you're playing. Deliberately focus on your playing, and ignore the dog, and you can expect that this will get easier because you're exercising the circuits that focus on the trumpet, and they will strengthen and expand, while the circuits that get stimulated by the dog's barking will become weaker by comparison. <u>Practice in concentration and focus will change your brain.</u> Attention, as Daniel Siegel says, is not some fixed process. In my terminology, it's a skill. Siegel has been able to show that attention is a learnable skill with an eight-week mindfulness awareness training program that has significantly improved attending skills, and reduced distraction and impulsivity, in adults and adolescents with ADHD.

In the same way, when you lose your cool in traffic and give in to road rage, you've just made it more likely you'll give in to road rage next time. The neuronal connections between traffic and yelling have fired together, and wired together. If you can instead learn to take a few deep breaths, you'll be wiring up a connection between traffic and calmness. Remember that learning takes place whether you want it to or not. If you don't want to learn to be more rageful, you have to deliberately learn to be more mindful.

The same principles are now being applied with stroke patients. For decades, medicine had assumed that the adult brain is incapable of change, and that if a stroke killed brain cells in a particular area, say those corresponding to use of the right arm, there was nothing you could do except use your left arm. Some scientists began to suspect, however, that it was a mistake to let that right arm atrophy. They began what's known as constraint-induced movement therapy—simply tying down the good arm and encouraging the patient to use the bad one. Now we see that, although the stroke-damaged area of the brain doesn't recover, other areas of the brain are "recruited" to step in and assume some of its functions.

If intensive practice can train new areas of the brain to take over the function of areas that have been knocked out by stroke, or get the brain to tune out some stimuli while focusing on others, then practice can enable us to learn how to be happy again. But it takes intense, focused practice. Focus is essential. What we pay attention to determines which of our brain circuits get strengthened and which recede into the background, as Merzenich's monkeys showed us. If you're in a crowd and you're looking for a friend's face, the facial recognition circuits in your brain are activated. If you're looking for a guy in a red shirt, it's the color recognition circuit. If it's some-body waving, the motion circuits fire, and so on. <u>If you're reviewing the events of your day, think of the times you felt good.</u> It will strengthen the circuits of good feeling. Think of what made you feel good, and the next day do more of that. In this way, we build happiness. You adjust your set point.

security and compassion

If we want to feel good, it helps to first feel safe. Our general sense of safety and security within ourselves and with the world turns out to have a lot to do with our early childhood experience. That shouldn't come as a surprise to anyone who's watched a generation or two grow up—we can see stable traits of temperament and personality that seem to begin in babyhood and endure throughout the life span. How anxious we are in general, how confident we feel about ourselves, an overall sense of self-esteem, and then how willing we are to extend ourselves to others—those are paradigms that seem to last. How much of it has to do with the child's genetic heritage and how much has to do with parenting is, of course, an open question. So for any particu-lar parent/child pair, we simply say that it's the interaction, the *fit*, between the child's innate temperament and the parent's ability and availability that impacts these paradigms.

Psychologists have been studying what's called <u>attachment</u> for almost fifty years. Observing how a mother and young child interact in a lab experiment called the strange situation—in which the mother leaves the child with a stranger for a few minutes, then returns—allows them to classify children into three groups:

- Securely attached children are happy to see mother return. They approach her for comfort and allow themselves to be comforted.
- Anxiously attached children may be in visible distress while mother is away, and when she returns, they cling to her, but their distress is not greatly alleviated.
- Avoidant attached children act as if they are in no distress while mother is away (though brain monitors register that they <u>are</u> in distress). When she returns, they ignore her. If she tries to comfort them, they may reject her.

Of course, a lot can change as the child grows up, but these attachment styles developed in early childhood tend to persist as adult personality types. There are reliable interviews and paper-and-pencil tests for measuring adults' attachment styles.

- Adults who are secure tend to form close, trusting, affectionate relationships. They are optimistic about the world and feel confident in their ability to manage life's ups and downs—and, when needed, they feel that they can turn to others for help. They tend to be generous, compassionate, and quick to volunteer.
- Emotionally anxious adults often seem desperate in their attempts to gain love and support from others, yet perpetually fear that they will be let down or abandoned. They don't have much confidence in their own abilities and tend to be needy, clingy, and manipulative. At bottom, they harbor grave doubts about their own self-worth,

reinforcing their fear that they will be rejected. If they act compassionately, it is to relieve their own distress at seeing another suffer, rather than to help the other person from motives of generosity or empathy.

- Adults who are emotionally avoidant tend to believe that others cannot help them. They are distant and uncomfortable with intimacy. Their aim is self-reliance but they try to attain it by ignoring their own weaknesses or needs, resulting in a very unrealistic and fragile self-image. They tend to lack compassion.

In large-scale tests, only a slim majority of young adult Americans are found to be securely attached. Another quarter are emotionally anxious, and about 20 percent are avoidant.

If security, confidence, and the capacity to form rewarding intimate relationships are a major component of happiness (and they are), it would seem that almost half of us are doomed. But in a fascinating series of experiments, Phillip Shaver of the United States and an Israeli researcher, Mario Mikulincer, have demonstrated that feelings of security can be heightened in anxious and avoidant adults. In one experiment, students who had been subliminally primed—exposed to words on a screen more quickly than they could be conscious of—with words associated with emotional security like *love, hug,* and *support* were found to express fewer prejudicial attitudes than students who had been primed with neutral words. The same reduction in prejudice was found with students who had been asked merely to imagine being in a difficult situation but surrounded by people who loved them and wanted to help. Those results were obtained even with subjects who had been found to be emotionally anxious or avoidant.

Expressing attitudes on a questionnaire is one thing, but actually feeling secure enough to help another person in trouble may be something else again. In another series of experiments, subjects were told that their role was to observe and score the behavior of another experimental subject, a young woman who was going to be asked to perform a series of distasteful or uncomfortable procedures—keeping a hand in ice water, petting a tarantula, touching a preserved sheep's eye, among other charming tasks. Actually, the "other" subject who was being observed was in on the experiment, and the scene was all on tape. As the naïve subjects watched the tape, the young woman expressed more and more distaste and reluctance, until she finally said she couldn't go on. The experimenter was seen to turn off the camera. After a few moments, he returned to the subject, and asked him if he would consider switching places with the young woman who had "dropped out." "The study can't go on unless someone actually pets the tarantula while someone else watches, and the next task is just as bad or worse, having cockroaches run up your arm."

As you might expect, subjects who had been rated as anxiously or avoidantly attached were less likely to offer to switch places and subject themselves to some personal distress. But again, when the subjects had been subliminally primed, or when they had been previously asked to think about another person who had once helped them in a difficult situation, they were more likely to volunteer—even the anxious and avoidant attached subjects.

Are we stuck with a set point of personal security? Do we have set limits on our compassion for others? These experiments, like almost all the social psychology research, were conducted with a mild, almost trivial, "mood inducer"—finding a dime in the copy machine, being given a free gift costing less than a dollar, getting a small bag of candy, seeing a word flashed on a screen, being asked to remember something—yet they find that the mood change lasts, at least for a while. Not only does the mood last, it may set in motion a positive feedback loop that will help sustain it. If you voluntarily offer to suffer for another, that one act may make a small permanent change in how you feel about yourself.

It's taken a hundred years for Western psychology to actually begin to test the hypothesis that what you do can make you happier, but the positive psychology movement (see Chapter 10) has finally provided the impetus. The early results are encouraging. One series of experiments showed that focusing on feelings of gratitude raises your happiness level, at least temporarily, improves your sleep, stimulates you to engage in more generous and helpful acts, and also somehow gets you exercising more. Another experiment asked subjects to perform five acts of kindness per week over six weeks; it concluded that, at least short-term, acting kindly toward others produced

positive change in subjective well-being. Still another found that simply reflecting on and reaffirming one's personal values lowered cortisol levels in the
blood (a reliable stress indicator) and lowered one's subjective feeling of
stress. A pioneer researcher, Michael Fordyce, had demonstrated some time
ago that simply teaching his undergraduate psychology classes about the
principles of happiness resulted in significant gains in their happiness
levels—but his results were largely overlooked until the past few years. His
fourteen-point program is generously available online, at www.gethappy.net.

Experiments like these provide strong evidence that when you find
yourself facing a situation that makes you uncomfortable or anxious, or
when you're feeling insecure for no particular reason that you can identify,
you can help yourself. None of these interventions require concentrated effort or a lot of work, certainly not the kind of focused practice that we want
to see in mindfulness training, nothing like the three months' practice I ask.
They're merely asking their subjects to answer a few questions or reflect for
a few minutes. How much more effective can you be if you make a sustained
effort? Here are some suggestions:

- Take a few minutes' quiet time and remember someone who loved
  you, someone who believed in you, someone who might be willing
  to suffer for your sake. Or think of someone who feels that way
  now. See how much you can remember of sensory details: their
  voice, their expression, their smell. The way they dressed. See if
  you can place them in context: a particular room, a particular time
  in your life. Remembering details like this is likely to jog your
  emotional memory and make it more powerful.
- Think of someone whose happiness and welfare you care deeply
  about, someone you'd be willing to sacrifice for. The emotional
  memory of this kind of connection will help you feel more secure.
- You might instead spend time thinking, or writing in a journal,
  about things in life that you are grateful for. Things that make, or
  have made, your life easier: lucky breaks, close calls, and learning
  experiences; moments of joy or satisfaction in the past. When
  someone in AA is feeling frustrated and bitter, it's a standard bit of

advice to have them draw up a "gratitude list." It usually makes a dramatic difference in their perspective.

- Both security and gratitude experiences also may be good memories to conjure up as you go to sleep at night.

sources of joy

Michael Argyle, a leading happiness researcher, has made a list for us of what most people say brings them good feelings. Here they are, not in any particular order:

- Eating
- Social activities and sex (Argyle considers humor a social activity)
- Exercise and sports
- Alcohol and other drugs
- Success and social approval
- Use of skills
- Music, the other arts, and religion*
- Weather and environment
- Rest and relaxation
  (Note that there is nothing here about money, possessions, or accomplishments.)

On the other hand, Dr. Barbara Ann Kipfer, a lexicographer by trade, has given us a book of *14,000 Things to Feel Happy About,* which is handy to have around. It consists of a very long list of little things, which represents more than forty years of recording what has made her happy. On the theory that when you think about something, you make it more likely you'll

---

* This is a very strange grouping; I can only think that Argyle puts religion together with art and music because they all can take us out of ourselves through an aesthetic experience, or inspire awe. But music (my own personal theory without anything to back it up) is different from other arts because rhythm and harmony get to the brain in a very direct, sensual way. And religion as a source of good feeling is not just about being moved, but also about having a purpose, a sense of community, perhaps a sense of being loved by a greater being. In any case, I'll discuss _awe_ shortly and _religion_ when we get to the chapter on finding meaning.

think of that thing again, it's probably a great book to scan at bedtime. Imagine how happy she must feel, being so mindful of happiness.

It's interesting that three of Argyle's top four happy-making activities can also be the source of misery—guilt, shame, and jail. But eating, sex, and drugs are such powerful, seductive sources of good feeling that they can easily tempt us to overindulge or transgress our own values. Only exercise and sports seem to be risk-free. Most of the other items are either not so inherently reinforcing or naturally self-limiting.

All joys are fleeting, and in fact, that is the very nature of good feelings. The feeling lasts as long as the experience lasts—if that long, we're so distractible. You won't be in a state of rapt attention for an entire movie, no matter how good Martin Scorsese is. The Nobel Laureate Daniel Kahneman suggests that the reason why we're so adaptable—why lottery winners and accident victims so quickly return to their baseline happiness levels—is that we have such short attention spans. At first, major life changes like these take up a lot of room in our heads, but it doesn't take long for us to be once again distracted by the minutiae of daily living. Rather like the mothers who report dissatisfaction with child-rearing because child care goes on continuously while they have to do everything else, we tend to forget about disability or being rich because they occupy our attention for only a diminishing fraction of our time. Once again, attention is the key. If we could train our minds to focus more on what's truly important and not be distracted by our next errand, we'd be much better off.

Greater mindfulness can help us focus. Mindfulness can help us stay aware of how transient and fragile good feelings can be. Mindfulness helps us accept those facts without being so frightened that we choose not to feel out of a fear of loss or disappointment. Of course, a mindful attitude makes us more sensitive to little pleasures—sunlight on our skin, good smells in the kitchen, or an e-mail from an old friend.

One reason we miss out on so much possible joy is that we rely too much on our paradigms. Whenever we see a familiar object, like a flower, there are actually two processes going on at the same time. Our eyes perceive an object of a certain color, size, and shape, and transmit that information to the lower levels of the cortex; that signal goes up through the layers of the cortex (there are six layers) to the higher levels, where apparently perception happens; we become conscious that we are seeing an object. But at the same time, the higher cortical layers are busy trying to identify the object. We know what a flower looks like from all our previous experiences with flowers. The higher layers are sending information downward to the sensory layers, saying essentially, *I got it. This is a flower. You don't have to pay attention anymore.* We have a paradigm of the category of flowers. Paradigms, as we've noted, are the superhighways of the brain; they are very useful in allowing us to quickly identify what's going on around us and move on to what we are trying to achieve. If we're weeding the garden, our minds can skip over all the details of the flowers because our purpose is to find weeds. But twenty-first-century life has us so busy that we're always in weeding mode. *Got to rush through the garden like every other task we have.* If we are trying to add joy to our lives, reliance on paradigms can blind us to the glorious detail of our experience.

THINK ABOUT HOW MANY THINGS YOU CAN FEEL HAPPY ABOUT.

When we're stuck in a hypervigilant state, feeling as if we have to keep busy merely because we have an unexamined fear of falling behind, all we're likely to see of life are those paradigms—including those of our children, our lovers, our bosses. Instead of seeing complex individuals with all their own feelings, we see only our stereotypes of them. Life zips by like cars on the interstate. Mindful meditation practice seems to help the higher cortical areas relax and slow down so that we are able to see beyond categories into the true novelty of our child on <u>this</u> day, at <u>this</u> age, with <u>this</u> expression on his face, with <u>this</u> concern.

savoring

In addition to learning how to recognize good feelings, we also must learn how to appreciate them. <u>Savoring</u> is a very popular subject in positive psychology, as well it should be. In the crush of today's world, always having too much to do, we develop the habit of quickly moving on from one mental subject to the next. But when the subject is feeling good, we need to stop and pay attention. Savoring is a skill to be learned and practiced.

Remembering luxuriating in a Jacuzzi is not the same as <u>being</u> in the Jacuzzi, unfortunately—but take a minute with me. My last Jacuzzi experience was in the winter eighteen months ago. I can remember the smell of chlorine, the intense humidity in my nose and sinuses, the bright sunlight in the room, the roar of the jets drowning out all other sounds in that confined space, the pleasant warmth of the water, the relief from gravity that buoyancy provides, and the pleasure of the water pressure massaging my aching muscles. It's amazing what you can remember when you focus. As I remember, my body remembers, too, and relaxes a little.

Here are some research-validated strategies for savoring.

- <u>Sharing.</u> Enlist others to share the experience with you. If you're being given an award, invite all your friends. Their good feelings for you are contagious. If you're bird-watching or visiting a museum, do it with friends, and talk about your impressions.

- <u>Memory building.</u> Take mental photographs (or real photographs, now that everyone has a camera phone) of the event. Take a physical souvenir. I bring rocks home from Civil War battlefields I've visited, from friends' homes, from beaches and mountains. When I go out on my deck and touch them, I'm reminded of the good feelings associated with each trip.

- <u>Self-congratulation.</u> As Christopher Peterson says, "Do not be afraid of pride. Tell yourself how impressed others are and remember how long you have waited for this to happen."

- <u>Sharpening perceptions.</u> Focus only on certain aspects of the experience and block out others. If it's congratulating yourself on the speech you gave, forget about how sweaty and nervous you were; remember how great you felt afterwards. If it's appreciating a good wine, focus on your sensory experiences and turn off thinking.

- <u>Absorption.</u> Let yourself concentrate on the good feelings, as you would focus on your breathing in meditation. Feel the effects of feeling good throughout your body. Stay with the experience.

- <u>Behavioral expression.</u> Laugh, dance, sing, jump for joy, cry, and verbalize your intense feelings. (*That cake was <u>so</u> good!*) We might suppress impulses like these because we worry about what "others might think," which is a reliable buzz kill. Let go and express your joy.

Considering all we know about the hedonic treadmill and other forms of adaptation that can bring us down, it seems like we'd all be very well advised to practice savoring in regard to any good feeling. Now that we know that our brain rewires itself based on what we pay attention to, we can make a strong case that savoring positive experiences will make it easier for us to experience good feelings next time around.

A common mindfulness exercise is to take five minutes to taste a single raisin. You may try this right now, if you want. Put the raisin in your mouth but don't chew or swallow. Explore it with your tongue. Notice the wrinkles and ridges. Do different parts of your tongue feel it differently? Notice how it may begin to soften a little as it absorbs your saliva. Then break it with your teeth, but don't chew any more. Notice the rush of flavor as it bursts. How would you describe the taste? What else tastes like this—cinnamon, wine, tea, chocolate? Think about this for a little while; then chew but don't swallow. Notice how the taste changes as you chew. Your saliva is having a chemical effect on the raisin, altering the taste somewhat. What other tastes are you tasting now? Then you may swallow, but notice the lingering taste in your mouth. Do you like this taste?

Most people are amazed at the richness and variety of experience that comes from eating one raisin mindfully. Think about adapting this to any sensual experience.

EXERCISE 11:
SAVORING

Make sure you have time available and won't be interrupted. Get comfortable.

Slow down. Take your time. Use mindfulness practice methods to focus on your experience. Instead of concentrating on the breath, concentrate on the taste of your food, the touch of your partner, the feel of the sun on your skin, the sound of the ocean—whatever it is you've decided to focus on. When you feel yourself distracted by other thoughts or feelings, just let them go and return to the sensation.

Take a mental picture. Step back and look at yourself, the position you're sitting in, the time of day, what's going on around you. Compose a picture in your mind of yourself as you are right now, and the sensual experience you're focusing on. Picture your brain burning this image into its memory, like the shutter of your camera exposes film. You will always have this picture, with its attendant sensations, to return to whenever you want to feel these feelings again.

Think of words and phrases you might use to describe this experience to another person. This will help make a memory. Don't judge yourself if words seem inadequate—they usually are, but they conjure up feelings in your listener that will help her understand.

There are many hidden flavors in any taste; allow yourself to go deep and explore them. In the same way, there are many hidden experiences in a touch, in a sound, in a visual scene. Practice changing your focus from wide-angle (watching yourself having this experience) to close-up (concentrating intently on a single detail), and back again.

KEEP A JOURNAL.
REVIEW THE JOURNAL
REGULARLY.
LEARN WHAT MAKES YOU
FEEL GOOD, AND DO
MORE OF IT.

When it comes to absorbing good feelings, it makes a big difference how we use our minds, as was shown in an experiment that highlighted the differences between thinking and remembering. Students were divided into two groups: one was to write about events in their lives in a logical, analytic way. The other was to write down details of memories about the events. When they were writing about happy events, the analytical students reported poorer overall well-being and physical health than those who were simply remembering. On the other hand, when it came to writing about negative events, those who wrote or talked analytically reported better well-being and physical health than those who were just remembering. It suggests that when we simply let our minds wander over past events, we are savoring or re-experiencing the event—and if it was a good one, we feel good; a bad one, we feel bad. But the analyzing, problem-solving part of our mind is most useful when turned on negative events; when we try to analyze happy events, we decrease our happiness. So don't dwell on bad feelings. Use your Wise Mind to reflect on negative experiences enough to learn how not to repeat them, absorb the lesson, and move on.

do: LEARN TO DETACH FROM NEGATIVE FEELINGS.

There is strong evidence of a virtuous circle (the opposite of a vicious circle) operating when it comes to experiencing positive feelings. Numerous studies have found that people who are happier than average are more successful in many fields of life: supervisory evaluations, work satisfaction, health, salary, relationships with friends, marital happiness, allergic reactions (happy people have fewer), social support, group leadership, physical attractiveness, estimated intelligence, "goodness," managerial potential, sleep quality, physical activity, medical visits, mortality rate (!), age at death, and immune system function, to name a few. In other words, bubblier, more extraverted people tend to be more successful in most areas of life than the less outgoing. Of course, this is a two-way street: the more successful, popular, and healthy you are, the more you have to be chipper about. All the more reason to be grateful for the research indicating that savoring positive experiences can reset your ability to be happy. It won't happen overnight, but with focused attention, you can expect to strengthen the brain circuitry that experiences good feelings, while those associated with negative feelings wither. Then you also can benefit from the virtuous circle wherein more positive feelings lead to greater success, better health, stronger relationships—the list is endless.

the best, and easiest, exercise in the book

Here's an exercise that can make a dramatic difference in your happiness level, yet is so simple and so easy, it requires almost no effort at all. Don't let that fool you. It's made a big difference in my life, in the lives of many of my patients, and (according to the research) for lots of other people as well.

EXERCISE 12:
THREE GOOD THINGS

Back when I wrote *Undoing Depression*, I suggested that people make a list at bedtime of three good things that had happened during the day. I thought I was passing along a common-sense idea that came from my wife. Turns out that the positive psychology researchers have been able to show experimentally that this is a good way to adjust the happiness thermostat. Christopher Peterson and others have demonstrated experimentally that focusing on only three things is better than trying to think of more, that the exercise is best performed in the evening, and that in addition to listing the items, it helps if people think about why each good thing happened. Thinking about it in this way makes us more mindful and makes the memory more indelible. They also showed that the exercise increases feelings of happiness and decreases symptoms of depression for up to six months, as long as people keep practicing. (Six months was the limit of the study; there's no reason to think that the exercise would be less effective over a longer time.)

Here's the research-based and tested version of the exercise:

- Each evening before bed, write about three good things that happened that day. Three things that went well, that made you feel good, that brought a smile to your face.
- These can be very small things or relatively big things. Something you liked for lunch, or getting a raise. Hearing a new song you enjoyed, or a productive day's work.

- These can be sensual pleasures, things you feel proud of, things you feel good about for others' sake—anything at all that yielded a positive feeling.
- For each item, answer the question "Why did this thing happen?" Just a simple answer, in your own words; nobody's judging your correctness.
- If you have a partner, you may want to do this exercise together at night and share your lists. You'll learn a lot about each other.
- You may want to do this in a journal that you keep, and review from time to time. Chances are that as you look back, you'll be very pleasantly reminded of things you've forgotten about. And you may see a pattern that suggests some change is in order: for instance, that you think about food more than you want to, or that it's rare for you to think of sensual pleasures.

And here's my lazy man's version:

- When you go to bed at night, clear your head of other thoughts. If you've got nagging worries, it may help to visualize taking each and putting it down in a small pile on the floor next to your bedside. Many of them will be waiting patiently there for you in the morning, though some may skulk off in the night.
- Now, think about three good things that happened during the day, as above; small or big, sensual pleasures, accomplishments, and the like.
- Focus in on your feelings about these things. Practice differentiating the subtleties of feeling. Do you feel proud? Excited? Joyful? *Naches?* Does the memory make you want to smile? Pay attention to the muscles on your face as they form a smile. Do you feel warm? Where? In your heart, your stomach, your whole body? Do you feel a pleasant lump in your throat? Does your heartbeat change?

- Visualize the neurons in your brain forming new happiness circuits—tiny little bulldozers widening the channels to happiness. Remember that brain cells form new circuits just because we're remembering. Visualize endorphins flowing into your joy receptors like fresh snowmelt flowing into those new happiness channels. Remember that doing this exercise regularly will change your happiness set point; you'll feel more joy, more easily.
- Let yourself go to sleep as you continue to savor, explore, and visualize.

One test of this exercise found that it increased happiness and decreased depressive symptoms for the entire six months of the study period, although participants had been asked to do it for only a week. Further exploration found that many of the participants continued to focus on three good things entirely on their own.

One effect of practicing this exercise may be to help you "be in the moment" more often and more easily, by cueing you to pay attention during the day to moments of beauty, pleasure, and pride. *My boss just gave me a compliment. I'll have to remember that!* When we talked about mindfulness, we didn't stress "being in the moment," but of course, that's what mindfulness is—focusing on our immediate experience, on what's happening right now, not being distracted by other thoughts or feelings, more thoughtful, more curious, more <u>aware.</u>

do: BE IN THE MOMENT.

the body

High on Argyle's list of sources of happiness are exercise and sports, rest and relaxation. And high on almost everyone's list of sources of misery are some feelings about their body: too fat, too short, too thin, too hairy, painful, out of shape—the list is endless. Hence our love–hate relationships with our bodies.

There is good reason to believe that the happier you are, the healthier you are. One now-famous study used the fortunate accident that the autobiographies written by young Sisters of Notre Dame when they were entering the order were still on file sixty years later. The researchers had a group of independent judges read each autobiography and count the number of words expressing positive and negative emotions. These counts were then compared with the individual sister's current health status. The study found that the more positive emotion the sister expressed when entering the order (average age of twenty-two), the healthier she was likely to be at present (age range of 75 to 95). This is generally considered to be an excellent natural experiment, since all the variables that might have affected health over the sixty-year time span of the study (eating, drinking, smoking, life partners, stress) were essentially the same for all the sisters. Since they all lived in essentially the same conditions, it's highly likely that the differences in their individual happiness set points caused their differences in robustness or vitality. <u>Happiness affects how long and how well we live.</u>

On the other end of the lifestyle spectrum, someone has noticed that Oscar winners live on average four years longer than losers. Less stress? More satisfaction? Innate vitality? Someone else has noticed that cosmetic surgery may be an exception to the adaptation rule. There is preliminary data to suggest that women who've had breast augmentation surgery gain a more-or-less permanent uplift in self-satisfaction. Maybe the prevalence of cosmetic surgery in Hollywood has something to do with greater overall happiness and better health. In a Pittsburgh hospital, it was found that among ten years' worth of patients recovering from gall bladder surgery, those patients who could see trees from their windows requested significantly less pain medication, got along better with the nurses, and had shorter hospital stays than those whose windows faced an airshaft.

So do we really need to talk about how the mind and body are interconnected? At this point in the research, it might be better to talk about how they are <u>the same thing.</u> The mind is not only in the brain, but in the endocrine and immune systems, the nerves, the muscles, the guts. When we feel an emotion, it's not just a passing experience in the mind; each emotional experience changes the brain and the body a little. Each time you feel happiness, you make it easier to feel happiness again, because you are reinforcing the happiness circuitry in your brain and the rest of your mind. Anxiety and depression not only shorten the life span, but they also have bizarre somatic effects. Somehow your surgical wounds heal more slowly if you're anxious or depressed. Unhappy people are more likely to catch colds. Chronic stress and long-term depression cause brain damage; big empty spaces appear where there used to be gray matter, and the receptor sites for endorphins, the chemicals of good feelings, just wither away. But when you have a happy experience, your body chemistry improves, and blood pressure and heart rate tend to fall.

My last book was all about how stress, and the negative emotionality associated with it, destroys the body. Obviously, controlling stress leads to better health, but I didn't realize that controlling stress in a positive way leads to better-than-better health. For instance, compared to control groups, people who simply write about their feelings have better health in a variety of ways. And Shelley Taylor has pointed out that—within limits—people whose thinking is unrealistically positive have better health than those whose thinking is more realistic. One study of HIV-infected men compared a group who had realistically accepted their illness and were preparing for death to a group who were holding on to unrealistically optimistic beliefs. The unrealistic thinkers lived an average of nine months longer (!). This is a very controversial subject in health psychology, and no one is suggesting you should cultivate delusions in order to be healthier, but comforting illusions can reduce your stress level, and that can affect your health. There are many pros and cons about looking on the bright side. We know now that a positive attitude has no effect on whether or not you develop cancer, but if you do have cancer, a positive attitude will have an impact on your quality of life and may have an impact on your chances of survival. Yet there's a point where rose-colored glasses become blinders, where a healthy defense like just deciding not to think about something upsetting for a while morphs into denial.

There are other ways, less dangerous than deluding yourself, to reduce your stress. Getting more endorphins flowing in your brain strengthens the immune system. Learning mindfulness, cultivating happiness, and exercise are three great endorphin producers. It's another virtuous circle: Happiness leads to better health, which leads to more happiness, ad infinitum.

Nowadays, about 60 percent of visits to primary care MDs are for psychologically related complaints, and all our most frequently used drugs treat the symptoms of stress. We are in the midst of a national epidemic of stress that is literally wearing out our bodies, and we have to take preventive measures—diet, exercise, restraint, learning how to de-stress. Tal Ben-Shahar says that not exercising is like taking depressants, that our bodies were meant to work, hard, every day, to chase down prey or tend the crops.

But—from the standpoint of happiness—how do we bring joy into the things we need to do to take good care of ourselves? Obviously, there are lots of forces within us that seem to oppose exercising regularly and eating right. We've talked about the need to develop will power as a skill, and the fact that using your will power feels good. But how do you start? Here's my advice:

- Exercise. Everyone knows about the runner's high, but there are
  some misconceptions. Many people believe that it's a state of near-
  euphoria you reach when you do a long run—an hour or more—but
  that's not it at all. It is true that exercise, especially aerobic activity,
  produces endorphins, the happy hormones that are the chemical
  messengers of good feelings in our nervous system. Chocolate, sex,
  and parties produce endorphins, too, so it's not only an exercise-
  related phenomenon. But any exercise will produce some endorphins. The more you exercise, the more endorphins; simply put,
  the more you exercise, the better you feel. On the other hand, you
  have to learn to pace yourself; you have to build up your strength
  and endurance gradually so that you don't hurt yourself by pushing
  too hard. As a lifelong member of the Lazy Man's Guild, I know all
  the tricks to make exercise more enjoyable: Do it with friends, do it
  in groups, do it with music, do it with the TV on, or do it
  mindfully. (There is a secret to exercise, too: Once you're past the

first five minutes, you're good to go for a while. Your body warms up, your negative anticipation about how awful this is going to be drains away, and you surprise yourself with the realization that this is not so bad after all.)

- <u>Physical skills.</u> One sure way to enjoy your exercise is to do something that involves growth in coordination and skill. You get lost in the game, and forget your aches and pains. Tennis, squash, swimming, basketball, cycling, dancing, an aerobics class at the gym. Not the July Fourth softball or volleyball game where you tear up your knee and spend three months recuperating; I'm talking about things you can do regularly, once a week or more. But, you have to do these things mindfully. You can't push too hard; you can't get too competitive. You have to be fully present in the game, and let those endorphins work on you.

- <u>Nutrition.</u> Our contemporary epidemics of obesity and eating disorders are problems of abundance. Human bodies weren't designed for plenty of food; we're basically grazing animals, programmed to make very efficient use of sparse resources. Animals that are allowed to eat as much as they want tend to die early. We've become conditioned to the idea that eating to the point of fullness is a source of comfort. Now there's evidence that filling ourselves up with rich comfort food is an effective, if self-destructive and temporary, antidote for stress. So how do we restrict our intake and remain happy? Some suggestions: Don't buy anything in a package; processed food is too full of empty calories, salt, and unhealthy stuff. Stay out of the middle aisles in the grocery store. Don't eat fast food or in chain restaurants. Stay with fresh meat and fish, vegetables, fruits, and a little bread. Olive oil and garlic. It doesn't take any longer to grill a piece of fish and steam some rice and a vegetable than to heat a frozen pizza. Snack on fruit and cheese. If you stick with this for a few weeks, you'll be cleansing your palate so that if you switch back to processed foods, you'll be overpowered by the salt, the additives, the artificially enhanced flavor. Most of all, <u>eat mindfully.</u> Eat slowly, and pay attention to the taste. You'll discover that moderation brings a richer kind of happiness than indulgence.

awe

I know a man who is a professional juggler. When I met him, he'd had some bad experiences, and said he was having trouble practicing the four to six hours a day he felt necessary to keep up with his work. With my brain in the grip of a gloomy Connecticut February, I thought, *Four to six hours a day? This guy is some kind of schizoid nut, retreating into his work to avoid the real world.* A few days later, still grumpy, feeling lonely, bored, and sorry for myself, I looked up his Web site, as he'd invited me to. I was transported. He does things that seem impossible, but more than that they are simply beautiful (or amusing, or both). There is some aesthetic to his work that I can't describe, but it has to do with creating a sense of wonder, or playing with our expectations, that is just awe-inspiring. My opinion of this man was changed utterly; if I could create that kind of magic with four to six hours a day of work, I'd do it, too. But more than that, my grumpy February mood was gone. Like C. S. Lewis, I was surprised by joy. I still get a faint glow when I think of the experience.

My question is, *How does that happen?* How does an experience with beauty make us stop feeling lonely and sorry for ourselves? How does it make us feel connected with a world that's worth living in? Understand, there was no thought process involved. I didn't think, *Oh, look, there's beauty in life after all!* I didn't think at all, I just had a mood transplant.

As far as I know, science doesn't have an answer for that yet, though I'm sure in a few years, we'll at least understand the brain mechanisms involved. When you think about it, it's a common enough phenomenon, just not usually so sudden and dramatic a reversal as mine. That is the appeal of music, of fine art, of fireworks, of dancing, of a double play, of natural beauty. These things grab our emotions, stop the train of thought, and take us on a trip to some place of pleasure. The effect on our mood can last for hours, even days, and we can get a little inward smile years later at recollecting the experience. So if our goal is to increase happiness, this phenomenon is obviously something we should capitalize on.

Though we don't know for sure how these things work, we do know that they are all right-brain experiences. It's the left brain (for most right-handed people) that's involved with logic, problem-solving, schedules, and facts. That's the part of the brain that's so overused in today's world. It's the right brain that thinks more impressionistically, holistically. It's tuned in to non-verbal and emotional communication. It may be what we commonly call the unconscious. Although we said that left-brain activity seems to be associated with greater happiness, that referred to a specific, small part of the frontal cortex; here we're talking about the hemispheres in their entirety. The evidence suggests that in the last few hundred years, since the invention of work, cities, and artificial light, we've lost much of what used to be the most common stimulus of right-brain thinking—that is, contact with the natural world. Even today, more people go to zoos annually than attend all sporting events combined; we desire a connection

do: STEP OUTSIDE AND VISIT NATURE.

to nature. Getting caught in a thunderstorm, going to bed in the dark and listening to the owls, watching your seeds grow—these are things that remind you of your place in nature.

If you're a city dweller, you don't have to drive two hundred miles to get a taste of this experience. Just try stepping outside with your senses open. Be a gawker for a while. Listen to the rush of traffic. Look at the people going by, without thinking of where you have to be. Be in awe of the thousands of different lives going on all around you, all the time, all the consciousnesses that you will never know. City dwellers generally have some armor up, with reason, most of the time, but you can let yours down deliberately for a while, and be reminded of how small you are.

The loss of intimate daily contact with the greater world has been a huge adjustment for mankind. For all of human history until very recently, people went to bed when it was dark and got up when it was light. Clock time wasn't a factor in our lives. We worked until we were tired, or until the job was done. We lived with dogs, cats, horses, cattle, swine, chickens, goats, camels—and we were intimately acquainted with a great many more species because we hunted them or were hunted by them. We were at the mercy of the weather and the seasons, just one more part of the natural world. Most of our time was spent making sure we had enough to eat, and we had a lot of time when we could slip into a reflecting state—waiting for the fish to bite, the sun to come up, the crops to grow. We've lost that humility and become very self-important. In our present world, we usually have to create the opportunity for transcendent experiences when we can be in touch with something larger than ourselves—the sea, the sky, the mountains, the wind blowing, the leaves falling, the bustle of the city. The loss has grown especially marked over the past fifty years, with our increased reliance on the automobile, air-conditioning, and television. If you look around, you'll see that even children don't play outside any longer. We're suffering from what at least one author calls nature deficit disorder.

No one, certainly not me, knows the impact of all this change. From the standpoint of happiness, it's not all bad. There's no benefit in putting up with fleas, lice, and bedbugs, or freezing winter nights. But we do lose many opportunities for awe. Our delusion that we can control the world gets reinforced. And that sense of connection with each other, with God, and with nature gave us some insulation from stress—we didn't think it was our job to master the universe.

Back to awe. It's not that hard to achieve, right? All I have to do is turn the stereo on loud and play Mozart's *Requiem,* or *Baez Sings Dylan,* or a Lucinda Williams album, and I'm there, <u>if I focus my attention</u>. Maybe you just have to look at a painting, or watch the sunset, or sing a favorite hymn in church. The hair on the back of your neck stands up, or you get a shiver or goose bumps. Awe is often inspired by coming into contact with something much bigger than ourselves—the ocean, the mountains, the city. We're reminded that we are a tiny speck in the universe. There's usually a mystery or surprise involved; if we get to analyzing what's going on, we lose our thrill. Here's a question: How many times have you felt transported like this watching television? My answer is almost never. I don't put down television entirely. Some programs are good for a real laugh, or for information, and that's important. But television just doesn't require the <u>involvement</u> on our part that seems to be required to take us someplace magic. Magic requires that our senses be overwhelmed, that we be put into a state of awe. So if we want to add more of this kind of joy to our lives we have to get up off the couch and turn off the television. Easy to say, hard to do these days. Television turns into a true addiction.

Beyond that, many of us often feel a resistance (to use that old psychodynamic term) to getting out of our humdrum selves and exposing ourselves to something different. *I just don't feel like driving an hour into the country today. . . . I've got too much to do. . . . What about dinner?* Let me tell you very directly what's behind those kinds of rationalizations: It's fear. We are, for many reasons, unconsciously afraid of exposing ourselves to something beautiful, breathtaking, or awe-inspiring; <u>we are afraid of intense emotional experiences,</u> largely because we know they can rock our world. They can challenge our safe, if semi-miserable, comfort in doing the same thing over and over again day after day. So my advice:

- Take every opportunity to learn about concerts, plays, art exhibits, walks in the country. Read the entertainment section of your local paper or the community calendar on the Web and let yourself daydream.
- Then when you start to rationalize why you can't do those things, face the fact that you're afraid. That's nothing at all to be ashamed of. We want to be safe and comfortable, but sometimes that desire conflicts with our desire for joy. We have to find a balance. So face your fear mindfully, take a deep breath, and do it anyway.

Daniel Gilbert refers to what he calls the "pleasure paradox." We have two coexisting motives—to be happy and to understand things. Sometimes understanding things takes away some of their happiness. His example is having a dozen roses delivered to your door, anonymously. If you find out they're from your sweetheart, chances are that within a few years, you'll have forgotten the incident. But if you never find out, chances are that this will be a memory that mystery will help keep alive for years and years. So I think this is a great deal to do with how awe works. I don't understand, with my left brain, what watching that juggler does to me, just as I don't understand what seeing a dinosaur skeleton or hearing Beethoven's *Eroica* does. The mystery keeps the magic alive.

play

We all need to make a deliberate effort to add play to our emotional lives—if it's not oxymoronic to be deliberate about play. Studies of infants show that among our most basic emotions are curiosity or surprise and joy. Play gives us the opportunity for both. It's very important for us stodgy adults to maintain the ability to play; without it, we just grow brittle and dry. Because we know now that the brain doesn't simply store our experiences, we realize that each experience changes the brain. When we play, we build up the circuits of joy, making it easier to experience joy in the future. Play requires loss of dignity, so we take ourselves a little less seriously. Play can unite a bunch of strangers into a group with an immediate intimate experience. It's pretend, it has you acting like someone else, so it stretches your perspective on life.

Small children and pets are very helpful aids to happiness, because they nag us to get up and play with them. Back in the old days before electricity, people used to set the baby in the middle of the room (tent, cave) and just watch it. It was fun. Our children do it now, playing with a kitten or a puppy.

Play is a unique, integrating experience; it gets the left and right hemispheres acting together. It can provoke a major change in our moods. I know that sometimes when I'm down, busy, preoccupied, sometimes I will resist my dog's attempts to get me to play fetch with her because I know it will change my mood—and then I'll feel foolish, having taken myself so damn seriously when it's so easy to change the way I feel.

Play is a uniquely mindful experience. It requires us to be spontaneous, to be in the moment. It takes us out of our usual roles, where we're concerned about looking dignified and important, and puts us in incongruous situations. Hopefully we forget all about our dignity and just have fun. It teaches us to more flexible, to be ready for the unexpected. It often gets us interacting with others in new and unfamiliar ways that lead to greater intimacy and self-disclosure. Of course, many forms of play get us practicing balance, coordination, and muscle skills, which get the two parts of the brain working together. Dance is especially good for this.

Humor is a special form of play. Humor is especially mindful, because it depends on shifting perceptions. We're provoked to laugh or smile because of a reversal; we're "set up" (in the comic's phrase) to expect one thing, and suddenly here's another, which makes us realize something about how we allowed ourselves to be set up, and we laugh at ourselves. Humor and wit are small examples of changing paradigms. They point out alternative versions of reality, and make us take ourselves much less seriously. Most humor presents a version of reality that is more subversive, absurd, or rude. In this way, humor is naturally mindful; it makes us change our perspective on reality.

PLAY EVERY DAY.

People with a good sense of humor are less affected by stress. Laughing is a mood-lifter. Humor is considered one of the most mature defenses, a way of taking the stress out of difficult feelings. It expresses conflict in a safe way. It promotes in-group solidarity.

The act of laughing—even the <u>anticipation</u> of laughing—has been reported to have health benefits for the immune system and the circulatory system. But even if the jury's out, why not laugh? One doctor in Mumbai, convinced of the beneficial effects of laughter, began a "laughter club" in 1995, and it's grown into a worldwide movement (see laughteryoga.org). All over the world now, there are groups of men and women getting together every day for a twenty-minute laughter workout. It's very simple— they just stand around being silly together. (They started out by telling jokes, but found that they ran out of good ones in a few weeks.) They've found that "forced" laughter quickly becomes genuine because it's being shared with others. In the same way, smiling will make you happy, but only if you are able to master the Duchenne smile,* the genuine smile that crinkles the eyes, and that isn't easy. We have a lot of ways to smile falsely. But if you can master the Duchenne smile, your body will send happy signals to your brain, your left PFC will light up, and you will experience positive emotions.

* After Guillaume Duchenne, a nineteenth-century French anatomist who generated false smiles by electrically stimulating muscles in his subjects' faces.

creativity

Cornell psychologist Alice Isen gave her experimental subjects a few small gifts—a few coins, some candy, a compliment—then asked them to do what they do every day. These subjects were experienced physicians, and they were asked to diagnose illnesses as a mock patient revealed his symptoms one at a time. The news about this experiment is that those small gifts were enough to get these doctors thinking more creatively; they reached the correct diagnosis using only half the steps that it took doctors who hadn't been treated specially.

Our stereotype is that calm, logical reasoning leads to the best decisions, that thinking should be separated from emotions. But at least in some situations, being in a positive emotional state seems to help us think more clearly, creatively, and flexibly. Intuition may be much more powerful than we realize. New research shows that the brain registers a pleasurable feeling when we merely read the right answer to math problems, grammatical questions, ethical problems—even before the logical brain "knows" the right answer. Positive affect seems to have beneficial effects on thinking and relating: It enhances creativity, flexibility, and problem-solving; improves negotiations; enables people to take different perspectives and think less defensively. It seems to help improve memory organization, and thus helps thinking and judgment. It gives us hints at the right answers. It helps us keep going at difficult tasks. It promotes helpfulness and generosity. Happy people are more generous and thoughtful. Find a quarter on the street, and you're more likely to help out someone who needs it. Listen to a comedy album, and you're more likely to lend money. I'm sure that if you think back over your own experience, you can see that there were times when you were in a good mood and gave a handout to a homeless person, or settled an argument more quickly and generously. Now the research scientists have the data to show that these effects are real and common.

On the other hand, we know for certain that having too much to do interferes with creativity. Although many accomplished multitaskers may believe they are at their best when overly busy, that's an illusion. Under time pressure, our thinking becomes more superficial and narrow, especially if we see the schedule as arbitrary or artificially imposed. And in fact there's a "pressure hangover," when creativity is decreased for days after an episode of spectacular busyness.

Want a more permanent boost in creativity than candy or a quarter can give you? Expose yourself to lots of stimulation. Mice raised in enriched environments (with toys and other mice, not in sterile lab cages) have 15 percent more neurons in the hippocampus. They learn more quickly, are less fearful, and more curious. Even older mice (the equivalent of sixty-five human years), when kept in an enriched environment, have three times the number of new brain cells in the hippocampus than their lab-raised age mates. And these new neurons seem to be structurally different from older cells, having much more densely branched dendrites, the receptor sites for new information.

Fred Gage, one of the researchers who recently proved that human brains do grow new brain cells (neurogenesis), believes that physical exercise is the primary factor in stimulating the development of new cells, but that the "enriched environment" has something to do with their survival. "Usually, 50 percent of the new cells reaching the . . . hippocampus die. But if the animal lives in an enriched environment, many fewer of the new cells die." Interestingly, forced exercise doesn't have the same effect; it's only voluntary exercise (in mice, the freedom to jump on or off the exercise wheel as they wish) that results in neurogenesis.

In mice, the new neurons migrate to a small, little-understood area of the hippocampus known as the dentate gyrus. This is fascinating because we know that in humans with depression, the dentate gyrus is often significantly shrunk. (We don't know whether this is a cause or effect of depression.) But these findings have led Gage, among others, to speculate that depression may be the inability to recognize novelty. "You hear this a lot with depressed people . . . 'Things just look the same to me. There's nothing exciting in life.' It turns out these individuals have a shrunken hippocampus." So depression may be partially a result of a failure of neurogenesis, leading to the loss of the ability to experience things as different or interesting. In fact, it's often observed that in depression, the most stubborn symptom is anhedonia, the loss of the ability to experience

don't: LET YOUR BRAIN SHRINK.

joy. The patient may be up and exercising, back to work, no longer obsessed with feelings of guilt and inadequacy, apparently fully engaged with life—but still not happy. That is when many patients discontinue their medication or drop out of treatment, feeling like they've made all the progress they're going to make—but it may be precisely the wrong time.

With the old model of the brain, a system of hard-wired circuits that was thought to represent everything we know, it's been hard to imagine that neuro-genesis would be any benefit. It would seem, to borrow Sharon Begley's image, rather like adding a box of wires to a computer. Now that we know neuro-genesis is the norm, and that learning stimulates it, we need a new model for the brain, one that takes into account continuous rewiring. But even without a new model, the message is clear: If you want to grow new neurons, if you want to keep your brain vital and resilient, exercise regularly and enrich your environment. For humans, I think that means read good books, do puzzles, engage in stimulating conversation, play, look for challenges in your work, try new recipes, expose yourself to new music and art, travel . . . use your imagination.

simple pleasures

An alternative title for this book was going to be *Happiness Is Smaller Than You Think,* because I firmly believe that we consistently overlook some of the greatest joys in life simply by not paying attention. We dismiss things as small or everyday when, if we focused, we might find ourselves in a state of intense pleasure. One good friend of mine puts sitting in the sun with her dog in her top ten,* and we've already referred to the really good grilled cheese sandwich. I've heard the following from other people:

- Solving puzzles
- Surprises (receiving and planning)
- Going back home
- All forms of correspondence—phone calls, letters, e-mails, instant messages, postcards

* By the way, fluctuations in sunshine levels in the city where the stock exchange is located is a reliable indicator of stock returns (Hirshleifer and Shumway, 2003).

- Singing
- Dancing
- Sex
- Birds at the feeder
- Your grown children are happy
- A baked potato with sour cream
- A favorite song on the radio
- A memory of love
- Children giggling
- The first robin (catbird, crocus, snowdrop)
- Cutting the grass
- The ability to find any weird thing in the world via Google and Wikipedia

The ability to derive joy from things like this is in grave danger in today's world, where we're constantly pressured to keep busy, to move right on to the next thing, to stay ahead of the curve. Then when we feel how empty we are, we turn to consumerism and buy ourselves consolation prizes, or we take an unnecessary antidepressant, or we turn bitter and hurt the people we love.

By now, you know that I've read a lot about what other people have to say about happiness. When I started to write about the pleasures of the senses, I was surprised to see how few notes I'd accumulated. So I looked again at all my happiness books and found that most didn't have much to say about small pleasures. In some, words like <u>sex</u> or <u>eating</u> were just absent from the index. And yet, most of the things that people commonly associate with good feelings involve sensual pleasure: eating, drinking, sex and love, touch, music and other arts, nature and beauty, physical activity and sports. These things are relatively free from the hedonic treadmill, too. If you really enjoy a cheeseburger today, you'll enjoy one just as much next week (maybe not tomorrow).

So that got me to thinking: Maybe what there is to say about small pleasures is obvious. Sex, eating, drugs, music, and so on, can be very enjoyable experiences, but they don't last. What more is there to say? Yet I do think it's worth talking about some things that interfere with our enjoyment, some things that deprive us of the opportunity, and some things we can do to heighten our pleasure. Remember that feeling good has so many side benefits: It makes you healthier, more creative, more interesting, more inclined to take care of yourself, more successful—the list is endless. So make yourself feel good in these little hedonistic ways as often as possible.

Sex

One survey has found that people say they would value a better sex life as much as about fifty thousand dollars more in income a year—which suggests there's something drastically wrong with our approach to sex. After all, how difficult is it? Unlike eating, for example, we don't need an expensive range, exotic ingredients, the latest utensils from Williams-Sonoma. All we need is some privacy, and maybe a partner. But of course, the difficulty with sex is mostly in our heads. When we're young, we're shy and inexperienced. Sex with new partners is always fraught with awkwardness and the potential for embarrassment and hurt feelings. When we get older, we get more embarrassed about our bodies, our flab and sags— and our bodies don't always work right. Then there's all the neurotic guilt we inherited from our Catholic (or Jewish or Protestant or whatever) upbringing. None of that should matter at all. Sex is good for you. It makes you feel happy. If it's not hurting anyone else, there's nothing to feel guilty about. Overcome your hang-ups and do more of it.

do: HAVE MORE SEX.

We've already talked about the Coolidge effect. The unfortunate fact of life is that new potential sex partners are inherently a lot more exciting than the same old body next to us in bed. But before you leave your spouse for the tennis coach, it's very important to realize that the excitement of novelty wears off very soon. We're quickly going to get used to the new partner as well, and we will have hurt and perhaps lost the love of our lives. Couples who've been together for a while need to accept that some of the spark is gone and find new pleasures in sexuality together, a sexuality that often may not lead to old-fashioned intercourse but a sense of mutuality, closeness, and fulfillment.

Taste and Smell

Eating is, of course, a great source of enjoyment. The smell of roasted meat or baking bread automatically releases endorphins, another example of how evolution uses positive feelings to guide us into useful behavior. There are more than a hundred thousand nerves connecting the tongue and the brain—and much of our sense of taste doesn't come from the tongue itself, but from smell receptors in the nose. We can cultivate the senses of taste and smell so that we become connoisseurs of more exotic and refined tastes as we grow older, combining novelty and adventure with the inherent pleasure of eating. Wine, and now beer, derive much of their pleasure power not from their intoxicating effects but from the complex blend of flavors and aromas that invite us to practice savoring.

Cooking for others is more fun than cooking alone. My wife puts it in her top five joys, which I suspect is true for many people. It combines the chance to practice your expertise with the opportunity to show love, caring, and generosity, plus you get to eat well. Sharing good food together makes everyone happy, gets everyone talking. One little study I love found that adding garlic bread to a family spaghetti dinner "decreased the number of negative interactions by an average of 0.174 per family member per minute or 22.7 percent (p = 0.05) and the number of pleasant interactions increased by an average of 0.25 per family member per minute or 7.4 percent (p = 0.04)."

do: LEARN HOW TO COOK SOME THINGS YOU REALLY LIKE. INVITE OTHERS TO SHARE WITH YOU.

One great benefit about cooking for others: If you invite people over for dinner, they'll invite you back.

Touch

Touching others, hugging, and caressing is much more important than cold people (like me) realize. Some depressed patients have been isolated so long that they develop skin hunger; when they're touched or hugged, they either freeze or melt. Many elderly nursing home patients suffer from the same condition, and experienced staff know that holding hands can go a long way toward helping someone who is scared and confused. Touch releases opioids, not only in people but in animals, too; that's why whining puppies stop whining if they're petted. It's the same process that helps a mother's touch soothe a cranky baby. If you're arguing with your spouse, you'll find it's hard to maintain your righteous indignation if you're holding hands.

An experiment showed the importance of touch for premature babies. These babies were more than two months premature, and weighed only about two pounds. They were given massage therapy three times a day for fifteen minutes, over ten days. That little bit of extra touch

do: HUG, HOLD HANDS, CUDDLE.

enabled them to gain 47 percent more weight than the babies who weren't massaged. On average, the massaged babies were discharged from the hospital six days earlier than the others.

Joy and Mindfulness

We've talked a lot about all the pressure society puts on us in today's world not to feel, to keep busy and constantly moving on to the next item on our list. We focused on mindfulness as a skill to help us learn to slow down, pay attention, and feel. In this chapter, you might say we've been talking about one result of greater mindfulness: a better ability to experience joy.

Yet joy and mindfulness are a two-way street. Experiences of joy make us mindful. They can, if we're not too distracted, grab us by the collar and make us pay attention. When we work on letting ourselves feel the simplest pleasures of life, we're also at work on dropping our character armor and changing our perspective. We're giving up some of our need to be in control and letting life happen to us. Inevitably, our values will change in the process; we'll start learning what really makes us happy and let go of some our beliefs about what should make us happy.

more satisfaction

While joys and pleasures are immediate and short-lived, satisfaction is a more sustained state that should be relatively independent of our momentary ups and downs. But when we come to talking about satisfaction, we may be at the most confusing and complex subsubject of happiness; yet so much about attaining more satisfaction in life seems to boil down to applied common sense. For instance, if you're not familiar with what AA refers to as the Serenity Prayer, you're missing out on a great deal of wisdom packed in a nutshell:

> God grant me the serenity to accept the things I cannot change,
> the courage to change the things I can,
> and the wisdom to know the difference.

In terms of life satisfaction, "knowing the difference" can make all the difference in the world. <u>Satisfaction</u> is defined as the state of having our needs or wants fulfilled; today, unlike for most of history, we can expect to have most of our _needs_ met without great effort on our part; but the list of our _wants_ can go on forever.

Satisfaction is really of two sorts, about the present and about the past. If we want to have feelings associated with satisfaction about the past, like having few regrets, it helps if we made what we feel were the right decisions. This is true also for satisfaction about the present. If we want to be pleased with the state of our marriage now, our work now, our children now, it requires that over the years we have built a good marriage, put effort into our career, and paid attention to our children. So we come back to our feckless grasshopper, who has not laid by his supplies for hard times. How do you balance immediate pleasure and long-term satisfaction?

calibrating the yardstick

One basic question about satisfaction is, _Am I using the right yardstick?_ If you're evaluating yourself and your life, what's your standard of comparison? If I'm comparing my book sales to Dr. Phil's, I'm going to feel just a bit dissatisfied with myself. But if I remind myself that nobody in my family ever published a book before, I feel a little better.

Consider personal income, perhaps the most common yardstick in Western cultures. Behavioral economics has now demonstrated that higher income aspirations reduce your overall life satisfaction. The greater the gap you feel between your actual income and what you want to make, the less happy you are. That's why rich people may, in fact, be slightly happier; after you reach a certain point, you don't especially want more money, so one big craving that other people feel is crossed off your list. And when you compare yourself to others, you feel okay because you are, in this respect, superior. But if you're not wealthy, it's the act of comparing that makes you unhappy with your income. The richer the people around you, the higher you want your own income to be, and the less satisfied you are with what you've got. Of course, "the people around you" may include the rich and famous, if you subject yourself to a lot of television or fan magazines, and if you're not part of a community. To some extent, you choose who you want to compare yourself to.

As David Myers, one of the great happiness experts, observes,

> What matters more than absolute wealth is perceived wealth. Money is two steps removed from happiness: Actual income doesn't much influence happiness; how *satisfied* we are with our income does. If we're content with our income, regardless of how much it is, we're likely to say we're happy. . . . This implies two ways to be rich: One is to have great wealth. The other is to have few wants.

In any other area of living you care to mention, aiming too high is a sure shortcut to misery. Call it perfectionism. For many years, someone I know well loved music but was embarrassed by what she considered her lousy singing voice. Recently, since she was welcomed by a group who get together regularly to sing—and are not too persnickety about anyone's ability—she's developed one of the greatest sources of pleasure in her life. Of course, the more she practices, the better her singing gets. How many things do we hold back on because we feel we just won't do well enough? A quick list of things I hear from my clients: cooking, painting, playing an instrument, writing (a book, a letter to the editor, any letter), any sport or game, any form of art, fixing the car (or anything else), taking care of a pet, building a deck (or anything else), public speaking, going after a promotion—love, marriage, children. If you're overly perfectionistic, you either won't try these things, and thus miss out on most of the greatest pleasures in life; or if you do try, you'll never be satisfied with your performance, and thus you'll turn what should be a joy into a misery.

don't: DON'T PUT YOURSELF UP AGAINST IMPOSSIBLE EXPECTATIONS.

So is the secret to happiness having low expectations? Yes and no. Back to the matter of what you can change and what you can't, what you want and what you need. I think it's very wise to reduce your expectations in areas where you have little control. Personal income is one. Having your kids get into Harvard. Your weight, to a degree. William James, the great founder of American psychology, said, "There is a strange lightness in the heart when one's nothingness in a particular area is accepted in good faith. How pleasant is the day when we give up striving to be young or slender. 'Thank God' we say, 'those illusions are gone.'" But in areas where you have some control, moderately higher expectations will motivate you to try a little harder, do a little more—and you'll end up with greater satisfaction.

The mere act of setting reasonable and concrete goals seems to improve both our experience and our performance. For instance, if—just to pick a topic out of the clear blue sky—you have to write a book, you'll do much better if you set yourself goals of X pages per day or Y chapters per month, than if you just vaguely write when you feel like it. Making a commitment focuses our attention on the target and helps us think more intently about how to get there. There is a lot of research to suggest that we feel happier as we are progressing toward our goals; we have a sense of purposeful involvement, we give ourselves mental pats on the back for being so good and industrious, our self-esteem is enhanced. We're put into a state like flow—more about that in a minute. But remember adaptation; those good feelings don't necessarily last once we've got where we're going. Instead of enjoying what we've achieved, we can just look around for the next mountain to climb. On the other hand, adaptation has its uses: We can fail to meet a goal, even though we've benefited from pursuing it, and get over our disappointment rather quickly.

As Tal Ben-Shahar writes, "the proper role of goals is to liberate us, so that we can enjoy the here and now." If we set out on a journey without purpose or direction, every fork in the road becomes another decision to make, another point where our ambivalence and anxiety can overtake us. *Will the scenery be better this way, or that way? Have we gone too far? What if there are no motel rooms? Should we stop at this battlefield, or that old cavern, or the antique center?* But if we know where we're going, our minds are saved all this hassle and we can enjoy the journey. *Should I be a doctor or a lawyer or an Indian chief?* The question of career is a very difficult one; to a great extent, a young person can't know how well he'll fit, how happy he'll be, in any profession—there are just too many unknowns. But having made a decision and committed to a path, you are freed from most of that uncertainty and doubt; and that allows most of us to find the joy available within the career we've chosen.

do your goals and values lead to happiness?

So let's assume that you're using the right yardstick, that you're neither unrealistically hard on yourself nor too easy on yourself. Let's assume also that, because you've absorbed the lessons about mindfulness and will power, you're relatively immune to craving. Does that mean greater life satisfaction? Those abilities will lead to less misery and greater joy, but they are only necessary-not-sufficient prerequisites for greater satisfaction. We come to the question of whether the goals and values you choose to pursue will effectively lead you to greater satisfaction.

Some goals are better than others when it comes to facilitating life satisfaction. There's a lot of research evidence that the more materialistic your goals, the less happy you are. One set of studies found that placing a high value on financial success was associated with less self-actualization, less vitality, more depression, and more anxiety. Other studies showed that making progress toward materialistic goals did not have any effect on subjective well-being, while progress on personal growth and improving relationships did. Still another study found that what's true for individuals is true for societies as well; those countries that place a high level of importance on money tend to have lower levels of well-being.

what's really satisfying

An interesting line of research gave subjects a list of ten possible life needs, based on several different historical theories of what leads to happiness and satisfaction. Subjects both in the United States and South Korea were asked to reflect on the most satisfying events in their lives and rate which needs were being satisfied in those events. The researchers found that the most satisfying events gave participants feelings of self-esteem, autonomy, competence, and relatedness. Ranked lower were needs like luxury, popularity or influence, and security. So the most satisfying events in your life probably led to these feelings:

- <u>Self-esteem.</u> Feeling you have many positive qualities, being satisfied with who you are, a strong sense of self-respect.
- <u>Autonomy.</u> Making choices that represent your true interests and values; able to do things your way, in a way that expresses your true self.
- <u>Competence.</u> Finding success in completing difficult tasks, mastering hard challenges, with a sense of capability.
- <u>Relatedness.</u> Feeling connected to a network of people you care for, who care for you in return, who are important to you; a strong sense of intimacy with the people you spend time with.

When you pursue goals that lead to these feelings, you benefit doubly. As you make progress on those goals, you experience more positive feelings and greater self-esteem. But in addition, in the future you will have grown in autonomy, competence, and relatedness from the exercise of pursuing these goals, leading to much greater life satisfaction. Being more skilled at life leads to greater joy.

That may be why lottery winners return so quickly to their previous levels of misery. <u>Winning</u> a million bucks is a lot different from <u>earning</u> a million bucks. To earn it, you've probably had to work hard, take risks, make tough decisions, work closely with others. You've been developing skills of competence and relatedness, and enhanced your sense of self-esteem and autonomy. But if you just happened to buy the lucky scratch-off at the Kwik-E-Mart, you haven't added to your life skills at all. Luck, as far as I know, doesn't add to self-esteem.

finding your priorities

Here's an exercise that will help you identify your priorities.

EXERCISE 13:
IDENTIFYING YOUR KEY VALUES

Take a few minutes' quiet time and put yourself into a mindful state. When you feel ready, write down a list of up to ten things that make life worth living for you. Don't worry about making the list perfect or complete, because you'll be doing this several times. Try not to think about what you feel are the "right" values; just write what comes to your mind, without judging. If being saintly doesn't make your list, but eating at good restaurants does, don't worry about it. This list is just for you; no one will ever see it but you, and you deserve to give yourself the most honest information you can. You can be general (nature) or specific (sunsets over the lake); that doesn't matter at this point. Don't be afraid to be individualistic or selfish; if playing Ping-Pong makes you happier than playing with the grandchildren, that's okay.

Put your list away for a few days, and do the exercise again. Don't look at your old list, start fresh. We assume you'll miss some obvious things the first time around, just because they're so obvious you can take them for granted. Or that you'll forget about some important values at first because your mind just isn't in touch with them at the moment. Then do this again, for a third time, after a few more days have passed.

Now combine the three lists, so that you have anywhere from ten to thirty items. If you have duplicate items, enter them only once but put a checkmark beside them for each additional time they come up. If you see that some items are just similar examples of a bigger concept (like dancing and going to concerts might be considered part of appreciating music), treat them as you would duplicates.

Now I want you to try to rank these items in order of their importance to you. These are going to be hard choices, but you're not locked in to them. Doing the exercise itself may change some of your ranking. Don't worry too much if you can't decide if sex is more important than eating well, or vice versa, but you should be able to put the items into a rough order to see, for instance, that both sex and eating well are more important to you than playing golf. Or not. It may help to imagine you're being forced to give up some of these activities. Which would you give up first?

Here's the painful part of the exercise: For the next few days, keep a little diary of your daily activities. Keep tabs on how much time you actually spend in activities or states of mind when you are actually in touch with your highest priorities. If you're like most people, you'll be dismayed when you see how much time is taken up with activities that are not on your list at all.

You will probably see that some of your low-value activities are necessary, for the present at least: Working and commuting come to mind. Schlepping the kids. But you may see that you're spending time in unnecessary low-value activities. Mowing the lawn or housekeeping, when you could pay someone else to do it for you. The classic example, watching television, takes up a lot of time for most people, though they don't rank it very high. But give yourself credit for needing some emotional downtime; we might wear ourselves out pretty quickly if we're constantly engaged in high-value activities.

Nevertheless, look mindfully at how you're spending your time, and try to add more value. Plan your evenings and weekends in advance. Get together with friends and family more than you're doing now. Exercise more so that you have more energy.

Finally, you can work on escaping or adding value to those necessary low-value activities. Develop a plan to change jobs, if it's really demoralizing, so you will enjoy it more or have less of a commute. Listen to recorded books when you're commuting. Sing with the kids while you're driving them around town. (They'll fuss mightily at first, but they'll get used to it.)

You'll notice that it's not so easy to change your old habits, even though it seems obvious that you can and should. Don't just give up, but look mindfully, without judging, at what's getting in the way. Are you afraid of change? Do you think if you extend yourself, you'll only get hurt? Are you just too tired? Talk about it with a trusted friend, or a therapist. We have a thousand ways of convincing ourselves we're too busy to do what we love and value. Challenging that is hard. Taking a chance is risky. But you get only one sweet and precious life—how will you spend it? If you keep the lessons of this exercise in mind, you can gradually, over the years, move your life in the direction you want it to go.

Remember, as John Lennon said, "Life is what happens while you're busy making other plans." The way we use our time may be the component of happiness that is under our greatest control. People who are battling cancer or other life-threatening illnesses find their priorities have changed drastically. They no longer waste time on unimportant things; they want to spend their time with loved ones or enjoying the simple pleasures of life—the seasons, the sunshine, eating, playing. Their lives are changed dramatically. As Tal Ben-Shahar points out, these are exactly the same people they were before their illness. They didn't learn anything new—no new skills, no new habits, no great revelations.

YOUR SCHEDULE IS YOUR LIFE.

They have only the same abilities that had seemed to be inadequate in making them happy before, but in truth, they always had within themselves the capacity to change their lives, reprioritize, and make themselves happier. We, too, have that capacity within ourselves. But, as one of Shelley Taylor's cancer patients observed, discussing how his illness had revolutionized his life for the better, "The trick, of course, is to do this without getting cancer."

However, getting people to change their schedules is not easy. James Hillman, the well-known Jungian analyst, says that he's found nothing harder to treat—that it's very hard to get people to see that your schedule is your life. Nothing is really going to change for you unless you're willing to make some changes in the way you spend your time. But the mindless, hard-charging, twenty-first-century go-getter wants a quick fix, a pill, something that won't entail stepping back and questioning himself.

If your goal is to build a happy life, then there are obvious steps along the way: get an education, train for a vocation, save money, find work that's personally meaningful, and develop rewarding relationships. Those goals require commitment and some sacrifice. That's where the balancing act begins. Every day, life forces us to choose between a current joy and a long-term satisfaction. Going to work every morning is the hallmark example, one that most of us do without much thought, except perhaps on a glorious summer day or on a snow day in the dead of winter. But there are hundreds of such choices every day: *Another drink and more fun tonight, or a clear head tomorrow? Go to the gym now? Turn off the television? Dessert?* This is where we leave psychology behind, because there are no rules; there is only judgment. Nevertheless, I'll jump in and give some principles for how to get some satisfaction:

do: IDENTIFY YOUR PERSONAL GOALS.

- Identify your own values, and follow them; if you're considering something that violates them, postpone it until you've had time to be sure.
- Make your decisions mindfully, as free from distortion as possible.
- Control what you pay attention to; don't allow yourself to be unduly tempted; distance yourself from craving and competition.
- Free yourself from categorical thinking; don't do any automatic judging.
- Use your whole mind—logic, emotion, and intuition.
- Accept the reality principle; see things as they are, not how you want them to be.
- Accept yourself as you are. Don't let the Inner Critic bully you into something you really don't want to do.
- Open yourself up to advice from friends, family, and mentors.
- Allow for adaptation; remember you'll soon get used to it, whether you like it or not.
- Control for dopamine: postpone it.

- Stay out of debt; it will raise your anxiety level to the point where you won't make the wisest decisions, and it may force you into making less-than-optimal choices.
- Try to anticipate buyer's remorse: the more expensive or frivolous something is, the worse your remorse will be.

Dukkha

What if you're feeling uneasy or dissatisfied and there's no reason for it? This is complicated. Sometimes it's depression, and you should do something about it. Sometimes it's what the Buddhists call *dukkha*—an unpleasant reality that's underneath the level of consciousness. Psychoanalysis also tells us that not every bad feeling is to be avoided or dealt with, but explored. Sometimes there's a nagging truth that we have to face. We might argue that it is only through facing necessary suffering—the harsh realities of life—that we can really experience joy and appreciate what we have. That through facing our demons, we find our greatest independence, creativity, or self-worth. Or *dukkha* may be a way of telling you to get off your high horse; stop being so arrogant about your own happiness, and have some empathy for the rest of the world. Or that we just got up on the wrong side of bed and tomorrow will be better. How do you know if it's depression and not *dukkha?* When it lasts a long time, when you feel hopeless, when you blame yourself, that's depression.

do: CULTIVATE FLOW EXPERIENCES THAT LEAD TOWARD YOUR GOALS.

don't: EXPECT TO BE CONSTANTLY HAPPY; SOMETIMES WE FEEL BAD AND JUST HAVE TO ACCEPT THAT IT WILL PASS.

work

Most of our satisfaction in life comes not from what we've achieved, but from what we do day to day. Thus work, leisure, and relationships are the areas where we find the most opportunities for satisfaction.

Some time ago, Mihaly Csikszentmihalyi published his famous book on *Flow,* a study of what makes people feel good. One of his most surprising findings was that people in general reported feeling better at work than at leisure. At work, people were much more likely to be in what Csikszentmihalyi called the "flow" state—feeling strong, active, creative, concentrated, and motivated. At leisure, people were much more likely to feel apathetic, passive, weak, dull, and dissatisfied. In most human activities, there is a thin line where the tasks we face are just challenging enough to bring out the best in our abilities—that's the state he called *flow*. In flow, we're highly involved, our attention is concentrated, our sense of time passing changes, we lose self-consciousness, all our other little worries and distractions recede to the background. When we're not in flow, either we're not being challenged enough, the task is too easy, and we're in a state of boredom; or the challenge is too great for our abilities, and we're in a state of stress and anxiety. Viewed that way, it's easy to understand why we're not often very happy. We vacillate between boredom and anxiety, with a narrow little balancing point in the middle where we're feeling good.

Yet flow is a controversial concept. Even Csikszentmihalyi found, as almost everyone else does, that people at work don't want to be there. They'd rather be somewhere else. Our list of common sources of joy in people's lives (Chapter 7) omits work altogether. People asked about positive life events rarely mention work at all, except for getting a raise or promotion; only a lucky few really enjoy the activities of their work. People with a lot of flow in their lives are less bored, but score no higher on measures of happiness. People in high flow occupations (musicians, artists, writers, therapists), in fact, are subject to frustration, depression, mood swings, and problems with addictions, which both motivate and hinder their self-expression. Kahneman and Krueger find that among their sample of women, work ranks next to last (just above the morning commute, just below the evening commute) in pleasurable activities. What's the story?

Voluntary choice explains much of why people may experience flow at work, but wish they were somewhere else. Most of us, unfortunately, are not in jobs that we find innately rewarding; we're there for the paycheck. We may find that while we're at work, time passes more quickly for us, we're less bored and more engaged, but because we feel forced to be there, we may not get that much joy out of flow experiences at work. Flow experiences we choose to participate in—developing our skills at a sport or an art, or being lucky enough to have work we find intrinsically rewarding—may be close to ideal sources of satisfaction. Part of the reason Csikszentmihalyi found his different results is that he used a different method: He actually interrupted people at different times during the day and asked them to assess their feelings then and there, while most studies ask people to remember their feelings. Remembering lets in more bias; if we <u>believe</u> we're unhappier at work, that's more likely to affect our answers when we're asked to remember, rather than biasing our present feelings.

Attitude Is Everything

Waiting for a bus at 7:40 A.M. in a dark January Chicago winter, with frozen slush ruining your shoes and the wind so cold you're afraid your ears might break off—no fun at all. But once in a while, you could get lucky and catch the Happy Bus. The driver would greet you with a huge smile and a booming voice: *Welcome to the Happy Bus!* Then he'd go on with his patter of songs, jokes, comments on the weather and the sports teams, flirting with the pretty girls, teasing the grouches, and the occasional *Jesus loves you!* You couldn't help smiling. And everyone in the bus became connected with each other, smiling, laughing, watching for the looks of amazement on the new riders who'd never met the Happy Bus driver before.

> LEARN A JOKE AND PASS IT ON. PEOPLE START TELLING <u>YOU</u> JOKES.

The point, of course, is the attitude you bring to work. The Happy Bus driver wasn't paid a penny extra for his personality, but he certainly enjoyed himself. Once you reach a certain basic level of expertise in your work, you can start to play with it. The Happy Bus driver was, I believe, quite sincere in wanting to spread his gospel of joy—but he also got a kick out of playing with people's expectations. Anyone whose job involves customer contact can do the same. Smile, and people smile back at you.

For all but a lucky few of us, work is a necessary evil, merely what we have to do if we want to eat regularly. But the flow studies and others have shown us that many people can find ways to make the most routine jobs somewhat enjoyable. We can enjoy work because it gives us structure and goals, and humans naturally are gratified by doing something well—or well enough. Even in the most boring jobs, people play games with themselves—*okay, I'll try to assemble twenty more widgets before break*—and make the time pass more quickly that way. We have a tougher time with leisure because we have to supply our own structure. We can have the toughest time of all if we're at work and there's nothing to do; we can feel both bored and guilty—or (if it only happens occasionally) we can feel tickled pink.

Unfortunately, changing conditions in the past thirty years have made it much more difficult for us all to enjoy work. The Gallup organization, which does a lot of business consulting, routinely asks employees, "Do you get to do what you do best every day?" and finds that no more than 20 percent agree. Even according to the Conference Board, a very business-friendly group, only half of U.S. employees say they are satisfied with their work.

That's largely because hours are longer, the workload is heavier, jobs are more insecure, and real wages have fallen. We're all working much harder now just to stay in place economically; the rat race is on steroids. But, wonderfully adaptable creatures that we are, we can get used to this, even make ourselves believe that working too hard is exciting or something to be proud of. Jobs with many deadlines, like publishing or broadcasting, or jobs that require highly focused attention under difficult conditions (finance, the law, the military) can create an "adrenaline addiction." Jobs where management creates an intense competitive atmosphere do the same thing. The challenge of the job creates a cycle of tension and relief, a very intense flow experience, which can feel rewarding even while it's destroying your brain and body with too many stress hormones. When someone has become used to this state and has to take time off because of an illness or injury, they frequently go through withdrawal and end up acting just like a junkie—depressed, angry, irritable, can't sleep. They actually <u>are</u> junkies, deprived of dopamine.

The same cycle is at the bottom of a lot of procrastination. By putting things off, the procrastinator is always raising the stakes on his deadlines, putting the task off so much that when it finally gets done, it feels like snatching victory from the jaws of defeat. It's a cheap thrill, though, and a hollow victory, because the final product would probably have been a lot better with more time and attention. You might get a more sustained, though less intense, kind of satisfaction from delivering a product you've really done your best on.

A highly competitive work environment, where bonuses are intensely scaled to performance so that some get rich while others get almost nothing, or where the threat of firing is always in the air, is management's way of getting you to kill yourself for the job, as well as to cheat and lie and betray your coworkers. It can be very exciting, but it's inherently demeaning. You're being manipulated in order to make management look good, or make more money for the owners, or both. You don't think you're being exploited, because you're making lots of money, or gaining a lot of prestige, but you are; in the process, you're turning into a monkey jumping on a string. Don't accept a job like that. Get out at the first opportunity. Job satisfaction is much higher when there is opportunity for social interaction and when people work as teams. In fact time-wasting horsing around can add to efficiency.

High demand and low control is a prescription for job unhappiness. To some extent, greater control is a buffer for high demand. If your employer can allow you to set your own schedule, it's a lot easier to put in fifty or more hours per week.

Working conditions have a direct effect on your health, but it can be a lot more subtle than being exposed to toxic substances or repetitive strain. One study found that those in the lowest grades of the British civil service had 3.5 times as many fatal heart attacks as those in the highest grade. This was largely due to the fact that these employees had less control and autonomy, which led to more stress hormones in the system, higher blood pressure, and so forth. It was also partly due to worse health-related behavior such as diet, exercise, and smoking in the lower grades—but smoking and a poor diet are partly a response to stress. No matter what their grade level, those who had the most routine work experienced the most clogging of the arteries.

The Happy Artisan/The Nature of Work

We want our lives to have meaning and purpose, to make sense, to add up. Some people think this desire is merely an artifact of how our brains work, and therefore we create gods or other kinds of belief systems to comfort us, to give us the illusion of meaning. That's not a question we're going to prove (unless the Rapture comes), so I'm not going to touch it. Still, the desire for meaning seems to be innate. People who consider religion an important factor in their lives tend to be happier. But because a rigorous religious belief system seems to be getting more difficult to maintain, we seem to be more and more on our own when it comes to creating meaning in our lives.

I have an individualism bias, which I think I share with a lot of writers and intellectuals—certainly almost all therapists. Take two men both making about the same money, with stable marriages and two kids each. One is a finish carpenter, a cabinetmaker. Every job is a little different, so he gets to use his creativity and problem-solving skills every day, and feels proud of the work he turns out. The other man works on an assembly line. His work is the same every day. There's very little challenge involved, no chance to feel a sense of mastery. My automatic bias is that the cabinetmaker is going to be a lot happier, more "fulfilled," more "self-actualized."

But the key word there is <u>self</u>. The cabinetmaker works alone. The assembly-line worker may have a group of buddies he works with, people he looks forward to seeing every day. They get together for beers after work, they play on the company softball team, their families spend time together. They support their union.

If we gave these men the standard questionnaires on happiness, the assembly-line worker might score a lot higher than the cabinetmaker. Here's where the bias really starts to work, because some of us intellectual types will think that's a false result: that the assembly-line guy just doesn't know what he's missing. He's not expressing himself, he's not leaving a mark on the world, he's not leaving anything to posterity. Compared with the cabinetmaker, his life lacks meaning.

Or does it? Maybe the cabinetmaker is kind of stressed by his work, the deadlines, the pressures of working for himself and making ends meet, the pressure to keep his clients happy. Maybe that makes him less available to his wife and children. Sure, he tries to attend his son's softball games, but maybe the assembly-line worker has time for batting practice with his son, golfing, or hunting. Now who's not leaving a mark on the world? Who's leaving something for posterity? Whose life has greater meaning? Who am I to say?

Individualism is a relatively recent arrival on the historical scene, coinciding with the Industrial Revolution. In the eighteenth century, a man was measured by how he fit in the community, not by how successful or creative he was. Vanity was a sin. Paris Hilton would have been burned at the stake. There was an emphasis on duty and responsibility, and on controlling desire and impulse. "The ideal man, then, was pleasant, mild-mannered, and devoted to the good of the community. He performed his duties faithfully, governed his passions rationally, submitted to his fate and to his place in society, and treated his dependents with firm but affectionate wisdom." After the Enlightenment and the American and French Revolutions, self-interest and individual initiative came to be more respected as manly virtues. The individual, not the community or even the family, came to be seen as the basic unit of society, and each individual was expected to find his proper place in the world through his own efforts.

That is the individualism bias. Much of the rest of the world still values good citizenship much more highly than in the United States. The Japanese and Chinese have a lot of trouble understanding American society because of this. The Chinese do not place a high value on individual pride. The British still queue up for buses.

Let's go back to the natural order of things. The notion of "a job" is a relatively recent phenomenon, a necessity of the Industrial Revolution. Before that, people worked, of course; they did a variety of things, but the notion of being tied to a particular employer with a "job" you might "lose" was something new. People worked as much as they needed to work, and no more; the rest of their time went into tending their land or cottage, hunting, fishing, growing crops, or hanging out at the pub. Unemployment did not exist. Even now the Kung people in Botswana hunt about six hours a week; the San bush people of South Africa work about a twenty-hour week. But the invention of mass production required people to change. As Tom Hodgkinson puts it, "The great problem of the Industrial Revolution was how to transform a population of strong-willed, independent-minded, heavy-drinking, party-oriented, riot-loving, life-loving Englishmen into a docile, disciplined, grateful workforce." And Juliet Schor pointed out in her classic *The Overworked American* (1991):

The claim that capitalism has delivered us from excessive toil can be sustained only if we take as our point of comparison eighteenth- and nineteenth-century Europe and America—a period that witnessed what were probably the longest and most arduous work schedules in the history of mankind.

So let's not assume there's something wrong with you if you don't love your job or thrill at the idea of spending all your adult life getting up with the alarm clock. But given that you're pretty much stuck with the situation, it's better to get to like it as much as possible rather than resent every day.

do: FIND WORK YOU FEEL PROUD OF, WITH CONGENIAL WORKMATES, THAT GIVES YOU A SENSE OF FLOW.
    FAILING THAT, CULTIVATE AN AVOCATION THAT PROVIDES THE SAME THINGS.

Attitude Adjustment

Return with me to the Happy Bus. Just what can you do about a low-satisfaction job? I have a few suggestions:

- Try to make something of your job. Work is one arena where we're given the opportunity to make a contribution, and that can be a major source of happiness. To create something new or unique, to solve a difficult problem, or to influence the future can add meaning to our lives. It may take a long period of learning or apprenticeship before you become expert enough to do something truly meaningful, but if you keep track of your own growing skill level, you will feel good in the meantime.

- If you have a job that really has no meaning to you other than a way to put food on the table, try to keep a mindful attitude about it. Don't take it too seriously. Try to show up like the Happy Bus driver, prepared to be friendly, to find something to enjoy every day. Try to add play to your work. Meanwhile, add meaning to your life in your leisure time—develop a skill, become an expert at something, learn to sing or paint or tie flies. Volunteer your time for community service.

- Try adopting a mindful attitude toward your coworkers, your customers, whomever you come in contact with. If you can make their day a little better, chances are good they'll return the favor when they have the chance. The whole work environment can become more pleasant just because you try to make a difference.
- If conditions are really miserable—if there's a bad boss or too much friction in the office—work on getting out before you become miserable, too. I've seen far too many depressed people stay stuck in terrible working conditions through fear of change; often that is the single greatest source of their unhappiness. Keep your résumé handy, and send it off every chance you get. Watch the want ads and the Internet. Think about relocating. Build up alternative skills, the so-called "portable" skills that are in demand everywhere— spreadsheets, databases, word processing. Customer service.
- Take advantage of the new economy. It's much more possible than ever to work from home, to work nontraditional hours, to schedule weeks off from work. Though there's a potential downside to each of those benefits, you can be your own boss and have much more time for family and leisure activities. Little things can add greatly to your overall happiness. For me, a perennial insomniac, the freedom to finally sleep till 9 A.M. is something I appreciate very much. Although it means working till 7 P.M., that schedule seems to suit my rhythm.
- Retired people, in general, are happier than those still working. But retired people miss the social interaction, the work itself, and the feeling of being useful. So while you're still working, pay more attention to those things. Make the social interactions more fun and supportive. Let yourself be mindful of your skills, and be as useful as you can be. Be a positive influence for others.

leisure

Psychology hasn't looked deeply into the question of what makes leisure activities fulfilling. Some posit that there are two aspects to satisfying leisure. One is that we get more out of activities in which we have a sense of mastery of a skill or knowledge base, like a golfer who continuously refines his game, or like a knowledgeable baseball fan who gets more out of watching a game than someone who has only a passing interest. The other aspect is that many leisure activities are pursued for a sense of moral purpose or social contribution—as in becoming active in politics, sponsoring the arts, or joining the volunteer rescue squad. While that is all very well, it leaves out relaxing in the hammock watching the clouds or curling up with a good book. Psychologists sometimes get a little carried away. I think that it's quite true that some of our most satisfying leisure activities require an involvement like flow, a certain challenge and mastery, and it certainly helps us feel good if we are making a contribution somehow—but still, we need to be able to enjoy doing nothing. *Dolce far niente.*

Without doubt, we need a balance. Too much of nothing leads to boredom and lethargy; too much drive, and we're not having fun anymore. The lack of balance probably leads to the contradictory findings in the research. On the one hand, the flow studies showed us a primary difficulty of leisure time. Though it obviously should be the most enjoyable time of the day, it often isn't, largely because we don't know what to do with ourselves and are bored or restless. On the other hand, many studies find that leisure activities are the strongest source of life satisfaction. Activities that involve exercise and group membership seem especially valuable. The opportunity for social interaction is perhaps most important. Michael Argyle reports that voluntary work is a source of joy just behind dancing, and provides greater joy than most other leisure activities. Of course, exercise, group membership, voluntary work, and dancing all are obviously flow-inducing activities.

So do you have to be good at leisure to enjoy it? With flow-centric activities, that seems obvious; there is a learning curve, and if you get stuck at a point before the activity seems fluid, or if you compare yourself negatively with others, you won't be happy. That is why television is the default leisure activity. But maybe we should think about developing skills for more passive activities—reading, playing, exercising your imagination, lying in the hammock, simply relaxing. These activities are so antithetical to today's world that we need reinforcement and practice in order to do them right, without feeling either guilty or the nagging sense that we ought to be doing something productive. These things are productive, but not as we usually think of the concept. They produce good health, an active mind, the opportunity to get in touch with our interior selves. They make us more at ease, more fun to be around, more at home in our skins, more comfortable with the concept of rewarding ourselves with what really matters.

There is also the question of *faux* flow. We can get completely absorbed in activities like gossip or video games, which have no redeeming social value and can, in fact, demean us. It's the same old voodoo that dopamine does so well, keeping us happy little hamsters in our exercise wheels, pleasantly preoccupied with getting somewhere while we don't think about where we're going. Do we feel as good as if we were doing something more "worthwhile"? The problem is that flow is morally and spiritually neutral. We'll return to this subject when we talk about meaning, but there are no easy answers.

What about teaching yourself to play the guitar, when you will probably never play for anyone else? Or any of a million other solitary pursuits— collecting Mr. Peanut memorabilia, hybridizing hostas, raising geckos? They're totally harmless, they're not going to make you feel guilty like video games might, they can be challenging and rewarding and add to your self-esteem.

IF IT MAKES YOU FEEL GOOD, IF IT HARMS NO ONE, IF IT RELAXES YOU—DO IT.

relationships

Jean-Paul Sartre, a well-known depressed guy, famously said, "Hell is other people." We don't know if his longtime companion, Simone de Beauvoir, took this personally. Maybe Sartre simply wasn't very good at getting along with people, because most of today's leading researchers believe that good relationships with others may be the single most important source of life satisfaction, across all ages and cultures. And if you mentally review the happiest times in your life, you'll probably agree that most of them intimately involved others—lovers, friends, parents, children. The research shows that people who feel connected to others live longer, happier, more productive lives, with fewer health problems than people who are isolated. People who care about others are happier than those who are preoccupied with themselves.

Relationships provide a double benefit for us. As much as we get from the love and support of others, we also gain from what being loving, thoughtful, and compassionate does to our character. When you practice being loving and compassionate, you become a loving and compassionate person. But having a network of relationships provides many other benefits as well:

- Relationships give us meaning and purpose. In a culture that overemphasizes cheap and shallow values, relationships give us the opportunity to make a difference in the lives of others; to be fruitful and generative.
- Relationships facilitate creativity. When we can see things from another's point of view, we can escape our constraining paradigms. The encouragement of friends can allow us to take risks and leaps that we could easily rationalize away if left alone. And, as members of a group, we can take risks that we'd never take on our own: sing for an audience, get up and dance, or march on Washington.
- Relationships challenge our paradigms. When we find that someone we care about feels differently than we do about something, we face cognitive dissonance, a creative challenge. When we see ourselves through others' eyes, we become both more honest and more modest, and we know when our defenses aren't fooling people.
- Relationships expand our minds and worlds. We can't read everything or be informed about everything of interest or importance. Having a network of friends who know your interests is like having a group of readers at your service, people who are in contact with the world, interested in finding out for you what you need to know.
- Relationships give us emotional depth. When we share an emotional experience with others, we strengthen our empathic connection. Sharing experiences with others makes them more real, somehow. Experiences are deeper and richer, too, because our feelings echo and resonate with those of others.

- Relationships give us playmates. It's not easy to play alone, but having partners and companions enables us to loosen up and have fun. Remember that laughter stimulates endorphins, as does dancing and socializing. Humor especially is difficult alone; we laugh much more often in company than alone. A good joke at the right moment can break up the most impacted bad mood, and wit can make us stop taking our worries so seriously.

- Relationships give us a sense of structure and belonging. The human race was designed to live in a tight-knit community, an extended clan or small village. Feeling a part of something like that gave us a sense of security that we don't even know we're missing now. But having a network of people in our lives who love and respect us can give us some of that old feeling. In today's culture, we need to make a deliberate effort to find or build those networks—through religious or voluntary organizations, self-help groups, clubs with similar interests.

The simplest, most honest and direct way to improve your relationships is to practice loving. Expressing affection, tender feelings, trust, support, attraction; empathizing and understanding—those are skills, too, which we can improve by practice. Of course, we can feel a lot of resistance or fear about extending ourselves; it's very painful to be rejected, and that fear makes many of us hold back. But you can start practicing with people you trust—your spouse, partner, child, workmate. Mindfulness meditation seems to increase empathy and the ability to cue into nonverbal communication by strengthening the brain areas responsible.

Practice compassion for the people you don't know well enough to love. Timothy Miller, in *How to Want What You Have*, says compassion is the intention to see every human being as no better or worse than yourself, worth no less and no more. Buddhism's loving-kindness meditation means wishing, for yourself, your loved ones, strangers and your enemies: *May you live in safety. Be happy. Be healthy, live with ease.* And, as the good teachers note, wishing is not enough. We have to put those wishes into practice with everyone we're connected to.

Practice extraversion. Reach out to people. Smile. Talk more. Extraverted people are much more likely to experience themselves as happy. Or is it that happier people are more extraverted?—we don't know, and it doesn't matter. A study of both types of college students found that everyone was happiest when they were acting extraverted, but even the introverted students were happiest when pretending to be extraverted, "implying that anyone who musters the will to be outgoing will be happy as a result."

> PRACTICE LOVING, COMPASSION, AND EXTRAVERSION. THESE ARE SKILLS YOU CAN DEVELOP THROUGH REPETITION.

Connections also provide us the arena for generosity and generativity, perhaps the two greatest long-term joys in life. Practicing kindness and thoughtfulness; trying to be a good parent and seeing the results as your children grow. Simply smiling at strangers and wishing them a good day, then noticing how they brighten. Allowing yourself to savor the glow of unselfishness. Life would indeed be nasty and brutish without those opportunities.

relationship skills

We have an unfortunate tendency to assume that, like happiness, relationships should be easy. On the contrary, relationships are full of conflict, whether it's out in the open or not. We want to be loved, but we fear being controlled. We want to be committed, but we cherish our freedom. Everyone wants to get their own way, whether it's how you like your eggs or how to raise the children. If there's no way to resolve conflicts, people walk away, either physically or emotionally. And hanging over every relationship is the possibility of loss or rejection, which makes many of us hold back from giving ourselves fully. So in all relationships, we're fighting each other and fighting our own fears. A little reflection will usually show you the mindful way to deal with those issues in a particular situation, but conflict and fear make it difficult to stay calm and mindful. So here are my tips—

<u>To build and maintain intimacy:</u>

- Express your love frequently and mindfully. Let the people you love know how you feel about them; let down your guard and act on your feelings in words and in gestures. Be generous with hugs and kisses. Be attentive and interested in the other person's world. Hold hands. Give compliments. Notice things. Get under your paradigmatic image of the other person and look at the details on this day, at this moment.

- Gifts and surprises are simply magical. They show you're thinking about your loved one when you're apart. They show you want to have fun together. They don't have to be expensive: a candy bar, a book, some flowers.

- Practice being thoughtful about the other person's needs and wants. Spoil them. Many of us now, from overstressed and too-busy families, have far too little experience of someone being genuinely interested in us, wanting to know about our thoughts and feelings just because they care about us and want to know more. Some people may feel initially scared of this because it's so powerful and unfamiliar, but don't hold back; this kind of love and attention promotes flourishing.

- Be gracious. Compromise and take turns. A trusting, intimate relationship is the safest place there is to practice being generous and magnanimous.

- Be generous in your praise and recognition. Pay attention to what your loved ones are doing, and look for opportunities to express your appreciation. Being grateful, as we've noted, makes you happier and healthier; and of course, it will give the recipient an endorphin rush, too.

- On the other hand, practice holding your tongue when you're in a bad place. Our loved ones can be sitting ducks for our irritability and thoughtlessness. Sometimes we want someone to blame, and who's the handy target? So if you let out a zinger, you're still in a bad mood and you feel like a jackass besides. Instead, be silent. Go for a walk. Your bad mood will go away more quickly, because you won't get into a fight or feel guilty. If your loved one wants to help but you find it irritating, explain politely that you need distance right now.

- Be open about what you're thinking and feeling. Believe it or not, people are interested. Letting someone into your interior world can seem like a wonderful gift, especially if you're usually pretty tight-lipped. Let your defenses come down and think out loud.

To add more joy in your relationships:

- Small gestures of thoughtfulness or affection
- Touch, hugs, and kisses
- Letting yourself completely relax into a mindful, meaningful conversation
- Sharing your daily lists of three good things
- Sharing excitement about ideas and experiences
- A weekly date
- Unselfishness in sex
- Letting the little things go
- Reliability; doing what you promise
- Always happy to see you or hear from you
- Dinner together, no TV
- Play
- Willing to listen, and to share yourself
- Laughing at the same jokes
- Overlooking your potbelly (or whatever it is that bothers you so much)
- Shared values
- Thoughtful surprises

To resolve conflicts:

- Remember validation. Don't not listen. Don't be dismissive. These are invalidating actions, and they can be very hurtful. The old advice about simply repeating back what you hear works because it's recognizing the other person's right to their feelings. You don't have to agree that the other person is right to show that you understand how she feels. When you try to understand her feelings, you get very important information about how this conflict developed. Ninety percent of the time, it's a misunderstanding, or due to a communications mix-up.

- Frame your messages with words. Talk about, don't just act out, how you're feeling. Partners frequently believe we're angry at them when we're really just frustrated with the way the discussion is going. Be direct about what you <u>are</u> feeling.

- Don't raise the emotional ante. Emotions are highly contagious. If I'm angry and nearly out of control, it's going to be very difficult for you to be calm and in control; but clearly <u>someone</u> needs to be. So don't use fighting words, don't make personal attacks, don't call names, don't make wild accusations. Don't use words like <u>always</u> or <u>never</u>, because they raise the stakes. They make the fight about who the other person is, not about something they did. No kitchen-sink arguments, into which you drag everything but. Stay with the subject at hand.

don't assume: "IF HE LOVES ME, HE'LL UNDERSTAND."

<u>To deepen our connection to society and the world:</u>

- Drop the habit of mindless judging and instead treat people with compassionate curiosity. Practice paying attention. Practice empathy and caring. In a too-busy world, there's a lot of pressure on us to rely on stereotypes and snap judgments, and that becomes a habit. We can break that habit by mindfully attending to our thinking processes, with a determination to look beyond the superficial.
- Strengthen and deepen your relationships. Friendships can provide the setting for some of the most joyful times of our lives—staying up late playing poker, going on trips together, simply having a stimulating conversation.

- Deepen your relationship with the natural world. Pay attention to how your environment affects you—sunny or gray days, interesting or monotonous locale, safe or threatening surroundings. The environment can make you feel stimulated or depressed, at home or estranged. Try to arrange your life so that you'll spend more time in settings where you feel comfortable and stimulated.
- Seeking a connection to the sacred is good for you and brings fulfillment into your life. So cultivate experiences that give you a sense of the profound, of meaning, of fitting in to a deeper purpose. This may be as simple as a brief daily meditation or as majestic as worship in a cathedral or a walk in the woods.

<u>Sometimes we have to know how to set limits in a relationship:</u>

- Trust your guts. If someone wants you to do something that feels weird, creepy, or inappropriate, don't do it.
- Don't let yourself be manipulated. Learn to identify guilt trips, veiled threats, and passive aggression.
- Don't try too hard to be liked. Don't be a people-pleaser; you compromise your own values in the process.
- Don't waste your time on difficult people. If you have to spend time with them, don't bother trying to change them. Extend them compassion, but don't get sucked in.

Mature Love

Though love is magical, the magic doesn't last. One researcher estimates that after about four years on average, the initial stage of infatuation has worn off the marriage, and the partners are secretly wondering if they made a huge mistake. Unfortunately, changes in divorce laws have made it too easy for couples to split when sometimes, especially if there are children, they would be better off to stick it out. For any marriage to work, romantic love has to be transmuted into companionate love (not that romantic love should entirely disappear). Companionate love is the affection we feel for someone whose life is deeply intertwined with ours. It's very important to recognize that this doesn't happen automatically; romantic love doesn't turn into companionate love without work from us.

The simplest way to cultivate this kind of love is to practice being nice. (I know, it's such a pedestrian concept, but it gets the idea across.) It's too easy to go "off duty" when we enter the front door and forget that we owe our spouse courtesy, respect, affection, and consideration. So:

- Listen.
- Talk.
- Help each other.
- Don't be critical.
- Don't raise your voice.
- Be thoughtful and generous.

When you do this, you're giving your spouse a reason to stick with you, and to treat you nicely as well.

Friends

Many of my depressed patients are lonely and isolated. Of course, it's partly that their depressed habits make them no fun to be around. But I find that many are isolated because they have no family, they're in a strange community, their work is solitary—plus they're shy and don't make friends easily. Depression takes that loneliness and adds self-blame to it, so people tend to see themselves as unattractive, worthless, or unlovable when they're really only shy.

For most of us, being with friends is a major source of joy. Overall happiness is correlated with satisfaction with friends, number of friends, number of close friends, frequency of seeing them, number of phone calls, visits, and parties. Much of advertising is built around the promise that if you drink our beer (drive our car, wear our clothes, use our toothpaste), you'll instantly be part of a cozy band of intimates.

Having friends inoculates us from stress. Robert Sapolsky, the great stress researcher, found that baboons who had more friendships—who spent more time together, who groomed each other, who watched from the sidelines as others jockeyed for status—had less stress hormones like cortisol in their bloodstreams. Many studies have found that the number of friends you have is one of the highest correlates with overall happiness, right up there with exercise, frequency of sex, success experiences, and simple sensual pleasures.

How to have more friends:

- Cultivate the friendships you have. Call people, invite them out with you. Just talk.
- Ask a lot of questions. People like to talk about themselves. Be sincerely interested.
- Share your enthusiasms. People may find raising geckos fascinating. Even if they don't, you let them see something that's important to you.
- Share your values and opinions, but do it in an open-minded way.

do: BE A JOINER—RELIGION, CLUBS, SUPPORT GROUPS, COMMUNITY ORGANIZATIONS.

By the way, this is one area where a more socially adept spouse can help out one who is more nerdlike. My extraverted wife has helped me feel more at ease, and thus enjoy many social situations where I would ordinarily run home as quickly as possible. Differences remain, however: at an annual retreat we attend with hundreds of people, she comes back to our hotel room bouncing off the ceiling while I melt into a puddle on the bed.

joy, satisfaction, and juggling

Remember that happiness isn't our natural state, that it takes work. Some of it requires facing some uncomfortable truths or making tough decisions—but if you don't do that, your life will keep on going down the misery trail. Fortunately most of the work in finding greater happiness is inherently pleasant or fun. Try to keep in mind that your brain is always making new connections. It learns whatever it is that you're paying attention to, and gets better at it, whether you want it to or not. So try to feed your brain just as much joy and satisfaction as you can. Learning to be happy requires some effort on your part, but once you've learned most of the skills, it requires a lot less effort to stay happy.

grief and pain

If you want to be happy, you have to let yourself be sad. Nobody gets a free pass, except maybe those Buddhist monks who have severed most of their connections to real life. The deepest joys in life come from our attachments—usually to other people—and life will take those other people from us at some point. Grief is an essential feeling, the natural emotional response to loss. There are other kinds of pain that seem inevitable; physical pain that as we age becomes debilitating, the mental anguish that comes with stress and with disappointment, the sympathetic pain we feel for our loved ones.

My day-to-day work is with people who are recovering from the bad things that life hands us—divorce, loss of a loved one, being stuck in a bad situation, chronic pain, even abuse and rape. Most of them wouldn't need me for long if it weren't for the mistakes they make in trying to adapt and cope. There is a popular saying among some psychologists now—*Pain is inevitable; suffering is optional.* While that feels a little glib to me, I understand the distinction. Life is hard, and pain is inevitable. But we can make our pain much worse and more prolonged if we're not smart about it.

Many of the depressed people I work with are that way because they were never able to completely grieve a loss that was especially traumatic for them—the death of a parent in childhood, parental divorce, or the loss of a spouse. They made an unconscious decision that the pain they felt was so overpowering that it would tear them apart—and then they tried to use their maladaptive defenses to try not to feel it. But they get stuck here; every subsequent loss triggers those fears and the associated attempts to deny or suppress their feelings. And in the process, they lose the ability to feel anything at all.

The awful truth is that when we're happy, we have a lot to lose. Some of us, because past losses have been so devastating, may stop trying to get what we want. As a deliberate, conscious strategy, this may work sometimes. Some people may choose never to remarry, but still enjoy committed, loving relationships. In general, however, people take that stance out of mindless fear, and it robs their lives of all joy.

We usually think of grief as our response to the death of someone we love, but there are many circumstances, some of which we don't recognize, that can trigger feelings of grief. We lose people in other ways, through divorce, through relocation, through inattention. People simply change. Our parents grow old, and before we know it, our roles are reversed and we're taking care of them. Our children grow up, and much as we love them as adults, we've lost our playmates. To complicate things further, contemporary society has given us opportunities for a new kind of loss, an ambiguous loss, where the person is still there in our lives but their meaning to us has changed. Divorce and Alzheimer's are the usual causes. There are no guidebooks and few examples for how to deal with this kind of loss. You have to be a supportive co-parent with someone who's just broken your heart. And Alzheimer's spouses are the favorite new lab rats of stress psychologists, because their role is inherently so difficult; the loss of a love, a partner, and the need to take care of a former lover who sometimes doesn't even recognize us.

Grief isn't always about the loss of a person. Our knees give out, and we can't play tennis any longer, something that's brought us great joy for fifty years. We change jobs, and find that the new one has less meaning to us. We move to a smaller house when the kids are grown, and find the new place never really feels like home. We commit

___

do: KNOW THAT GRIEF DOESN'T LAST FOREVER.

___

ourselves to a course of action, and find that we miss the sense of endless opportunity that we didn't even know we had before. Terrorists strike in New York, and we no longer feel as safe and secure.

Grief takes time. We have a natural healing process, rather like any kind of adaptation. At first, the loss is the biggest thing in our lives, but with the passage of time, other experiences gradually push it into the background. Time is essential, but in today's world, there is tremendous pressure to get on with things. Our friends want us to be over it long before we're ready. Our job certainly expects us to be fully attentive again. Driving down the road at 65 miles per hour demands a degree of concentration we didn't need riding in the buggy; life just goes faster, and there's no time to reflect.

We have to learn the skill of mindfully sitting with pain. As with other feelings, we have to learn to experience them without feeling overpowered by them—but this is different, more difficult, because it can hurt so much, you fear you can't stand it. This is where meditation practice really helps; as in meditation, we can see our feelings as raindrops falling on a tranquil pool—they splash, they make ripples, but that's all. They don't harm or destroy the pool; in fact, they add to it, as all our experiences, even pain, add to our lives.

Dr. Kübler-Ross developed her model of the stages of grief almost forty years ago, and most of us have some awareness of it by now. It's still valid, even if it sometimes irritates us because it seems so pat. Judith Viorst, in her priceless book *Necessary Losses,* refers to the sense that there is a Julia Child of sorrow trying to give us a recipe for the perfect grief. Yet the model is helpful largely because it reminds us we need time; that we're caught up in a process that has a natural flow, and we can't hurry it along. Something bigger than ourselves has taken over, and it won't let go till it's through with us. But we can be reassured that we'll come out okay—in fact, better, for some kinds of grief. When we lose someone we love and admire, once we're past

the initial devastation, we unconsciously begin to take into ourselves some
of our loved one's strengths. Confronted with a decision or a stressful situation, we almost can't help thinking about
what our loved one would want us to
do—viewing ourselves with the same love,
patience, and understanding in the process, and adding to our reserves of inner
strength.

don't: AVOID
APPROPRIATE SADNESS
AND GRIEF.

blessing the past

What is there to do other than letting time take its course? For many of us,
remembering the past is associated with such a powerful sense of loss that
we try <u>not</u> to remember. We hear a song on the radio that we listened to with
our first lover; we see a child who bears a striking resemblance to our now-
grown daughter; we see a book that our father loved—and there's a sharp
pain, as if we've touched a sensitive tooth, that makes us suck in our breath.
We don't even have to regret that we broke up with the lover; we can be very
proud of our daughter; we can be happy that our father died in a state of
grace. None of that matters. We know we'll never have those experiences
again, and that in itself can feel unbearable.

What if we <u>do</u> regret? What if we were estranged when father died? What
if we feel we were total idiots to break up with that girlfriend? What if our
daughter is lost to us now? How much sharper is loss coupled with regret? It
takes great courage, a very old-fashioned virtue, to be able to face these experiences. But we have to remember. If we keep recoiling, we live by our defenses;
we're fundamentally dishonest with ourselves, and we lose self-respect. We
can't be in the present, we can't attain mindfulness, if we don't face the past.

Here are three qualities that I think help us accept these painful memories:

- <u>Forgiveness.</u> Both for ourselves and for people who've wronged us.
  When we did something we regret, we were acting on the best
  information we had at the time, with all our feelings at the time. We
  can't put ourselves back into that emotional state, but if we could,

we'd do the same thing all over again, because that's the best we knew how to do. Patients often ask me how they could have stayed in a destructive relationship (or job, or family, and so on) as long as they did. I tell them they are forgetting about hope. Back then, they always had a glimmer of hope that things would turn around. How can you beat yourself up for being hopeful? And the people who hurt us? They, too, were acting on the best information they had. It's really quite rare for someone to actively desire to hurt another person. It's much more common to be full of anger, living in a distorted paradigm, hurt and defensive and wanting to get justice for a perceived injury. That's how we hurt people, and others hurt us. You have to forgive people for merely being human.

- Gratitude. That experience we look back on now must have been terribly important to us, or we wouldn't be so affected by the pain. We have to be grateful that we were permitted to experience it. The terrible truth about life is that opening ourselves up to joy also makes us vulnerable to loss. Would you choose no joy? We've talked in other places in this book about how, in lab experiments, expressing gratitude has been found to make us happier and healthier. I think even more important is that it makes us a grateful person—someone who appreciates past loves, past experiences, their youth. Someone who looks forward to living, even when it hurts.

- Determination. If there are regrets, we won't make the same mistake again. If we didn't savor our experience enough at the time, we won't let that happen again. We can't rewrite the past, but we can make sure we get the most out of the present. We can't protect ourselves from loss, but we can enjoy life to the fullest now.

other kinds of pain

There are other kinds of pain than the loss of a loved one, some of them even more difficult in their ways. Though humans are in general wonderfully adaptable, in researching this book, I've noticed that different investigators have identified several conditions that we may not be able to completely adapt to. Daniel Nettle identifies two things, and I add three more:

1. <u>Lasting disability.</u> Although it's true that many studies have found that our happiness levels do bounce back admirably after a disability, we don't usually bounce back all the way.
2. <u>Noise.</u> People who live near new sources of noise (new roads, increased air traffic, and so on) believe they will get used to it, but they don't. It remains a constant irritant.
3. <u>Physical pain.</u> People do adapt to chronic pain and learn how to get on with the business of living. But it slows you down, makes you cranky and preoccupied. It may not interfere with satisfaction, but it can take away from joy.
4. <u>Divorce.</u> Even though we have no-fault divorce, we have psychological winners and losers. The loser is usually the one who was left and is financially worse off. Much of the bitterness of divorce battles is about jockeying for "winner" status. The loser can suffer a permanent blow to self-esteem, and remain prone to depression.
5. <u>Unemployment.</u> Some argue that the loss in happiness due to unemployment is actually worse than that due to divorce. It can lead to passivity—a lot of television watching—and alcohol consumption. Even in countries like Holland and Sweden, which give the unemployed good financial support, there is still a drop in happiness, health, and mental health. And you don't get used to it, even after two years; and when you go back to work, there is a scar, some permanent damage to our capacity to enjoy our work.

So we may not adjust perfectly to these things. My advice is to take that into account, do whatever you can about it, and don't blame yourself. Move away from noise, if you possibly can. If you have chronic pain, use physical therapy, acupuncture, kinesiology, and if you have to, take painkillers. Our society is far too paranoid about drug abuse, so paranoid that dying patients are sometimes deprived of the drugs that would alleviate their suffering. If opiates are the only relief from your pain, use them and learn how not to abuse them; see a physician qualified in pain management. Do everything you can to recoup from a disability and avoid becoming demoralized. Remember that unemployment exists to help maximize profits, not because you're not a good enough worker; don't let self-blame drag you down into passivity. And educate yourself about the psychological effects of divorce; don't let yourself be steamrollered into the loser role.

There are some common traps that can seduce us with the promise of relief from suffering. But they don't work, and in fact only make it come back later in spades:

- <u>Stuffing</u>. Pretending it doesn't matter, denying the pain, moving on too quickly. When we do that, we develop a fault line; we become more vulnerable to similar experiences in the future. We'll turn cold. As I said before, you can't turn off negative feelings without turning off positive ones as well. You'll lose the capacity for happiness.

- <u>Blaming</u>. *It's my fault. It's his fault. It's the government's fault.* There's a big difference between assigning responsibility and blaming. Blaming is an expression of anger. Anger is tempting when we're in pain, because it makes us feel righteous and powerful. But it's only a temporary distraction; we have to allow ourselves to feel the damage.

- <u>Obsessing</u>. *If only (we'd caught it earlier, taken a different flight, checked the brakes)*. This is a mind trap that will keep your left brain so busy that you won't be able to really feel anything other than panic.

- <u>Giving in to fear</u>. *I can't handle it, I'm not strong enough, I'm going to fall apart*. These reactions may be unavoidable sometimes, but we have to guard against giving in to them. They are the beginning of depression and despair. In fact, humans are amazingly adaptable creatures, and chances are that you <u>can</u> handle it, you <u>are</u> strong enough, and you <u>won't</u> fall apart.

- <u>Turning to alcohol or drugs.</u> Possible temporary relief but will only complicate your troubles.

Remember that whatever happens to you, your magnificent mind has the power to make it much worse. Try blaming yourself. Try wallowing in bad feelings. Overeat and don't exercise. Snap at people who try to help, and then avoid them. Be sure to keep comparing yourself to everyone who's luckier. Stay inside and avoid contact with anything beautiful or awe-inspiring. Watch a lot of TV, and don't skip over the commercials. Make some impulsive purchases to add to your guilt. Stay up late and oversleep in the mornings. Eat more junk food. <u>Pain is inevitable, but suffering is optional.</u>

facing the worst

Trauma doesn't necessarily lead to post-traumatic stress disorder. If you have the resources to master it, trauma can lead to growth. Our basic assumptions are shaken, but that can be beneficial. We all know of people who have come out of catastrophes better off than before.

I think two or three real, honest-to-goodness breakdowns are about average per lifetime nowadays. Circumstances become simply overwhelming, and you stop sleeping, start crying, your mind starts racing, and you feel like you're going crazy. I'm making light of it right now, but when you're feeling this way, there's no joking around; you really don't know if you're going to survive it. Even if you survive it, there's a very good chance you'll be permanently damaged by it—demoralized and scared—unless you make it a good breakdown. From the standpoint of preserving your future capacity for happiness, this is essential.

Fortunately, my friend Bill O'Hanlon has written *Thriving Through Crisis,* and if you follow his advice you can turn this breakdown into a breakthrough. Here's my take on some of his main points:

- <u>You're having the breakdown because stress has beaten down your defenses.</u> Everyone needs defenses, ways of coping with stress. Yours worked fine up until now, but nobody's perfect. This is a signal you need to learn new ways of coping.
- <u>It's not your fault, so make it a good breakdown.</u> Don't waste time feeling inadequate, guilty, or ashamed. Life simply got too hard for a

while. But take the opportunity to learn the <u>best</u> ways of coping with stress, rather than putting on Band-Aids.

- <u>Use the breakdown as a time to reexamine basic assumptions, rather than buttressing your defenses.</u> One or more of your basic paradigms didn't work; hence the crisis. Look mindfully at yourself and your circumstances to figure out what this was: The idea that you were perfect? The idea that your job would last forever? The idea that you could stuff your feelings?

- <u>Work on telling the truth and face lies, self-deception, and inauthenticity.</u> Lies, including those we tell ourselves, grow one on top of each other exponentially, until the house of cards collapses. Telling the truth is much simpler; you have to remember only one version of the story, the right one. And you'll gain immeasurably in self-respect.

- <u>Make permanent, not temporary, necessary changes.</u> Like I said, adopt the <u>best</u> ways of coping. Learn mindfulness. Learn to let yourself feel. Learn to make decisions with logic, emotion, and intuition. Learn to be honest, loving, and compassionate.

- <u>Find your own voice, and use it</u>. Identify your own values, and put them into practice. Stop following, and speak up.

- <u>Develop compassion for yourself and others</u>. Remember that the world's a mess and we're all just doing the best we can.

- <u>Make a contribution to the world.</u> Do good things for other people. Karma is real; there will be a payoff for you. In the meantime, you'll feel better about yourself.

If you can follow these rules, chances are that your breakdown, instead of permanently damaging you, will actually do you some good. Maybe you'll only have to have <u>one</u> breakdown, instead of two or three in your lifetime.

happy pills

There's no such thing as a happy pill, except for a few illegal substances that are so addictive they <u>have</u> to be illegal. But there's a frightening trend in

Western culture right now to give people whatever pills they ask for—principally antidepressants, the SSRIs like Prozac, and SNRIs like Cymbalta—to help them "cope."* They're enormously popular drugs, but they raise an important question about the nature of illness. Alcohol is a very effective drug for social anxiety disorder. Does that mean that social anxiety is the result of a deficiency of alcohol? Yet that's the reasoning behind why "antidepressants" are believed to be good for depression; there has yet to be any independent confirmation that these drugs are correcting a chemical imbalance in the system.

There are some alarming signs that antidepressants interfere with emotional vitality. I have a patient, a musician, who had to go on Lexapro because his intense social anxiety would lead to severe asthma attacks. The medication helped a lot, but he noticed that he stopped getting goose bumps when he was really moved by music. When he stopped Lexapro, he was able to get goose bumps again. It wasn't just the physical manifestation of his appreciation of music that he lost, he felt he lost some of his ability to immerse himself in the music. He's not the only patient of mine who's reported that they just feel a little numb on SSRIs. One found he stopped feeling guilty about his sexual conquests. Their experience is similar to that of a group of patients who reported sexual dysfunction as a result of taking antidepressants. The researchers found that these patients also reported significantly less ability to cry, care about others' feelings, erotic dreaming, surprise, creativity, anger, and ability to express their feelings.

Then there's a study in which "normal" (not depressed) volunteers were given Paxil or another antidepressant for a week. They were then shown slides of human faces expressing different emotions. (Psychologists have developed a standard set of slides that most people agree on, which can be used to test empathy or emotional sensitivity or certain kinds of brain damage.) After medication, these normal volunteers had a significant amount of trouble identifying negative emotions, especially anger and fear. Another study of normal volunteers found that four weeks of Paxil significantly reduced their

* I have the same concerns about the overuse of medications for ADHD and, recently, mood stabilizers for adolescents. Do we really need to have these drugs advertised all over the place?

level of negative feelings. It may be that antidepressants derive some of their efficacy from blunting depressed people's overreaction to negative emotion—but how much blunting do we want? Do people who are not depressed really need protection from negative feelings?

Don't get me wrong. As a therapist, I'm very very glad we have the new antidepressants. I think they've saved thousands of lives and certainly helped millions of people find their way out of depression. But depression is a serious illness, and most patients taking these meds don't have it.

Emotional blunting seems to be part of how antidepressants work. They make people less sensitive. They help us stop worrying about what other people think. Peter Kramer pointed these effects out, way back in <u>Listening to Prozac.</u> Depending on the circumstances, that may be a good or a bad thing. But are they helping us cope with a world we shouldn't cope with? Go through any nursing home, and you'll find that 90 percent of the patients are being given an antidepressant to help them tolerate the boredom and loneliness of their lives. Those of us out of nursing homes—are we taking them to help us tolerate the stress and emptiness of our lives? Suppose it's antidepressants, rather than the absence of a draft, that accounts for the difference in protest level between Vietnam and Iraq?

So—if you're genuinely depressed, find a therapist and a doctor and by all means try an SSRI. But if you're merely unhappy, stressed out, or grief-stricken—stay away from the pills. Work on changing your circumstances and attitudes instead. Grief, sadness, and anger are all necessary, if uncomfortable, parts of ourselves. We can't eliminate them either by using our own defenses or by taking pills inappropriately. We might want to, but that choice will lead to a flat and empty life.

TEN

the meaning of life*

We've reviewed many strategies for reducing misery and promoting joy and satisfaction. But there's another dimension to happiness, which is usually called <u>meaning</u>—a sense of purpose, of making a contribution, of leaving something behind, a belief that our lives make sense, if only in some way known to God alone. Obviously, some of our choices in life are dictated by a desire for this feeling: It's why people go to church, why I'm writing this book, a great part of why people choose to have children. These are activities that may bring us some joy or satisfaction, but those rewards are incidental to the main purpose of the activity. There is another kind of reward; we decide to do these things because, I think, there is an inborn, instinctual desire for our lives to have meaning. And without that, we will be lacking a certain quality that makes for happiness.

---

* I have to add an asterisk after that chapter title, just to be sure that everyone understands it's a joke. I don't <u>really</u> know the meaning of life; sorry to disappoint.

We have to be more self-conscious about this quest nowadays. We have lost the world humans were designed for, of structure and interconnection, where we had daily contact with nature and the sacred, where both religion and an intricate web of relationships and expectations told us who we are and why we are here. Now we're faced with the problem of <u>creating meaning for ourselves</u>—a challenging task, a yawning abyss opening up suddenly at our feet, the very definition of the existential crisis. Mindlessness—consumerism, multitasking, escapist fantasies, staying busy—is a way of distracting ourselves from this need. We can stay busy until we keel over—and then, will that matter to anyone? Most of us, regardless of how busy we are, occasionally face the dark night of the soul when we wake up at 4 A.M. and wonder if we <u>matter.</u> We want to matter. We can't be truly happy unless we feel we matter, that our lives have meaning and purpose.

If you could take a drug every day that would keep you in a state of bliss, would you choose to? Most people say no. We want genuine, not artificial, experiences. Much of our good feeling about ourselves comes from a sense of achievement, of having overcome obstacles. Much of our creativity is about struggle and conflict.

Carol D. Ryff has been working for decades on what constitutes genuine happiness—not just joy, satisfaction, and the absence of misery, but what constitutes a life of fulfillment and meaning. Her work is the best basis I have found for organizing our thoughts in this chapter. She outlines six factors:

1. <u>Self-acceptance.</u> Liking yourself, generally approving of yourself.
2. <u>Positive relations with others.</u> The ability to love, to feel empathy, to be connected.
3. <u>Autonomy.</u> The sense that you are making your own choices, that you are relatively free of a need for approval or permission.
4. <u>Environmental mastery.</u> The ability to advance in the world and change it to suit your needs.
5. <u>Purpose in life.</u> A sense of direction, of goals, a belief that life has meaning.
6. <u>Personal growth.</u> The intention to continue to grow, to take in new ideas and information and change your paradigms.

Let's assume that we've covered the first two areas adequately already, and focus on the last four.

autonomy

Mindfulness meditation, or any type of meditation, holds a seductive promise, the idea that we can rise above craving, that we can become so detached, such good observers of ourselves, that we can no longer be seduced by our wants.

"I don't get it," one of my patients asked me provocatively. "Are we supposed to accept emptiness, or are we supposed to fill it?" It was her shorthand introduction to what, to me, is a central question of happiness. On my suggestion, she'd been reading a lot about mindfulness. A therapist herself, the Jewish mother of demanding adolescents, married to a depressed husband, she spends all her waking hours trying to help others fill themselves up. *Unhappy? Do something about it: take a pill, get into therapy, get married, get a divorce, join a gym, go on a diet.* Now my suggestion: *Learn about mindfulness.* Mindfulness, in a tradition that goes straight back to the Buddha, tends to suggest a different solution: *Wanting is the cause of all human misery. Learn to want less. Accept that life is painful. Face the existential emptiness that is an essential part of our nature.* In the terms I've used in this book, are we to <u>discard our defenses</u> entirely and try to face life naked, to feel all our feelings without protection, or are we to <u>improve and bolster our defenses</u> so that we can function better? Be a mystic, or a success? Fortunately for us all, I think this is a false dichotomy, but let's explore this question a little further.

Buddha and, three thousand years later, Freud, both said essentially the same thing: Misery is part of the human condition, and desire is at the heart of misery. Trying too hard to fix misery, mindlessly pursuing our desires or trying to stuff them away, just makes things worse, leads you into a world of self-delusion, of frenzied, meaningless activity. Paradoxically, accepting the fact that we are all fundamentally alone, that we face death and the great cosmic void naked and defenseless, leads to a certain comfort.

Mark Epstein, in his valuable book *Going to Pieces Without Falling*

Apart, captured the fundamental difference between Buddhism and the secular* Western view of man:

> In Western theories, the hope is always that emptiness can be healed, that if the character is developed or the trauma resolved that the background feelings will diminish. If we can make the ego stronger, the expectation is that emptiness will go away. In Buddhism, the approach is reversed. Focus on the emptiness, the dissatisfaction, and the feelings of imperfection, and the character will get stronger.

Barry Magid, in *Ordinary Mind,* puts it this way: "the common goal of Zen and psychoanalysis is <u>putting an end to the pursuit of happiness.</u>" By that he means that the belief that we'll be happy if and only if we get what we want is the path to misery—especially if what we want is to be free of misery. Many religions promise a way out. *God is with you. Death leads you to a destination where your questions about life will be answered. Life is not empty or meaningless; we can't understand it yet, but we will.* In the twenty-first century, with faith in all institutions breaking up all around us, that kind of faith is difficult to maintain. Yet in America and in other societies, political and religious fundamentalism seems to appeal to more and more, perhaps in response to the emptiness of Western culture. But if you have a strong faith in God or the government and are still reading this book, I suspect all your questions haven't been answered yet.

So why is this a false dichotomy? One reason is that both goals are impossible. Is it possible not to want to fill the emptiness? Biologically, it seems to make more sense to talk about craving, the dopamine system that keeps us always wanting more. Yet we're also talking about fear, the existential anxiety of meaninglessness. <u>Emptiness</u> is a word for how we experience the craving and the fear. So no, we can't fill emptiness—the emptiness is a perception, a feeling, an expression of craving and fear that's part of human

---

* Western thought is not necessarily secular. Jesus and the early Christian church talked about giving up this world much like Buddhism; and elements of mysticism and renunciation remain strong in some Christian and Jewish traditions.

nature. But we can learn to feel less fear, to control our desires. We can structure our lives so that we feel a greater sense of meaning and purpose, but we can't fill the emptiness completely.

Is it possible simply to accept empti-ness, to stop craving? Again, craving is part of human nature. Where would we be if we stopped trying to better ourselves, to improve our condition? Yet we can learn to love ourselves better as we are.

WOULD YOU RATHER BE A MYSTIC, OR A SUCCESS?

This is a very real issue in psychotherapy. You can caricature two camps. One camp is the experts. Whether it's a psychiatrist who'll give you pills, or a cognitive psychologist who'll tell you exactly what's wrong with how you think, or a social worker who'll give you all kinds of advice about how to run your marriage and family (I'm guilty here), these people firmly believe, with more or less reason, that they have expert knowledge and their role is to use that to help you. The premise is that you can fill the emptiness by perfecting yourself. The other camp is those who firmly refuse to give advice. They can be orthodox Freudians (a dying breed) whose goal is to help you come to grips with your unconscious desires; or more mindful practitioners who will help you face that misery is caused by craving. These different camps of no-advice-givers are not that far apart, though the Freudians will probably be less warm and fuzzy, and charge more. The premise is that you can't fill the emptiness, no matter how hard you try; just face your fears, and you'll become stronger. My patient's dilemma, and mine as a therapist: Reinforce your defenses, learn better ways of coping, learn better cognitive and emo-tional control—or just sit down and confront your demons.

No matter which way we choose, we can run headfirst into irony. My suggestion to my patient, to learn more about mindfulness, while meant to help her accept emptiness, can turn into another attempt to fill it. *If I just get really good at mindfulness, then I'll be happy. If I can find more time for meditation—maybe an hour a day? Maybe three? Then I won't be so dissatis-fied.* Yet mindfulness is supposed to teach us to live with dissatisfaction. We could turn the pursuit of mindfulness into another mindless quest. It may be true that Davidson's Buddhist monks, who spend their whole lives in meditation, are the happiest people in the world—by some standard. Would we exchange our lives for theirs? No relationships, no attachments, no love. Bliss without fun, without involvement.

To try to thoroughly enrich our lives, even in the wisest way, can mean turning our backs on our basic nature. Positive psychology, so squarely American and Can-Do, would provide us with a formula for happiness that seems to erase doubt, ambivalence, regret. Is this really possible? Or is it an attempt to keep us busy and distracted until we die? What good is being in flow if we're only playing video games?

So I come down firmly in favor of straddling the fence. Don't stop trying to perfect yourself, but at the same time recognize that you'll never get there. Learn to distance yourself from your cravings and fears, but don't expect that you can totally rise above them. Recognize that the voices of insecurity and self-doubt are your frightened inner child at work, and that you'll be happier in the long run if you cultivate independence, even if it's scary.

It's interesting to me that the researchers have found that, when you're under stress, simply reflecting on your personal values reduces the cortisol response, and your subjective feeling of distress. It's also interesting that happiness generally increases with age, despite declining health. There are no positive explanations why. I think it has to do with becoming wiser; the fires of youth (ambition, competition, revolution) decline, and people are more able to listen to the still, small voice inside that says *This is the right thing to do.*

Positive Psychology

The subject of autonomy leads directly into a brief discussion of positive psychology. Martin Seligman, a true giant of American psychology, who revolutionized the field with *Learned Helplessness* among many other valuable contributions, challenged the profession in the year 2000 to focus more on what makes the good life, not merely on helping the disturbed. Since then, he and many collaborators whom I've already cited here—Mihaly Csikszentmihalyi, Christopher Peterson, Jonathan Haidt, Carol Ryff, among others—have already made huge contributions to our understanding. Seligman's Authentic Happiness Web site is a rich trove of information and self-tests.

The ultimate goal of positive psychology is what's called the autotelic

<u>personality</u> (autotelic = determining one's own purposes and goals). The autotelic person:

> Needs few material possessions and little entertainment, comfort, power or fame, because so much of what he or she does is already rewarding . . . they are less dependent on external rewards that keep others motivated to go on with a life composed of dull and meaningless routines. They are more autonomous and independent, because they cannot be as easily manipulated with threats or rewards from the outside. At the same time, they are more involved with everything around them because they are fully immersed in the current of life.

As Daniel Nettle points out, there are many virtues and benefits associated with this state, but increased happiness is not necessarily one of them. People who measure high on flow in their lives are indeed less bored than others but they do not score any higher on measures of happiness. People in high-flow occupations describe themselves as no more happy than anyone else, and indeed are subject to frustration, depression, mood swings, and problems with addictions, which both motivate and hinder their self-expression. In fact, the relationship between autonomy and happiness is murky because many of the people who consider themselves very happy need a lot of social contact and approval. I prefer Ryff's point of view, that autonomy is one of several components of a rewarding life. But even she acknowledges that this formulation largely omits qualities like joy in living or capacity to accept change. In this book, I wanted to stick more to happy feelings, whether of joy or of a more long-lasting state of satisfaction or peace; but you can't talk about happiness without talking about our conceptions of the good life.

Seligman is forthright about using the terms <u>happiness</u> and <u>well-being</u> to mean positive activities <u>that have no feeling component</u> (and obviously he's using his own definition of "positive"). He seems to assume that trying to change the individual set point for cheeriness is not an especially effective strategy; thus positive psychology focuses more on eudaimonia than simple pleasures. I prefer (perhaps for selfish reasons) not to make that assumption. One reason is that I think the evidence is there that the brain, and the set point for happiness, is much more mutable than positive psychology has considered so far.

The primary way that positive psychology proposes to increase happiness is to focus on one's own strengths (called Signature Strengths); to develop them and stop trying to do things that are just inherently difficult for you. Seligman has a list of 24 Signature Strengths, and a self-test to measure your standing. The idea that you can build on your strengths, like learning new skills, is of course very congenial to me. But one of the major weaknesses here is the reliance on a self-test, which may or may not be very valid. I am also concerned with the message that if, for instance, you score low on "kindness and generosity" (a Signature Strength), you may give up trying to make yourself better in this regard and focus more intently on your leadership skills. This stance is of course a vast and perhaps unfair characterization of the method, but one I am afraid some people will take away.

So I have some quibbles with positive psychology, but I thoroughly endorse the direction and the movement. I privately suspect that the shift in the field of psychology is a response to greater unhappiness, stress, and lack of meaning among the masses of us, not just those who have a diagnosable condition. God knows we need to find ways to be happier and healthier, without pills. The world today is tough, and we need new tools and ways of thinking in order to cope.

mastery

In order to be happy, we need first to be masters of ourselves, then masters of our environment. Total mastery in either sphere is impossible, of course, and aiming too high will cause us misery, but it's a pretty simple function: The more we feel in control of things, the better we feel. Doing something well brings us joy, and the better we are at it, the better we feel. If you pick up the guitar, the first weeks are very frustrating, but pretty soon you'll be strumming out "Red River Valley" (or something else relatively easy). Then you'll probably polish that tune for some time, because it feels better to see continuous improvement than to move on and try new chord changes.

"Locus of control" is a psychological variable, a trait: some of us inherently feel we are in control of our lives, and some of us (especially the depressed and the traumatized) feel continually battered by fate. The belief that you are in control of events in your life is to some extent independent of how much objective control you have; nevertheless it is highly correlated with feelings of subjective well-being. You can take a test and see how much you think you're in control. Yet being in control of your life is not simply an illusion. People who make realistic plans, who save for the future, who pursue tangible and concrete goals, who use practical methods for attaining their goals, who build productive and supportive relationships, are obviously at an advantage compared with those who are pursuing impossible dreams or following the whims of the moment. As Admiral James Stockdale (an American POW during the Vietnam War) famously observed, the optimists died first. "They were the ones who said, 'We're going to be out by Christmas.' And Christmas would come, and Christmas would go. Then they'd say, 'We're going to be out by Easter.' And Easter would come, and Easter would go. And then Thanksgiving, and then it would be Christmas again. And they died of a broken heart." But as Viktor Frankl, a concentration camp survivor from World War II, observed, the ones who survived were the ones who focused on what they could control—on living day by day, on keeping themselves clean, nourished, and fit, on helping others.

Remember Ellen Langer's nursing home patients? Those who were given greater responsibility lived longer. Those who were told to rely on the staff grew more and more dependent, and died sooner. Mindfulness is good for you, but it's not always the comfortable, easy choice. It means facing up to our own self-deceptions, including the idea that we can depend on others to make our decisions.

Feeling that we're in control of ourselves is very important to our overall sense of well-being. One of the most upsetting things about depression or anxiety is the feeling that no matter how hard we try, we can't stop our disturbing thoughts, feelings, and impulses. We fear that we've lost control of our own minds, and that seems like the definition of crazy. Shelley Taylor, a respected psychological investigator, argues that it's our _feeling_ of being in control more than the actual degree of control that's important to us. This is good news, in a way; lots of things can help us feel in control. Most patients

with serious illnesses are helped greatly when they know as much information as they can about what's going to happen to them. Lamaze classes
demystify childbirth. Predictability adds greatly to our sense of being in
control, even if there's nothing we really can do to change the course of
events.

Increasing our sense of control is a key reason why cultivating a mindful
attitude is comforting to us. We may see that there's not really much we can
do to control our thoughts and feelings, but we also may see that they make
more sense than we ever realized. Remembering that our brains were designed for a different time, when the world was simpler, when our primary
focus was *Do I get to eat today?*—this places our stress and confusion in context. It's not so much that we're out of control, but that we shouldn't expect
so much to be <u>in</u> control. There is quite literally too much information to
process today, and our circuits get overloaded trying to keep up. Mindfulness suggests that we keep working to simplify our lives, to think as clearly
as we can, and extend a little patience to ourselves.

Luxury car makers are hip to the importance of control. That's why
their cars are packed with so many little servomechanisms. You can adjust
the temperature by tenths of degrees, separately for the driver and the pas-
senger and the backseat. (At least it says you can; who knows if the ther-
mometer is accurate?) You can adjust your seat six hundred ways through
four dimensions, and heat and cool it besides. You can have the sound come
from the radio, a CD, your iPod, and you can have it come at you from up,
down, and sideways, with infinite adjustments of treble, bass, and midrange.
On some models, you can probably adjust the volume to 11. All this gives
you the comfortable illusion of control, even if what you're controlling is
rather trivial. You may be stuck in traffic burning gas at twenty dollars per
hour, but you sure <u>feel</u> in control.

That's one illusion of control. Another is to get good at things that, in
themselves, are not very good. Remember *The Bridge on the River Kwai?*
The morale of the British POWs was great because they were building a really keen bridge. It was hard work that achieved tangible results every day.
They managed to forget that the bridge would carry a Japanese railway that
would help the enemy's war effort considerably. I'm sure the Nazis were

proud of their efficiency. And the most ghastly example of all, suicide bombers have very clear and concrete goals that provide them with almost unimaginable motivation.

This brings us to some reservations about flow. In my mind, flow can be dangerously close to mindlessness; we can get completely absorbed in something and lose sight of whether what we're doing serves a purpose or is good for us or others. Video games are designed with flow in mind; there is a careful balance between boredom and anxiety as the player gains points and moves through levels. Skills are definitely being built, and time definitely slows down. The positive psychologists like to call this *faux* flow, but there's nothing *faux* about it. You can experience flow at a beautiful church service, a rock concert, or a neo-Nazi rally (if that's your value system). I think, along with Dan Siegel, that it's best to retain a portion of our attention devoted to mindfulness, to keep looking at the direction we're going, not just how rewarding the activity seems to be.

So I think that <u>pride</u> is an important component to add to flow. We may spend hours online playing video games, and reach the highest levels of expertise. We may feel in a total state of flow, lost in the moment, time standing still, our reflexes hyperperfect; we can get really pumped up, full of adrenaline and the neurotransmitters of joy and engagement. But we're unlikely to tell our friends about it, at least if we're older than eighteen. No matter how involved we are, we're a little ashamed because we know that this is a trivial pursuit. In order for us to take real satisfaction in what we do, we have to feel that we are doing something worthwhile. This can be as bereft of real benefit to the world as a game of golf, but because the golfer presumably lives in a culture that respects his accomplishments, he develops a measure of pride in his game.

Still, pride doesn't solve the problem of values; our neo-Nazi may feel just as immersed in flow as a yogi in meditation. Unfortunately, for most of us, happiness is value-neutral. I <u>believe</u> that for most of us, lies and bad acts are ultimately bad for us—we suffer with guilt and, to the extent we fight the guilt, we twist our character into something worse than it is already. I've seen a lot of this; therapists deal with this every day, but not everyone is susceptible to guilt. Some value systems endorse things I find appalling, like blowing yourself and other people away in the name of religion. I'd <u>like to believe</u> in bad karma—that lies and bad acts will ultimately be punished, in this life or the next—but I haven't seen a lot of evidence for this. And I <u>know,</u> unfortunately, that there are many people out there who feel no guilt, suffering, or punishment for their bad acts.

So I believe that mindfulness can be the savior here. I don't believe that it's possible to develop true mindfulness and blind ourselves to the needs of others, to act on prejudice or hate. I know, unfortunately, that some people follow what they believe is a mindful path selfishly. In Sharon Salzberg's metaphor, they forget to untie the rowboat. They buy the boat and start rowing intently—or meditating intensively—but they don't notice that they continue to yell at the kids. They think that meditation alone is enough. But true mindfulness, the kind that comes from learning to detach from impulse and emotion, from looking at yourself and your world with compassionate curiosity, allows you to keep on being observant. You can get immersed in flow but continuously monitor your values. You can have a feeling of mastery and a sense of direction as well.

Remember that in Chapter 6 I asked you to make note of something you'd really like to change about yourself? You might start your happiness campaign with one of those things. You may want to go back to Chapter 6 and review how to develop the skills of will power.

EXERCISE 14:
LASTING CHANGE

Identify one thing about yourself you really want to change. It can be something that is contributing unnecessary misery to your life, or it can be learning something that will bring more happiness. This need not be a huge thing, but it shouldn't be trivial either. In the misery category, you might think of smoking, eating better, getting organized, drinking less, being more thoughtful or less irritable. In the happiness area, you might think of finding a new job, developing a new skill, getting into an exercise program, becoming more assertive, asking someone out on a date, practicing mindfulness meditation. So it can be kicking a bad habit or learning a good one.

Set a date when you're going to start this, or, if it's a one-time only activity, start and finish. If you need to gather information, allow time for that. For instance, if you want to change your diet, you should talk to your doctor, and you may want to consult some of the many diet books out there. Just don't make learning about your options a way to procrastinate.

Commit yourself to three months. Even if you slip up on the second day, start again on the third. If you slip again in the second month, hang in there. Remember that you're building new brain circuits, even if you're not able to be perfect.

If we're reducing misery here:

- Think about all the ways this thing has hurt you and made you unhappy. At this point, and only at this point, really wallow in misery. Add guilt if you can—how it's hurt others, how you've chosen your bad habit over more important things in life. Just pile it on.
- Now start thinking about how good you will feel once you've licked this thing. All the ways it will make you happier and healthier. How it will simplify your life. How it will improve your relationships.
- And next think about how beating this habit will add to your self-esteem. How good it will feel to be in control of yourself.
- Visualize the bad habit as a superhighway in your brain. You're going to shut it down, set up roadblocks at the ends, take jackhammers to the pavement. In the meantime you're going to be exploring some less familiar paths. They're there in your brain— you know how to do what you need to do—but you haven't spent much time on these paths.

If we're adding happiness by learning a new skill or habit:

- Think about all the ways accomplishing this will bring joy and pleasure to your life. You'll have a brand new skill, one that by definition will bring good feelings. It may also be something you can share with others, that other people will enjoy about you. You'll feel proud of yourself for mastering something difficult. You'll feel good about your self-discipline. Three months is a long time to stick with anything; you really should be proud of yourself.
- Visualize a little pathway in your brain getting bigger and easier with use. At first maybe only the rabbits and deer can squeeze through. But then here come the people, beating it into a firm path with their feet. Soon there's a farmer with a team of oxen. Then little yellow bulldozers. Before you know it, your new habit is a nice paved road in your mind, an easy journey.
- Once you're past a certain point in practice, it starts to get automatic. You don't have to think about it anymore.
- Now do it.

life purpose

All of us experience a desire for life to have meaning or purpose. Religion often fills that need. In some cultures, religion is an intrinsic part of everyday life. Preparing a meal has to be done in a certain way. There are elaborate rituals about cleanliness, about contact between the sexes, about the right way to pray. It provides a sense of meaning and purpose to even the most humdrum aspects of life. There are a couple of million people in Brooklyn today who live this way. Some are Jewish, some are Muslim, some are Christian, some are something else. But most Americans, unlike these Brooklynites, have disconnected the sacred from everyday life, which means they've lost one possible avenue for finding meaning.

Religion is slightly but consistently correlated with happiness. Religion usually offers a sense of community, sometimes quite a strong bond, and that's one factor making for greater happiness. But there is also the sense of a personal relationship with God as a friend, mentor, or protector, the wonder and ecstasy of religious experience, and the satisfaction associated with life making sense. My aunt on her deathbed saw Jesus, her deceased sisters, her mother, all welcoming her. It certainly helped her approach her death with equanimity, even joy. Religious belief can relieve some powerful negative emotions, such as fear of death, guilt, grief, and deprivation, thus raising overall happiness.

We omitted from our list of happy feelings a difficult-to-describe feeling that Jonathan Haidt describes as elevation—elevation because it means a rising away from involvement with the dirty, the beastly, the profane. (This is a different meaning from what Paul Ekman gives the word in Chapter 7; he means being motivated to become a better person.) Haidt argues that the human mind is built to appreciate a feeling of divinity or sacredness— whether or not God exists, we're wired to feel this feeling. Contemporary culture has created a profane world, where very little is left as sacred; but, as Haidt notes, even atheists have feelings of elevation, sacred places in their hearts, experiences that are especially meaningful to them—they just don't attribute their feelings to God at work. I, an agnostic, am moved when in St. John the Divine in New York, in European cathedrals, in a Shaker meetinghouse, even in the bare ruined choirs of the Irish abbeys. It's partly the beauty of these places but it's also partly because I know that there is so much collective faith at work there; I feel connected to a community.

When people attend church or religious services, they have a collective experience in elevation—contact with the sacred, singing, meditation, ritual, and stories about love, generosity, and altruism. They feel together what Christians call _agape_—love without an object, love for their fellow human beings, perhaps the loving-kindness that Buddhist meditation focuses on. These feelings are quite real and, if you lean toward faith, it seems natural to attribute them to the action of God within you.

Haidt has been investigating elevation in his lab at the University of Virginia. He'll show one group some videos about heroes or altruists, and show his control group some comedy videos. Compared to the controls, the experimental group reports more warm, calm, and loving feelings; they want to better themselves. In one of his more interesting studies, one of his graduate assistants found that nursing mothers lactated more when watching the elevated videos. There's obviously something very deep at work here, something that gets stirred up not only by religious experiences but also simply by witnessing acts of virtue.

Religion is not by any means the only source for a sense of purpose in life. Scientists and scholars may have a deep feeling of purpose in the advancement of knowledge. Mothers may get it from raising their children well. Artists from self-expression. Builders from making something that will last. Others get it from contributing to a cause—a political agenda, environmental cleanup, helping the homeless. And purpose can change as our lives change. For many years, my greatest sense of purpose came from being sure my children were raised better than I had been. Once they were grown, that purpose was largely gone, and I began writing. In a secular world where we're facing death without a comforting belief in the afterlife, we want to leave something behind.

personal growth

Fulfillment is the sensation of personal growth. Whereas joy is an immediate sensation of pleasure or gratification that makes us want to smile, laugh, or sing, I mean by fulfillment a more quiet state. It's the state that we feel when we've worked hard for something and finally attained it. It may be that we've reached a goal that's important to us, something that expresses our aspirations and values. We feel a sense of accomplishment, of having arrived at a milestone. We may have achieved some recognition, and be taking the time to savor it; or it may be that we have simply been proved right to ourselves in a way that no one else will ever know about. Pride as well as joy is part of fulfillment. But fulfillment can also come from reading a good book or hearing a good sermon or watching our children grow in independence and accomplishment, so it can be somewhat vicarious. It may be that fulfillment engages both the thinking and feeling parts of the brain more than simple joy does, because there is often an element of thoughtful reflection in fulfillment. More eudaimonia, living up to one's potential, than simple hedonism.

There is a value system inherent in the concept of fulfillment; fulfilling activities accomplish something we feel is useful or good. That doesn't mean necessarily that fulfillment is more important to our happiness than joy. We need lots of both. There are people who pursue fulfillment exclusively and don't know how to dance, or get down on the floor and roughhouse with the dogs, or be charmed by a catbird; they are missing out on a great deal. But a sense that we are doing something that will stretch us and challenge us is at times also an essential for happiness.

When I'm giving a presentation—am I happy? Chances are I spent the last two days in a state of anxiety, that I didn't sleep much the night before, that I'll spend the next couple of days picking over all the little faux pas I made and gaps in my knowledge I displayed—yet just give me a chance, and I'll do it again, gladly. This is partly because I feel very alive when I'm speaking. Somehow the mental act of juggling what I'm saying now, what I want to be saying next, how much time is left, the connection I feel with the audience, is one of the biggest thrills of my life. It's a peak experience, in Csikszentmihalyi's terms. "Some types of happiness—possibly the most profoundly gratifying ones—are not dependent on positive outlook, jolliness, or comfort."

In a study of forty HIV-infected men who had recently lost a close friend or partner to AIDS, the ability to find meaning in the experience had a marked effect on the immune system. Men who reflected on their loss, who indicated that it had changed their paradigms in some way (usually by making them more attentive about relationships), were able to maintain the CD4 T helper cell level in their immune systems over a two- to three-year follow-up, while those who did not had reduced levels of these immune cells. Half of those who had not found meaning died within five years, while less than 20 percent of those who had found meaning died.

So fulfillment is not necessarily joyful; in fact, it can come from tragedy. It can be the source of those life-changing events that people have after a brush with death. When we feel fulfilled, it's usually the result of mindful, deliberate activity. We've used our creative juices, we've met a challenge, we've taken a chance. We've changed a paradigm and we're seeing things from a new perspective. We've satisfied our curiosity. We've gained control.

don't: DO THINGS YOU WOULDN'T WANT (YOUR MOTHER, GOD, YOUR CHILDREN) TO KNOW ABOUT.

Fulfilling activities can put us into a state of flow, absorbing us completely, but that's not a precondition to fulfillment. Fulfillment, like flow, can come from reading a good book, having a rewarding conversation, or fixing the lawnmower. But fulfillment can also come from long-term activities that can recede to the background of our lives while we deal with the minutiae of everyday living: finishing your dissertation, finally getting the promotion you deserve, taking an active part in social or political causes, or raising the children mindfully.

Fulfilling activities require the whole brain, and maybe that's what makes them uniquely rewarding: They require our best reasoning skills as well as our emotions, values, and intuition. When you put your whole self together like that, and it works, that's the nature of fulfillment. It gives us a sense of coherence, of being all of one piece, not unfocused or in conflict.

the story of your life

One more thing about meaning that Ryff doesn't talk about is a sense of identity. We discussed in Chapter 4 how the child develops a sense of himself as a complete unit, consistent within himself and over time, through good-enough parenting. Daniel Siegel's hypothesis in *The Developing Mind* is that we build a coherent autobiographical narrative—an identity—through knitting together the left and right hemispheres' pictures of ourselves; the left brain's ability to explain things and link facts in a linear fashion combined with the right brain's emotional and autobiographical processing. Our emotional selves and our factual, historical selves need to align and cohere. When we put the two together successfully we get a complete and fairly accurate set of beliefs about the self. With that, when something happens to upset us, we know why it did. Our paradigms are consistent, without contradiction. We'll wake up tomorrow in pretty much the same mood and mind-set we woke up with today, and if we don't, we'll understand why. We're able to make decisions using our minds, heart, and intuition. <u>The brain and the mind are able to work together to create a coherent identity, making us genuinely secure, and able to be happy.</u>

This stable identity is founded on the self-image that the mother and infant develop together in their earliest interactions. It's largely the adult caregiver's ability to form a coherent narrative of his or her own childhood experience that determines whether their child will be able to form a secure attachment. In other words, having a coherent identity enables one to be empathic and connected. Based on that foundation, we continue to add to our identity through our interactions with other people throughout our lives. When we feel validated by others, that they understand and respect our point of view, we gain coherence. When we feel ignored or disrespected or disliked, we lose coherence. Coherence happens not only in our feelings, but also in the physical structure of the brain.

But if you missed out on it in childhood, the compassionate curiosity of mindfulness allows us to provide that essential validation for ourselves. As we said in Chapter 5, when we're able to look at ourselves thoroughly and honestly, without fear, we feel deeply connected, deeply held. We're able to examine the structure of ourselves, and in the process we deepen our feelings of acceptance and affection for ourselves. Not that we forgive ourselves for everything we've done, but we see ourselves without the distortion of our defenses and paradigms, we understand, and perhaps resolve to do better.

do: WORK ON THE STORY OF YOUR LIFE; THERE'S A NARRATIVE FLOW.

IT'S YOUR JOB TO CONSTRUCT MEANING FOR YOUR LIFE. WHAT ROLE DO YOU PLAY, WHAT ROLE DO YOU WANT TO PLAY?

SET SOME GOALS AND WORK TOWARD THEM.

EXERCISE 15:
YOUR OWN EULOGY

Put yourself into a mindful state and turn your compassion and curiosity on yourself.

Think about the end of your life. In your final moments, you are at peace and your thoughts are clear. Think back over the course of your life. What brought you the greatest satisfaction, the greatest happiness? What were your biggest disappointments and regrets? What were your strengths? Do you feel you did your best? Do you feel you were loved, and loved others? Did you make a contribution to others? How would you evaluate your life as a whole?

Most likely you can get in touch with a number of regrets—missed opportunities, ways you wasted precious time. But fortunately it's not yet the end of your life. You have the time to correct for some of the problems and regrets this exercise has brought to your attention.

Fast-forward again to your life's end. You successfully made most of the important changes you wanted to make. You readjusted your life so you could put more time and energy into the things that matter to you most. Now think about your eulogy. What would your spouse, your best friend, your son or daughter, say to memorialize your life? Take a piece of paper and write this out.

Here's an example:

He wasn't perfect but he did his best. He started out with some terrible handicaps that would have made many people bitter and selfish. But he deliberately turned the other way and spent his life helping others. He did his best to be patient, kind, and loving. His wife and children knew he loved them deeply.

He made a project of being more warm and outgoing. It wasn't easy but he made some real progress on that. It brought him more joy but more important to him was that it helped others along.

He also deliberately worked on appreciating life. His work showed him how tragically blind to everyday beauty and simple pleasures so many people can be, and he knew he didn't want to die regretting that he didn't pay attention. He learned to love good writing, good music, the beauty of nature, the pleasures of laughter. He tried to get others to pay attention, too.

ELEVEN

staying happy

Here we are at the end. When I started to write a book on happiness, I thought I could turn out something about half this length. Maybe you wish I had. Happiness is smaller than you think, but there is a lot to think about the subject. So if you have made it this far, pat yourself on the back. But if you have made it this far, it would be foolish to just put the book aside. I urge you to try a happiness campaign for three months. I want to emphasize again that experience changes the brain, and that by choosing our experiences we can have some control over the way the brain grows. Remember those jugglers and their three months of daily practice before the changes in their brains were observable. Our goal is to adjust your happiness set point, move whatever's normal for you on the gloomy–cheerful scale toward the cheerful side. If you will seriously work on happiness for three months, you'll have a different brain, and be a different person.

We just gave you an assignment in the last chapter, to address one of the ways you make yourself more miserable, or take on learning something new.

But you can scrap that right now if you're willing to apply the same commitment just to making yourself more happy—by enjoying small pleasures more, by strengthening your relationships, by practicing mindfulness meditation. Remember that it helps if goals are concrete, and a mild stretch, not impossible.

So how do you do this? Here are my suggestions:

- Give yourself an hour a day, half for exercise and half for meditation. If you give meditation a good college try and decide it's not for you, use that half hour instead to read some of the books on my Contemplative Reading List (at the end of this chapter). An hour a day, five days a week. You can do more than that if you want, but keep it reasonable.

- Wake up! There's incredible beauty all around you. I'm absorbed in writing this book but I managed to look closely at a tiger swallowtail butterfly in the garden yesterday. Did you know there are gorgeous shades of red and blue among the black streaks at the bottom of the wings? It looks like nothing other than cathedral windows, a quarter inch high. Yet if you'd asked me, I would have said that butterfly is yellow with black stripes. If I can see that, with less than two weeks to go before my deadline, you can discover something beautiful today, too. Open up to your senses. Become a connoisseur of small pleasures.

- At bedtime, let yourself go to sleep thinking about three things to be grateful for, things that made you happy, or simply the best memories of the day. As you do this, pay attention to the feelings in your body: the smiling reflex, a warmness in your heart, the flow of tension out of your neck and shoulders. Whenever you feel good, let your body express it.

- Work on wanting what you have. Look around you and try to appreciate your possessions and possibilities as if you were Ben Franklin popped into the twenty-first century. *Central heating, air-conditioning, indoor plumbing, a stove and refrigerator. A vehicle that will take you six hundred miles in a day, in comfort, on paved roads. An orchestra you can carry in your pocket.* If Ben Franklin doesn't do it for you, simply look carefully at your surroundings. Your furniture, books, possessions. There's beauty and memories there. Savor them.

- Remember that <u>happiness is not our normal state of mind.</u> We were bred to be tense and restless. The world today is not a great garden of bliss, either. Cultivating happiness takes deliberate attention. Don't expect that you're going to turn into Pollyanna; but do expect that you can find more occasions to feel good, and feel even better on those occasions.

- On top of that, <u>contemporary living conditions are not what we were designed for;</u> we're constantly in fight-or-flight mode, and that makes us stressed, anxious, and depressed. So don't buy that this is the best of all possible worlds; take as much control as you can, and create the world you want.

- Remember that <u>getting what you want won't make you happy.</u> The more you value financial success, the less happy you're likely to be. Arm yourself against consumerism and competition. Learn about advertising. Learn what they're teaching in business schools, because it's going to be used to manipulate you. Practice thrift.

- Still, <u>happy feelings are a clue to solutions.</u> We seem to have an aesthetic appreciation for the right answer to a math problem, an ethical dilemma, a grammatical question, that registers even before the logical brain has done its problem-solving. Pay more attention to these hints from your intuition.

- <u>Your brain learns whether you want it to or not,</u> so pay attention to what you want it to learn. If you obsess and worry about all the character defects that you've never been able to change, chances are you won't fix them, but you'll become more depressed and stressed by them. Get up and do something different.

- <u>Pay systematic attention to what makes you feel good.</u> Take notes, talk about it with friends and loved ones. Remember that we assume we know what makes us feel good, but our brain has all kinds of ways of tricking us into doing what's good for the species. You have to outsmart your own brain. Learn what makes you feel good, and do more of it.

- The same goes for misery. <u>Learn what makes you feel bad, and do less of it.</u> Again, you have to pay systematic attention to outsmart yourself, to get under your defenses and distortions.

- <u>Happiness is smaller than you think.</u> Cultivate small pleasures. Learn to cook. Eat well. Cook for friends. Expose yourself to awe and beauty; get out in nature, and <u>pay attention.</u> Watch less television. Play more. Get a dog. Join a laughter club. Get more touching into your life.

- <u>Learn to be mindful, in every way you can.</u> Catch yourself judging, and slowly you'll begin to stop. View yourself and the world with compassionate curiosity, the desire to understand and the belief in your own worth. Learn to be noncategorical, detached, willing to let go, willing to think independently, willing to take responsibility. Do a lot of reps, and give it three months. Go back to "A Simple Mindfulness Meditation," page 114, and keep it up.

- <u>Take the effects of adaptation into account.</u> Use the peak-end rule for your own good; save the best for last. But don't get fooled. Use time and variety to avoid adaptation—don't have your favorite meal every night, but once a week. Learn every trick in this book to increase your happiness quotient.

- Considering the effects of buyer's remorse, and then the fact that if you lose something it costs you more happiness units than getting it gave you, it seems that <u>acquisitions open the door to a lot of misery.</u> It probably makes most sense to buy as little as possible.

- You certainly shouldn't buy anything big until you <u>get out of debt.</u> Somehow we've been brainwashed into believing it's normal and acceptable to be in debt. But in my office I hear over and over that's the fear keeping people up at night. Being in debt causes devastating and totally unnecessary stress.

- When you have to buy, <u>be a satisficer, not a maximizer.</u> Know what you want, know a fair price, get it and get out of the store as quickly as possible. Don't use your credit cards; you'll be willing to pay twice as much if you do. The easier way to be rich is to have few wants.

- Practicing thrift like this will allow you to <u>save money for what it's really good for: security, freedom, and the time to enjoy life.</u> Security will give you some protection from stress when there's a fire and you suddenly need a new house. Financial freedom gives you the ability to quit your job, if you hate the boss; or to take time off and explore the world. And time means just that; what we used to have in abundance, before the invention of work. The time to hang out with friends, look at the sunset, watch the crops and children grow.

- Consider that <u>you may be a stress or trauma survivor.</u> This may make it more difficult for you to be happy, but nowhere near impossible. If you think you have ADHD, it may be that you're dissociating. If you're depressed or anxious, you probably have good reason for it. Take the advice in this book, but if it's not enough, go find a good therapist.

- <u>Pretend you're an extravert.</u> Extraverts have more fun. Even introverts have more fun when they're pretending to be extraverts.

- Remember that <u>will power is a skill;</u> practice it and watch it grow.

- <u>Check your self-defeating behavior</u> for a healthy desire to rebel. But it probably means you're bored or have no goals right now or feel trapped. Try to turn that energy into something that will change your circumstances, instead of taking it out on yourself.

- <u>Get a new attitude toward that Inner Critic of yours.</u> It's just the voice of your fears, of your parent in a bad mood, of a little bully you brought home from the playground in fifth grade. It doesn't know the truth about you, it just knows how to manipulate you. You're a grown-up now; treat the Critic with your best adult skills, some compassion and detachment, and it will wither like the Wicked Witch.

- <u>Learn to detach</u> from obsessive thoughts, mindless craving, the voice of the Inner Critic, sticky feelings. Detachment is a skill you can learn, and mindfulness will help.

- <u>Detachment means a different perspective with your thoughts and feelings:</u> that these merely are the contents of your mind, changeable at a moment's notice, not the truth they feel like.

- <u>Don't wait until you're motivated.</u> Take a step, and motivation will follow. Doing something is the single best way to change how you feel.

- Watch out for the hedonic paradox—by <u>worrying too much about whether you're happy, you can make yourself more miserable.</u> You have to practice, but don't worry. Don't expect to be happy all the time.

- <u>Don't work too hard.</u> Don't work more than forty hours per week, if you can possibly avoid it; and if you can't, start making plans to shake up your life. We know that the more hours you work, the less satisfied you'll be with your life. Don't work too hard at any one sitting, either. Schedule yourself breaks when you can clear your head. You'll end up working more efficiently.

- <u>If you're bored or anxious, it probably means you don't have a goal right now.</u> But it's very difficult for most of us to jump right out of that emotional state and into a new project. Instead, give yourself a week to research and daydream about what you're going to do.

- <u>Try to make your work flow.</u> Find challenges. Improve the atmosphere. Make it meaningful, playful. Make it bring joy to others.

- <u>Be a complex person.</u> The more ways you define yourself, the less vulnerable you are to setbacks in any area. If you're only a writer, and your book doesn't sell, you're sunk. But if you're a writer and researcher and a teacher and a wife and mother and gardener and volunteer EMT and singer in the choir, it's easier to bounce back from disappointments. The more sources of joy and pleasure in your life, the better.

- <u>When you find yourself judging, yourself or others, move on to something else.</u> It's a hallmark symptom of mindlessness to be constantly classifying our experiences, including how we experience other people, into simple black-and-white categories. When we do this we miss out on all the rich detail of life. And we act on prejudices and stereotypes. If you learn to stop judging, you will start to undermine your most ingrained paradigms.

- Activities are more likely to be rewarding if they are <u>out</u> of the house, <u>involve</u> other people, and <u>require</u> physical activity. If it's in the house, solitary, and sedentary, you're more likely to be lethargic and bored. There are a few exceptions, like reading a good book.

- Assume that <u>karma is real: what you give, you get back.</u> If you treat people well, you'll be treated well. If you spread happiness, you'll reap happiness. If you are generous, you'll be rewarded with generosity. Practice loving, compassion, and extraversion.

- <u>Develop good rituals and habits,</u> especially around things you find difficult. Deprive yourself of the opportunity to think about it and to let ambivalence demotivate you. This is one area where you can be mindless: Just start doing your morning workout before you have time to let anything interfere. Just find a way to save money automatically.

- <u>Organize yourself.</u> Happy people feel in control of their lives. Don't allow yourself to be a victim of inefficacy and clutter. Accept the fact that there is just too damn much to do nowadays, so give up on being perfect. Take another hour. Start in one corner, and move on only as you finish. Don't stop until the hour is up.

- <u>Don't try to avoid necessary grief.</u> You can't stifle unpleasant feelings without stifling the good ones, too. So, if you've lost something or someone important to you, let yourself feel it. Don't be afraid. Remember how adaptable we are, and that grief itself doesn't last forever.

- We are what we do. <u>Your schedule is your life.</u> Far too many of us spend much of our lives in dreamland, waiting for a miracle, or in the past, looking for justification for being stuck right now. Or in a mindless frenzy, trying to keep up with too many commitments. We think that good intentions count, but they really don't. Don't waste any more time waiting for your happiness.

Now, if you'll excuse me, it's August in Connecticut. I'm going to go weed my garden, play with the dogs, and pay attention to my wife.

APPENDIX: FURTHER READING

Begley, Sharon. *Train Your Mind, Change Your Brain*. New York: Ballantine, 2007.

Borysenko, Joan. *Minding the Body, Mending the Mind*. New York: Bantam, 1987.

Chödrön, Pema. *When Things Fall Apart*. Boston: Shambhala, 2000.

Cushman, Philip. *Constructing the Self, Constructing America: A Cultural History of Psychotherapy*. Cambridge, MA: Perseus, 1995.

Csikszentmihalyi, Mihaly. *Living Well: The Psychology of Everyday Life*. London, UK: Weidenfield and Nicholson, 1997.

Dalai Lama and Howard Cutler. *The Art of Happiness*. New York: Riverhead, 1998.

Davis, Martha, Elizabeth R. Eshelman, and Matthew McKay. *The Relaxation and Stress Reduction Workbook*. 5th ed. Oakland, CA: New Harbinger Publications, 2000.

Dominguez, Joe, and Vicki Robin. *Your Money or Your Life*. New York: Penguin, 1999.

Epstein, Mark. *Going to Pieces Without Falling Apart*. New York: Broadway Books, 1998.

Frankl, Viktor. *Man's Search for Meaning*. New York: Washington Square Press, 1967.

Gilbert, Daniel. *Stumbling on Happiness*. New York: Knopf, 2006.

Goleman, Daniel. *Emotional Intelligence*. New York: Bantam, 1995.

Haidt, Jonathan. *The Happiness Hypothesis*. New York: Basic Books, 2006.

Hayes, Steven C., with Spencer Smith. *Get Out of Your Mind and Into Your Life: The New Acceptance and Commitment Therapy*. Oakland, CA: New Harbinger, 2005.

Herman, Judith. *Trauma and Recovery*. New York: Basic Books, 1992.

Hodgkinson, Tom. *How to Be Idle*. New York: HarperCollins, 2005.

Kabat-Zinn, Jon. *Full Catastrophe Living: Using the Wisdom of Your Body and Mind to Face Stress, Pain, and Illness.* New York: Delacorte, 1990.

Kasser, Tim. *The High Price of Materialism.* Cambridge, MA: MIT Press, 2002.

Kornfield, Jack. *After the Ecstasy, the Laundry.* New York: Bantam Books, 2000.

Lamott, Anne. *Bird by Bird: Some Instructions on Writing and Life.* New York: Anchor Books, 1994.

Langer, Ellen J. *Mindfulness.* Reading, MA: Addison-Wesley, 1989.

Layard, Richard. *Happiness: Lessons from a New Science.* New York: Penguin, 2005

LeDoux, Joseph. *The Emotional Brain: The Mysterious Underpinnings of Emotional Life.* New York: Touchstone, 1996.

Louv, Richard. *Last Child in the Woods.* New York: Algonquin Books, 2006.

Lykken, David. *Happiness: The Nature and Nurture of Joy and Contentment.* New York: St. Martin's Griffin, 1999.

Lyubomirsky, Sonja. *The How of Happiness.* New York: Penguin, 2007.

Magid, Barry. *Ordinary Mind: Exploring the Common Ground of Zen and Psychotherapy.* Somerville, MA: Wisdom Publications, 2002.

Miller, Timothy. *How to Want What You Have.* New York: Avon, 1995.

Myers, David G. *The Pursuit of Happiness.* New York: Avon, 1992.

Nettle, Daniel. *Happiness: The Science Behind Your Smile.* Oxford (UK): Oxford University Press, 2005.

O'Connor, Richard. *Undoing Perpetual Stress.* New York: Berkley, 2005.

O'Hanlon, Bill. *Thriving Through Crisis.* New York: Perigee, 2005.

Paul, Marilyn. *It's Hard to Make a Difference When You Can't Find Your Car Keys.* New York: Penguin, 2003.

Safran, Jeremy (ed.). *Psychoanalysis and Buddhism.* Somerville, MA: Wisdom Publications, 2003.

Sapolsky, Robert M. *Why Zebras Don't Get Ulcers.* New York: W. H. Freeman, 1998.

Schor, Juliet B. *The Overspent American.* New York: Basic Books, 1998.

Schwartz, Barry. *The Paradox of Choice: Why More Is Less.* New York: HarperCollins, 2004.

Schwartz, Jeffrey, and Sharon Begley. *The Mind and the Brain: Neuroplasticity and the Power of Mental Force.* New York: HarperCollins, 2002.

Segal, Zindel V., Mark Williams, and John Teasdale. *Mindfulness-Based Cognitive Therapy for Depression.* New York: Guilford, 2002.

Seligman, Martin E. P. *Authentic Happiness.* New York: Free Press, 2002.

Siegel, Daniel J. *The Developing Mind.* New York: Guilford, 2001.

Taylor, Shelley E. *Positive Illusions.* New York: Basic Books, 1989.

Thich Nhat Hanh. *The Miracle of Mindfulness.* Boston: Beacon Press, 1999.

Trungpa, Chogyam. *The Myth of Freedom and the Way of Meditation.* Boston: Shambhala, 2005.

Viorst, Judith. *Necessary Losses.* New York: Free Press, 1998.

Wansink, Brian. *Mindless Eating.* New York: Bantam, 2006.

Weiner, Eric. *The Geography of Bliss.* New York: Twelve, 2008.

NOTES

INTRODUCTION

3   *Western psychology is only beginning to investigate whether that kind of intentional, focused practice can change something like feelings of happiness:* The earliest results are encouraging. See Fordyce (1983), and Lyubomirsky, Sheldon, and Schkade (2005).

4   *the hedonic treadmill:* Brickman and Campbell (1971).

4   *After observing three months of daily practice, the researchers could identify measurable growth in gray matter in certain areas of their subjects' brains:* Draganski et al. (2004).

ONE: LEARNING HAPPINESS

6   *A famous study compared lottery winners and accident victims a year later:* See Peterson (2006, 55); the study is actually more complex, and the results not so simple: Brickman, Coates, and Janoff-Bulman (1978).

8   *Those juggling college students are just one example among hundreds of studies that have shown us how life experience changes the physical structure of the brain:* See Pascual-Leone et al. (2005), for an authoritative discussion of plasticity in the brain.

8   *Now we know that the brain is constantly forming new brain cells:* Eriksson (1998).

9   *The brains of London cabbies are enlarged and enriched in the areas associated with navigation and orientation:* Maguire et al. (2000).

9   *The area of the brain that controls the left hand is greatly enlarged in violin and other string players:* Elbert et al. (1995).

9   *Successful psychotherapy results in brain changes that are visible on PET scans:* Schwartz et al. (1996).

9   *Merely rehearsing a task mentally results in the same kind of brain changes that actual practice does:* Pascual-Leone et al. (2005).

9   *People who are hopeful have better health after heart transplants, etc.:* See O'Connor (2005), for a more complete discussion of stress, health, and the brain.

10   *Recently I took a test that measures how happy you are:* Lykken (1999, 35).

14   *This "meaning" dimension of happiness complicates everything, and science certainly doesn't know very much about it:* See Diener and Scollon (2003) for a thoughtful discussion of this subject from the point of view of a happiness researcher.

16   *These results are found, with some slight variation from country to country, all over the world:* Nettle (2005).

17   *the experimenters arranged to have half of a group of subjects find a dime in a copy machine just before taking the SWB quiz:* Schwarz and Strack (1999).

17   *Olympic bronze medalists report higher satisfaction than silver medalists:* Medvec, Madey, and Gilovich (1985).

17   *subjective well-being is worth talking about because the same person will tend to answer the same way fairly consistently over time:* Myers (1992).

19   *thoughtful reflection made him withdraw that opinion:* (Lykken and Tellegen, 1996).

19   *there is good reason to believe that the set point is changeable:* See, for example, Fujita and Diener (2005), who found that, over a seventeen-year period, 24 percent of 3,400 people experienced significant change in their set point. Almost 10 percent changed three or more points on a ten-point scale.

20   *They found that one twin's score on happiness was very closely related to the other's:* Lykken (1999).

20   *about half of an individual's subjective well-being set point is determined by genetic heritage:* Lyubomirsky, Sheldon, and Schkade, 2005.

TWO: CONTEMPORARY INSANITY: THE CULTURE

27   *Western society has been operating on the assumption that eliminating the causes of suffering will result in greater happiness:* This theme owes a lot to Nesse (2004).

29   *when you look at the PET scans of people who suffer chronic stress, you see big white spaces where there used to be brain tissue:* Sheline et al. (1996).

29   *Victims of child abuse and combat veterans have shrunken hippocampi:* LeDoux (1996).

30 *Eight out of ten of the most commonly used medications in the United States treat conditions directly related to stress:* Servan-Schreiber (2003).

31 *Young male elephants, traumatized by witnessing their elders "culled" by poachers:* Bradshaw et al. (2005).

31 *infant rats who receive more licking and grooming from their mothers are less fearful and more intelligent as adults:* Champagne and Meaney (2001).

31 *All it takes is for us to stress a mother rat out for a while to turn her into an ineffective and inattentive mother:* Francis et al. (1999).

31 *A recent UNICEF survey ranked the United States next to the bottom of all wealthy countries in terms of overall child well-being:* UNICEF report (2007).

32 *Robert Sapolsky . . . refers to the Bushmen as the original affluent society:* Sapolsky (1998).

32 *they work only two to four hours per day, as is the norm in hunter-gatherer societies:* Lee (1984).

33 *As the Rev. Andrew Townsend, a nineteenth-century management consultant, wrote:* The quotation is in Hodgkinson (2005, 23).

34 *Stressful jobs lead to a marked increase in major depression and anxiety disorders in previously healthy young people:* Melchior et al. (2007).

34 *In 2004, 45 percent of college students reported feeling depressed to the point of having trouble functioning:* Kadison (2004).

34 *In 2006, Americans spent an estimated $76 billion a year on antidepressants:* Handler (2006).

34 *the World Bank and the World Health Organization predict that soon depression will be the world's single biggest public health problem:* Murray and Lopez (2006).

34 *Many are noting that gross domestic product was a meaningful measure of social value as countries were emerging from poverty:* e.g., Diener and Seligman (2004).

34 The Economist, *analyzing the world country by country:* The Economist (2005).

34 *In China during the period of 1994 to 2005, average real income rose by an astounding 250 percent, but the percentage of those reporting themselves happier with their lives decreased, and unhappiness increased:* Kahnemann and Krueger (2006).

35 *less and less contact with neighbors, and less and less trust of each other, of the government, of schools, religion, medicine, the media:* See, for instance, Richard Layard, *Happiness: Lessons from a New Science* (New York: Penguin, 2005); Robert D. Putnam, *Bowling Alone* (New York: Simon & Schuster, 2000); Robert E. Lane, *The Loss of Happiness in Market Democracies* (New Haven: Yale University Press, 2000).

35 *since the 1950s, the neighborhood has been slowly dying:* Putnam (2000).

35 *Golf clubs are in trouble because people don't have time for golf anymore:* Vitello (2008).

35 Eric Weiner, in *The Geography of Bliss:* Weiner (2008).

36 *people in 2006 were walking an average 10 percent faster than they were in 1994:* Henderson (2007).

36 *In America over the past twenty-five years, the average citizen has increased his working hours from forty to fifty:* Greenhouse (2001).

36   *French workers . . . are actually more productive per hour than Americans, giving a full dollar's-worth more value per hour:* Bennhold, 2004.

36   *New immigrants to America undergo an automatic rise in blood pressure:* Steffen et al. (2006).

36   *the fifth year in a row of stagnant median household income . . .* Greenhouse, 2008.

37   *34 percent of us check in with the office so much on vacation that we come back just as stressed as when we left if not more:* Fisher, 2005.

37   *those of us who have "time affluence" rather than material affluence report greater overall life satisfaction:* Kasser and Brown (2003).

37   *49 percent of marriages end in divorce:* Divorce Magazine.com.

37   *the choice of a more flexible and less intense work schedule:* Kasser and Sheldon (2008).

37   *half of Americans would trade a day's pay for the opportunity of a four-day week:* http://www.newdream.org/live/time/timepoll.php.

37   *a growing worldwide happiness gap between men and women:* Stevenson and Wolfers (2008).

38   *Suburban sprawl leaves everyone dependent on automobile travel, adds to obesity and health problems, and leads to isolation:* Ewing et al. (2003).

40   *Sixty-six percent of Americans report that they enjoy shopping as a leisure activity:* Setlow (2001).

40   *if you use your credit card instead of cash when you go, you're likely to be willing to spend twice as much on each purchase*: Prelec and Simester (2001).

40   *people with materialistic values tend to be less happy, unless they are rich (and even then they are not necessarily happier than average):* Diener and Biswas-Diener (2002); Kasser and Sheldon (2008).

40   *people who've watched a sad movie are willing to pay up to four times more:* Cryder, Lerner, Gross, and Dahl (2008).

43   *rates of depression, alcoholism, and crime have increased dramatically in almost all Westernized countries:* Layard (2005).

43   *Most people, when asked what they need to be happier, answer first that they need more money:* Myers (1992).

44   *there's only a slight tendency for the actually wealthier to be actually happier:* Myers (1992).

44   *scientists estimate you'll need fourteen thousand dollars more next year to experience the same pleasure as ten thousand dollars this year:* Layard (2005).

44   *We think, "I know it's endless. I know it's painful. . . .* Mipham (2004, 23).

45   *those on the bottom rungs of the economic ladder who feel they have greater personal control are much happier than those at the top without it:* Nettle (2005).

46   *The vast majority of people decided they'd like to make more than average, even though it meant they'd have a lot less:* Solnick and Hemenway (1998).

46   *one of the basic functions of wealth in our society is a way of keeping score:* Kahnemann and Krueger (2006).

46   *the proportion of people who say they are satisfied with their income has actually fallen:* Layard (2005).

46 *relative income seems more important than actual income when it comes to happiness:* Kahneman, Krueger, et al. (2006).

48 *Consumers "know," without being told or convinced, that they are not adequate:* Cushman (1995, 85).

49 *the more television you watch, the less happy you become:* Layard (2005).

50 *When Bhutan began to allow television in 1999, it experienced a crime wave:* Scott-Clark and Levy, 2003.

50 *Repeated exposure to images of attractive or powerful members of your own sex makes you feel worse about yourself:* Buss (2000).

50 *In 1976, the richest 10 percent of Americans controlled:* Collins and Yeskel, (2000).

52 *In 1997, indebtedness was 95 percent of income:* Henwood (1998).

THREE: INNATE FOOLISHNESS: THE BRAIN

54 *It is quite possible that people could get so preoccupied with wanting things that they could forget to do things they enjoy:* Nettle (2005, 153).

54 *It makes us feel "motivated, optimistic, and full of self-confidence":* Klein (2006, 88).

55 *Getting what we want gives us relief from desire, but that's also only temporary. Pretty soon we'll desire something else:* Nettle (2005).

55 *dopamine doesn't make rats or people happy at all, but it gets them activated and craving:* Nettle (2005).

55 *the "happiness system" is . . . always on the lookout for something better, and it makes us pursue those things:* Nettle (2005); Gilbert (2006).

56 *Pleasure is a message, and once the message is delivered, the messenger departs:* Klein (2006).

56 *Daniel Nettle . . . points out that most of the primary emotions initiate a specific hard-wired program in our brains and bodies:* Nettle (2005).

58 *losses have more than twice the impact of equivalent gains:* Schwartz (2004).

58 *another example, this one from Barry Schwartz:* Schwartz (2004).

59 *consumers served the same wine at different prices liked it better the more it cost:* Plassman, O'Doherty, Shiv, and Rangel (2008).

59 *"The things we want in life are the things that the evolved mind tells us to want. . . ."* Nettle (2005).

59 *People who judge their success by material goods are generally found to be less happy than others:* Argyle (2001).

60 *subjects preferred a longer colonoscopy that had a relatively painless interval at the end:* Kahneman (2000).

60 *Findings like that have been repeated in many other situations, like watching funny movies:* Nettle (2005); Peterson (2006).

61 *Daniel Gilbert sums up the research:* Gilbert (2006, 202).

62 *"time and variety are two ways to avoid habituation, and if you have one, then you don't need the other."* Gilbert (2006, 131).

62 *But most people would rather have twenty dollars a year from now than nineteen dollars in a year less a day:* Van Boven and Loewenstein (2003).

63   *When a male rat sees a new female behind a pane of glass, his dopamine level rises
      by 44 percent:* Fiorino, Coury, and Phillips (1997).

63   *sports-related injuries are the second-most common reason for visits to the doctor:*
      NBC Nightly News, Sept. 27, 2006. http://www.msnbc.msn.com/id/15031753/

64   *"In the long run, people of every age and in every walk of life seem to regret
      not having done things much more than they regret things they* did:" Gilbert
      (2006).

65   *"We make a kind of best guess . . .":* Nettle (2005).

67   *heavy viewers . . . actually enjoy their TV watching less than light viewers:* Kubey
      and Csikszentmihalyi (2002).

FOUR: UNNECESSARY MISERY: THE MIND

70   *We'll start to deny, or rationalize, or any of a hundred other defenses:* Literally, a
      hundred: Blackman (2004).

71   *"Each group denied that they were experiencing stress, and their bodies believed
      them."* This example is from Vaillant (1993).

74   *The Department of Veterans Affairs now estimates that more than 30 percent of the
      men who served in the Vietnam theater experienced full-blown post-traumatic stress
      disorder (PTSD) in later life:* Kulka et al. (1990).

74   *10 percent of women and 5 percent of men in the United States general population
      also suffer from PTSD:* Kessler et al. (1995).

74   *Helplessness to change the outcome may make the difference between acute PTSD
      and normal stress reactions:* van der Kolk (2002).

74   *PTSD occurs even among those who choose to expose themselves to trauma, such as res-
      cue workers:* Fullerton, Ursano, and Wang (2004).

76   *Chronic trauma syndrome:* Herman (1992).

76   *In a well-known study of seventeen thousand largely white, middle-class people, 22
      percent reported that they'd been sexually abused as children:* Felitti (2002); Felitti
      et al. (1998); Edwards et al. (2003).

78   *Abuse and neglect are much less common when children are part of an extended
      family:* Buss (2000).

80   *imprinting: "a very rapid form of learning that irreversibly stamps early experi-
      ence upon the developing nervous system":* Schore (1994, 118).

80   *A disturbing recent study found that mothers ranked child care as one of their least
      preferred, most frustrating activities:* Kahneman and Krueger (2006).

80   *The researchers noted by way of explanation that these mothers were likely en-
      gaged in other activities and found child care distracting:* University of Michigan
      Press release: http://www.umich.edu/news/index.html?Releases/2004/Dec04/
      r120204c.

80   *a tribe of Cherokees began to receive an average of twelve thousand dollars each per
      year:* Costello, et al. (2003).

81   *Allan Schore and Daniel Siegel, the leading researchers in this growing field, agree:*
      Schore (1994, 2003a–b); Siegel (2001).

81   *in mice, attentive mothering leads to better survival of new neurons in the hip-pocampus:* Bredy et al. (2003).

82   *Barbara Fredrickson and her colleagues have been investigating the effect of posi-tive emotions on coping and thinking:* Fredrickson (2001).

91   *Men who are unable to feel fear (because of brain tumors) trust everyone and get taken advantage of:* Bechara et al. (2007).

FIVE: A NEW PILOT

100   *Steven Hayes, the architect of Acceptance and Commitment Therapy, makes a fasci-nating point:* Hayes, Strosahl, and Wilson (1999); Hayes (2005).

101   *all that rumination just perpetuates the feeling state of depression, so they feel worse, more immobilized and helpless:* Segal, Teasdale, Williams (2004, 50).

101   *the "fundamental attribution error":* Slusher and Anderson (1989).

105   *A recent survey of clinicians: Psychotherapy Networker* article "The Top Ten" (March/April 2007).

106   *Langer gave each member of a group of nursing home residents a plant for their rooms:* Langer and Moldoveanu (2000, 2).

107   *Langer has written extensively . . . on how to modify our environment to stimulate mindfulness, creativity, and curiosity:* Langer (1989); Langer (2005).

108   *Exercise 6. A Taste of Mindfulness:* This exercise is based on Austin (1998).

112   *Jon Kabat-Zinn's Mindfulness-Based Stress Reduction Program . . . has been shown to have some remarkable benefits both for the mind and body:* See Segal, Williams, and Teasdale (2002); Kabat-Zinn (1982); Kabat-Zinn et al. (1992); Kristeller and Hallett (1999); Kabat-Zinn et al. (1998); Goldenberg et al. (1994); Kutz et al. (1985); Speca et al. (2000); Shapiro, Schwartz, and Bonner (1998); Davidson et al. (2003); Carlson et al. (2003).

113   *Its practice improves interpersonal relationships and an overall sense of well-being:* Grossman et al. (2004).

113   *A mindfulness-based program of treatment for depression has been proved to be much more effective at preventing relapse than conventional treatment:* Segal, Williams, and Teasdale (2002).

113   *This is similar to the process psychologists call* extinction: McEwen (2002, 38).

113   *what Daniel Goleman calls the "high road" through the logical brain and overrides the "low road" connection from the amygdala directly to mindless relief seeking:* Goleman (1995).

113   *That apparently leads to greater integration of the left and right hemispheres, the "logical" brain and the "creative" brain, as shown by structural changes in the con-necting areas of meditators' brains:* Lazar et al. (2005).

116   *You can get a tape or CD with nothing on it but temple bells:* For instance, Jon Kabat-Zinn's *Guided Mindfulness Meditation* CD.

116   *Christian Centering or Contemplative Prayer:* See, for example, centeringprayer. com or the works of Abbot Thomas Keating.

117   *"Trying to focus on the breath is like trying to balance on a beach ball":* Paul

Fleishman, remarks, Conference on Meditation and Psychotherapy, Boston, MA, June 1, 2007.

117 *Meditation may achieve most of its effect because it is primarily practice in learning how to pay attention:* Cahn and Polich (2006).

120 *When we're asked to think of sad events, the corresponding area on the right lights up:* Nettle (2005); Davidson (2000).

120 *If you're afraid of public speaking, and made to give a speech, the right PFC lights up like the Fourth of July:* Klein (2006).

121 *Those who tend to have more activity on the right side of the brain are more likely to cry when mother leaves than those who are more active on the left:* Fox and Davidson (1986).

121 *Apparently, the more activity in the left PFC, the better your immune response:* Rosenkranz et al. (2003).

121 *Davidson and some colleagues developed an eight-week mindfulness training program for Westerners:* Davidson, et al. (2003).

122 *both secure attachment and mindful meditation practice are associated with better regulation of body systems, balancing emotions, attuning to others, modulating fear, responding flexibly, and exhibiting insight and empathy:* Siegel (2007).

SIX: LESS MISERY

127 *Learn Will Power Like Juggling:* Some of these ideas were suggested by Polivy and Herman (2002).

132 *"Nothing in life is quite as important as you think it is when you are thinking about it":* Schkade and Kahneman (1998).

133 *Jeffrey Schwartz, a psychiatrist at UCLA:* Schwartz and Begley (2002).

133 *"The week after patients started relabeling their symptoms as manifestations of pathological brain processes, they reported the disease was no longer controlling them":* Begley (2007)

134 *Anne Lamott, who has chronicled her battles with life in a hilarious series of essays and memoirs:* Lamott (2003).

137 *the correlation between subjective well-being and IQ is .06:* Lykken (1999).

138 *"You come to see these activities of the mind as waves at the surface of the mental sea":* Siegel (2007, 19).

139 *The gratitude group experienced several benefits:* Emmons and McCullough (2003).

139 *women who are exposed to repeated images of other women who are unusually attractive—for instance, when they read a lot of women's magazines—feel less attractive themselves, and their self-esteem is diminished:* Buss (2000).

140 *the link between thinking and unnecessary misery:* The major resources here are Beck et al. (1979), Ellis (2005), and Burns (1980). You might also see my review in O'Connor (2001).

140 *Those depressed people who are the most perfectionistic generally have the worst outcomes in treatment:* Blatt (1998).

144 *some experienced cognitive therapists who have been rethinking how their method*

really works and using more mindfulness-based techniques to improve it: Segal, Williams, and Teasdale (2002); Williams, Teasdale, Segal, and Kabat-Zinn (2007).

148 *"Learning to Control Emotions":* These suggestions are a distillation of a lot of reading and my own clinical and personal experience, but the last four points specifically are from Linehan (1992).

149 *the more you regain self-control and mastery from putting the trauma in context, the better the improvement in your immune system:* Pennebaker, Mayne, and Francis (1997).

149 *Bargh has gone on to document what he calls the "chameleon effect":* Chartrand and Bargh (1999).

150 *My best advice about using money wisely is to read* Your Money or Your Life: Dominguez and Robin (1999).

151 *Barry Schwartz argues that when we make decisions, we fall into one of two groups, "maximizers" and "satisficers":* Schwartz (2004).

152 *"The more options there are, the more likely one will make a nonoptimal choice and this prospect may undermine whatever pleasure one gets from one's actual choice":* Schwartz et al. (2002).

152 *Only in America did a majority of people say they preferred the wider choice:* Weiner (2008).

152 *Taking care of the children was ranked as one of the most frustrating, least enjoyable activities:* Stone, Schwartz, et al. (2006).

152 *many women—35 percent, in a recent poll—think of child-rearing as the most enjoyable, satisfying aspects of their lives:* Wallis (2005).

153 *The lower the number they were asked to memorize, the more likely people were to make the healthier choice:* Zweig (2007).

154 *The number of people in the United States who say there is no one with whom they discuss important matters tripled between 1985 and 2004.* McPherson, Smith-Lovin, and Brashears (2006).

SEVEN: MORE JOY

161 *Paul Ekman . . . has a pretty long list of good feelings:* Ekman, 190.

164 *Within half an hour, the nerve cells began to grow new dendritic spines:* Engert and Bonhoeffer (1999), cited in Klein (2006).

164 *some experiments by Mike Merzenich that bear directly on your problem:* Rencanzone, Schreiner, and Merzenich (1993).

165 *"Experience coupled with attention leads to physical changes in the structure and future functioning of the nervous system. . . .":* Begley (2007, 159).

165 *Siegel has been able to show that attention is a learnable skill:* Siegel (2007).

166 *although the stroke-damaged area of the brain doesn't recover, other areas of the brain are "recruited" to step in and assume some of its functions:* Begley (2007).

166 *If you're in a crowd and you're looking for a friend's face, the facial recognition circuits in your brain are activated:* These findings are reviewed in Begley (2007).

167 *Psychologists have been studying what's called "attachment" for almost fifty years:* For an excellent review of this literature, see Karen (1994).

168 *In large-scale tests, only a slim majority of young adult Americans are found to be securely attached:* Begley (2007).

168 *in a fascinating series of experiments, Phillip Shaver of the United States and an Israeli researcher, Mario Mikulincer, have demonstrated that feelings of security can be heightened in anxious and avoidant adults:* This is all reviewed very cogently in Begley (2007, 183–211).

169 *"The study can't go on unless someone actually pets the tarantula while someone else watches, and the next task is just as bad or worse, having cockroaches run up your arm":* Begley (2007, 206).

169 *yet they find that the mood change lasts, at least for a while:* Isen (2003).

169 *focusing on feelings of gratitude raises your happiness level:* Emmons and McCullough (2003).

169 *acting kindly toward others produced positive change in subjective well-being:* Lyubomirsky, Sheldon, and Schkade (2005).

170 *reflecting on and reaffirming one's personal values lowered cortisol levels in the blood:* Creswell, et al. (2005).

170 *simply teaching his undergraduate psychology classes about the principles of happiness resulted in significant gains in their happiness levels:* Fordyce (1983).

171 *Michael Argyle . . . has made a list for us of what most people say brings them good feelings:* Argyle (2001).

171 *Dr. Barbara Ann Kipfer, a lexicographer by trade, has given us a book of* 14,000 Things to Feel Happy About: Kipfer (2007).

172 *Daniel Kahneman suggests that the reason why we're so adaptable . . . is that we have such short attention spans:* Kahneman and Krueger (2006).

174 *some research-validated strategies for savoring:* Peterson (2006); Bryant and Veroff (2007); Bryant (2006).

174 *"Do not be afraid of pride. Tell yourself how impressed others are and remember how long you have waited for this to happen":* Peterson (2006).

176 *an experiment that highlighted the differences between thinking and remembering:* Lyubomirsky et al. (2006).

177 *people who are happier than average are more successful in many fields of life:* All reviewed in Lyubomirsky, King, and Diener (2005).

178 *Peterson and others have demonstrated experimentally that focusing on only three things is better than trying to think of more:* Seligman, Steen, Park, and Peterson (2005).

180 *many of the participants continued to focus on three good things entirely on their own:* Seligman, Steen, Park, and Peterson (2005).

181 *One now-famous study used the fortunate accident that the autobiographies written by young Sisters of Notre Dame when they were entering the order were still on file sixty years later:* Danner, Snowdon, and Friesen (2001).

181 *Oscar winners live on average four years longer than losers:* Redelmeir and Singh (2001).

181 *women who've had breast augmentation surgery gain a more-or-less permanent up-lift in self-satisfaction.* Argyle (2001).

181 *those patients who could see trees from their windows requested significantly less pain medication, got along better with the nurses, and had shorter hospital stays than those whose windows faced an airshaft:* Ulrich (1984) cited in Sapolsky (1998).

182 *surgical wounds heal more slowly if you're anxious or depressed:* Kiecolt-Glazer et al. (2002).

182 *Unhappy people are more likely to catch colds:* Cohen et al. (2003).

182 *when you have a happy experience, your body chemistry improves, and blood pressure and heart rate tend to fall:* Ryff and Singer (2003).

182 *controlling stress in a positive way leads to better-than-better health:* Larsen et al. (2003).

182 *people who simply write about their feelings have better health in a variety of ways:* Pennebaker (1990).

182 *The unrealistic thinkers lived an average of nine months longer:* Taylor (2005).

182 *There are other ways, less dangerous than deluding yourself, to reduce your stress:* O'Connor (2005).

183 *about 60 percent of visits to primary care MDs are for psychologically related complaints:* Servan-Schreiber (2003).

183 *not exercising is like taking depressants:* Tal Ben-Shahar, remarks, Conference on Meditation and Psychotherapy, Boston, MA, June 1, 2007.

184 *there's evidence that filling ourselves up with rich comfort food is an effective, if self-destructive, antidote for stress:* Dallman et al. (2003).

186 *more people go to zoos annually than attend all sporting events combined:* Weiner (2008).

187 *We're suffering from what at least one author calls nature deficit disorder:* Louv (2006).

188 *Daniel Gilbert refers to what he calls the "pleasure paradox":* Gilbert (2005).

190 *The act of laughing—even the anticipation of laughing—has been reported to have health benefits for the immune system and the circulatory system:* Berk et al. (1989), Berk and Tan (2006).

190 *if you can master the Duchenne smile, your body will send happy signals to your brain, your left PFC will light up, and you will experience positive emotions:* Klein (2006).

191 *they reached the correct diagnosis using only half the steps that it took doctors who hadn't been treated specially:* Isen, Daubman, and Nowicki (1987).

191 *the brain registers a pleasurable feeling when we merely read the right answer:* Cabanac et al. (2003).

191 *being in a positive emotional state seems to help us think more clearly, creatively, and flexibly:* Isen (2003, 185).

191 *Listening to a comedy album makes you more likely to lend money:* Myers (1992).

191 *Under time pressure our thinking becomes more superficial and narrow, especially if we see the schedule as arbitrary or artificially imposed:* Amabile et al. (2002).

192 *Mice raised in enriched environments (with toys and other mice, not sterile lab cages) have fifteen percent more neurons in the hippocampus:* Begley (2007).

192 *"Usually, 50 percent of the new cells reaching the . . . hippocampus die. But if the animal lives in an enriched environment, many fewer of the new cells die"*: Begley (2007).

192 *"It turns out these individuals have a shrunken hippocampus"*: Begley (2007).

194 most of the things that people commonly associate with good feelings involve sensual pleasure: Argyle (2001).

195 One survey has found that people say they would value a better sex life as much as about fifty thousand dollars more in income a year: Klein, 2006.

196 adding garlic bread to a family spaghetti dinner: Hirsch (2000).

197 On average, the massaged babies were discharged from the hospital six days earlier than the others: Field (2003).

EIGHT: MORE SATISFACTION

199 higher income aspirations reduce your overall life satisfaction: Stutzer (2004).

200 What matters more than absolute wealth is perceived wealth: This quote is from Myers (1992, 39).

200 *"There is a strange lightness in the heart when one's nothingness in a particular area is accepted in good faith. . . ."*: William James, quoted in Nettle (2005, 159).

201 The mere act of setting reasonable and concrete goals seems to improve both our experience and our performance: Ben-Shahar (2007).

201 *"the proper role of goals is to liberate us, so that we can enjoy the here and now"*: Ben-Shahar (2007, 70).

202 the more materialistic your goals, the less happy you are: Kasser (2002).

202 placing a high value on financial success was associated with less self-actualization, less vitality, more depression, and more anxiety: Kasser and Ryan (2003).

202 making progress toward materialistic goals did not have any effect on subjective well-being, while progress on personal growth and improving relationships did: Kasser (2002).

202 those countries that place a high level of importance on money tend to have lower levels of well-being: Diener and Biswas-Diener (2002).

202 Subjects both in the United States and South Korea were asked to reflect on the most satisfying events in their lives and rate which needs were being satisfied in those events: Sheldon, Elliot, Kim, and Kasser (2001).

206 these are exactly the same people they were before their illness: Ben-Shahar (2007).

206 *"The trick, of course, is to do this without getting cancer"*: Taylor, 1989, p. vii.

206 James Hillman . . . says that he's found nothing harder to treat—that it's very hard to get people to see that your schedule is your life: Ventura (2006).

208 it's what the Buddhists call dukkha—an unpleasant reality that's underneath the level of consciousness: Wallace (2005).

209 Mihaly Csikszentmihalyi published his famous book on Flow, a study of what makes people feel good: Csikszentmihalyi (1991).

209 People asked about positive life events rarely mention work at all, except for getting a raise or promotion; certainly not the activities of work: Argyle (2001).

209 People in high flow occupations (musicians, artists, writers) in fact are subject to frus-

tration, depression, mood swings, and problems with addictions, which both motivate and hinder their self-expression: Nettle (2005).

209   *among their sample of women, work ranks next to last (just above the morning commute, just below the evening commute) in pleasurable activities:* Kahneman and Krueger (2006).

211   *The Gallup organization . . . routinely asks employees, "Do you get to do what you do best every day?" and finds that no more than 20 percent agree:* Peterson (2006).

211   *Even according to the Conference Board, a very business-friendly group, only half of U.S. employees say they are satisfied with their work:* Ben-Shahar (2007).

212   *those in the lowest grades of the British civil service had 3.5 times as many fatal heart attacks as those in the highest grade:* Marmot (2005).

213   *People who consider religion an important factor in their lives tend to be happier:* Myers (1992).

214   *"The ideal man, then, was pleasant, mild-mannered . . ."* Rotundo (1993).

214   *The Chinese do not place a high value on individual pride:* Eid and Diener (2001).

214   *the Kung people in Botswana hunt about six hours a week; the San bush people of South Africa work about a twenty-hour week:* Schumaker (2007).

214   *"The great problem of the Industrial Revolution was how to transform a population of strong-willed . . ."* Hodgkinson (2005, 21).

215   *The claim that capitalism has delivered us from excessive toil can be sustained only if we take as our point of comparison eighteenth- and nineteenth-century Europe and America:* Schor (1993, 6).

216   *Retired people, in general, are happier than those still working:* Argyle (2001).

216   *Some posit that there are two aspects to satisfying leisure:* Wrzesniewski, Rozin, and Bennett (2003).

217   *many studies find that leisure activities are the strongest source of life satisfaction:* Argyle (2001).

217   *voluntary work is a source of joy just behind dancing, and provides greater joy than most other leisure activities:* Argyle (2001).

218   *the question of* faux *flow:* See Peterson (2006).

218   *good relationships with others may be the single most important source of life satisfaction, across all ages and cultures:* Reis and Gable (2003).

218   *people who feel connected to others live longer, happier, more productive lives, with fewer health problems than people who are isolated:* O'Connor (2005).

219   *People who care about others are happier than those who are preoccupied with themselves:* Layard (2005).

220   *Mindfulness meditation seems to increase empathy and the ability to cue into nonverbal communication by strengthening the brain areas responsible:* Siegel (2007).

220   *compassion is the intention to see every human being as no better or worse than yourself, worth no less and no more:* Miller (1995).

221   *A study of both types of college students found that everyone was happiest when they were acting extraverted:* Fleeson, Malanos, and Achille (2002).

225   *One researcher estimates that after about four years on average, the initial stage of infatuation has worn off the marriage, and the partners are secretly wondering if they made a huge mistake:* Lykken (1999).

226 *Overall happiness is correlated with satisfaction with friends, number of friends, number of close friends, frequency of seeing them, number of phone calls, visits, and parties:* Argyle (2001).

226 *baboons who had more friendships—who spent more time together, who groomed each other, who watched from the sidelines as others jockeyed for status—had less stress hormones like cortisol in their bloodstreams:* Sapolsky (1998).

227 *the number of friends you have is one of the highest correlates with overall happiness, right up there with exercise, frequency of sex, success experiences, and simple sensual pleasures:* Argyle (2001).

NINE: GRIEF AND PAIN

230 *Dr. Kübler-Ross developed her model of the stages of grief almost forty years ago:* Kübler-Ross (1997).

230 *Judith Viorst . . . refers to the sense that there is a Julia Child of sorrow:* Viorst (1998).

233 *Nettle identifies two things, and I add three more:* Nettle (2005).

233 *it [pain] slows you down, makes you cranky and preoccupied. It may not interfere with satisfaction but it can take away from joy:* See Kahneman and Krueger (2006).

233 *Even though we have no-fault divorce, we have psychological winners and losers:* Wallerstein and Blakeslee (1989).

233 *Some argue that the loss in happiness due to unemployment is actually worse than that due to divorce:* Layard (2005).

237 *there has yet to be any independent confirmation that these drugs are correcting a chemical imbalance in the system:* Moncrieff and Cohen, (2006).

237 *these patients also reported significantly less ability to cry, care about others' feelings, erotic dreaming, surprise, creativity, anger, and ability to express their feelings:* Opbroek et al. (2002).

237 *a study in which "normal" (not depressed) volunteers were given a Paxil or another antidepressant for a week:* Harmer et al. (2004).

237 *four weeks of Paxil significantly reduced their level of negative feelings:* Knutson et al. (1998).

238 *Peter Kramer pointed these effects out, way back in* Listening to Prozac: Kramer (1998).

TEN: THE MEANING OF LIFE

240 *If you could take a drug every day that would keep you in a state of bliss, would you choose to? Most people say no:* Diener and Biswas-Diener (2003).

240 *Carol D. Ryff has been working for decades on what constitutes genuine happiness:* See, for example, Ryff (1989).

242 *In Western theories, the hope is always that emptiness can be healed:* Epstein (1998, 19).

242 *"the common goal of Zen and psychoanalysis is putting an end to the pursuit of happiness":* Magid (2002, 82). Emphasis in the original.

244 *simply reflecting on your personal values reduces the cortisol response, and your subjective feeling of distress:* Creswell et al. (2005).

244 *Martin Seligman . . . who revolutionized the field with* Learned Helplessness: Peterson, Maier, and Seligman (1995).

245 *Needs few material possessions and little entertainment, comfort, power or fame:* Csikszentmihalyi (1997, 114), quoted in Nettle (2000, 26).

245 *there are many virtues and benefits associated with this state but increased happiness is not necessarily one of them:* Nettle (2005).

245 *People in high-flow occupations describe themselves as no more happy than anyone else:* Nettle (2005).

245 *she acknowledges that this formulation largely omits qualities like joy in living or capacity to accept change:* Ryff (1989).

245 *He seems to assume that trying to change the individual set point for cheeriness is not an especially effective strategy.* Seligman (2002); see Nettle (2005).

247 *The belief that you are in control of events in your life is highly correlated with feelings of subjective well-being and, to some extent, is a matter of belief:* Argyle (2001).

247 *As Admiral James Stockdale (an American POW during the Vietnam War) famously observed, the optimists died first:* Wikipedia main article, Stockdale, James.

247 *the ones who survived were the ones who focused on what they could control:* Frankl, 1967

247 *Shelley Taylor . . . argues that it's our feeling of being in control more than the actual degree of control that's important to us:* Taylor (1989).

249 *The positive psychologists like to call this* faux flow: e.g. Peterson (2006).

249 *it's best to retain a portion of our attention devoted to mindfulness, to keep looking at the direction we're going, not just how rewarding the activity seems to be:* Siegel (2007).

250 *they forget to untie the rowboat:* Sharon Salzburg, remarks, Conference on Meditation and Psychotherapy, Boston, MA, June 1, 2007.

253 *a difficult-to-describe feeling that Jonathan Haidt describes as elevation:* Haidt (2006).

254 *In one of his more interesting studies, one of his graduate assistants found that nursing mothers lactated more when watching the elevated videos:* Haidt (2006).

255 *"Some types of happiness—possibly the most profoundly gratifying ones—are not dependent on positive outlook, jolliness, or comfort":* Schumaker (2007, 36).

255 *Half of those who had not found meaning died within five years, while less than 20 percent of those who had found meaning died:* Taylor et al. (2000).

256 *Daniel Siegel's hypothesis in* The Developing Mind *is that we build a coherent autobiographical narrative:* Siegel (2001).

258 *Exercise 13. Your own eulogy:* This exercise is based on Peterson (2006), Chapter 1.

ELEVEN: STAYING HAPPY

265 *the more hours you work, the less satisfied you'll be with your life:* Kasser and Brown (2008).

BIBLIOGRAPHY

Amabile, Teresa M., Constance N. Hadley, and Steven J. Kramer. "Creativity Under the Gun." *Harvard Business Review*. August 2002 (special issue).

Argyle, Michael. *The Psychology of Happiness*. 2nd ed. New York: Taylor & Francis, 2001.

Austin, James H. *Zen and the Brain*. Cambridge, MA: MIT Press, 1998.

Bechara, Antoine, Hanna Damasio, Daniel Tranel, and Antonio R. Damasio. "Deciding Advantageously Before Knowing the Advantageous Strategy." *Science* 275 (1997): 1293–95.

Beck, Aaron T., A. John Rush, Brian F. Shaw, and Gary Emery. *Cognitive Therapy of Depression*. New York: Guilford, 1979.

Begley, Sharon. *Train Your Mind, Change Your Brain*. New York: Ballantine, 2007.

Ben-Shahar, Talil. *Happier*. New York: McGraw-Hill, 2007.

Berk, Lee, and Stanley A. Tan, "[beta]-Endorphin and HGH Increase Are Associated with Both the Anticipation and the Experience of Mirthful Laughter." *FASEB Journal*, 20 (2006): A382.

Berk, Lee, Stanley A. Tan, William F. Fry, et al. "Neuroendocrine and Stress Hormone Changes During Mirthful Laughter." *American Journal of Medical Science* 298:6 (1989): 390–96.

Blackman, Jerome S. *101 Defenses*. New York: Brunner-Routledge, 2004.

Blatt, S. J. "Contributions of Psychoanalysis to the Understanding and Treatment of Depression." *Journal of the American Psychoanalytic Association,* 46:3 (1999): 724–52.

Bradshaw, G. A., Allan N. Schore, Janine L. Brown, Joyce H. Poole, and Cynthia J. Moss. "Elephant Breakdown." *Nature* 43:24 (2005): 807.

Bredy, Timothy W., Rebecca J. Grant, Danielle L. Champagne, and Michael J. Meaney. "Maternal Care Influences Neuronal Survival in the Hippocampus of the Rat." *European Journal of Neuroscience* 18:10 (2003): 2903–09.

Brickman, Philip, and Donald T. Campbell. "Hedonic Relativism and Planning the Good Society." In Mortimer H. Appley, ed., *Adaptation Level Theory: A Symposium* (287–302). New York: Academic Press, 1971.

Brickman, Philip, Erik J. Coates, and Ronnie Janoff-Bulman. "Lottery Winners and Accident Victims: Is Happiness Relative?" *Journal of Personality and Social Psychology* 36:8 (1978): 917–27.

Bryant, Fred B. "Finding Joy: The Art and Science of Savoring." *Alternative Medicine* (May 2006): 63–66.

Bryant, Fred B., and Joseph Veroff. *Savoring: A New Model of Positive Experience.* Mahwah, NJ: Lawrence Erlbaum, 2007.

Burns, David D. *Feeling Good: The New Mood Therapy.* New York: Avon, 1980.

Buss, D. M. "The Evolution of Happiness." *American Psychologist* 55:1 (2000): 15–21.

Cabanac, Michel, Jacqueline Guillaume, Marta Balasko, and Adriana Fleury. "Pleasure in Decision-Making Situations." *BMC Psychiatry* 2:7 (2002): http://www.biomedcentral.com/1471-244X/2/7.

Cahn, B. Rael, and John Polich. "Meditation States and Traits: EEG, ERP, and Neuroimaging Studies." *Psychological Bulletin* 132:2 (2006): 180–211.

Carlson, Linda E., Michael Speca, Kamala D. Patel, and Eileen Goodey. "Mindfulness-Based Stress Reduction in Relation to Quality of Life, Mood, Symptoms of Stress, and Immune Parameters in Breast and Prostate Cancer Outpatients." *Psychosomatic Medicine* 65 (2003): 571–81.

Champagne, Frances A., and Meaney, Michael J. "Like Mother, Like Daughter: Evidence for Non-Genomic Transmission of Parental Behavior and Stress Responsivity." *Progress in Brain Research* 133 (2001): 287–302.

Chartrand, Tanya L., and John A. Bargh, "The Chameleon Effect: The Perception-Behavior Link and Social Interaction." *Journal of Personality and Social Psychology* 76:6 (1999): 893–910.

Cohen, Sheldon, William J. Doyle, Ronald B. Turner, Cuneyt M. Alper, and David B. Skoner. "Emotional Style and Susceptibility to the Common Cold." *Psychosomatic Medicine* 65:4 (2003): 652–57.

Collins, Chuck, and Felice Yeskel. *Economic Apartheid in America: A Primer on Economic Inequality and Insecurity.* New York: New Press, 2000.

Costello, E. Jane, Scott N. Compton, Gordon Keeler, and Adrian Angold. "Relationships Between Poverty and Psychopathology." *Journal of the American Medical Association* 290 (2003): 2023–29.

Creswell, J. David, William T. Welch, Shelley E. Taylor, et al. "Affirmation of Personal

Values Buffers Neuroendocrine and Psychological Stress Responses." *Psychological Science* 16:11 (2005): 846–51.

Cryder, Cynthia E., Jennifer S. Lerner, James J. Gross, and Ronald E. Dahl. "Misery Is Not Miserly: Depressed and Self-Focused Individuals Spend More." *Psychological Science,* June 2008.

Cushman, Philip. *Constructing the Self, Constructing America: A Cultural History of Psychotherapy.* Cambridge, MA: Perseus, 1995.

Csikszentmihalyi, Mihaly, *Flow.* New York: Harper Perennial, 1991.

———. *Living Well: The Psychology of Everyday Life.* London, UK: Weidenfield and Nicholson, 1997.

Dallman, Mary F., Norman Pecoraro, Susan F. Akana, et al. "Chronic Stress and Obesity: A New View of 'Comfort Food.'" *Proceedings of the National Academy of Sciences,* 100:20 (Sept. 30, 2003): 11696–701.

Danner, Deborah D., David A. Snowdon, and Wallace V. Friesen. "Positive Emotions in Early Life and Longevity: Findings from the Nun Study." *Journal of Personality and Social Psychology,* 80:5 (2001): 804–13.

Davidson, Richard, Jon Kabat-Zinn, Joel Schumacher, Melissa Rosenkranz, et al. "Alterations in Brain and Immune Function Produced by Mindfulness Meditation." *Psychosomatic Medicine* 65 (2003): 564–70.

Davidson, Richard. "Affective Style, Psychopathology, and Resilience: Brain Mechanisms and Plasticity." *American Psychologist* 55:11 (2000): 1214–30.

Diener, Ed, and Christie N. Scollon. "Subjective Well-Being Is Desirable, but Not the Summum Bonum." Paper presented at University of Minnesota Interdisciplinary Workshop on Well-Being, Oct. 23–25, 2003. Available at http://www.tc.umn.edu/~tiberius/workshop_papers/Diener.pdf.

Diener, Ed, and Robert Biswas-Diener. "Findings on Subjective Well-Being and Their Implications for Empowerment." Paper presented at the World Bank Conference, "Measuring Empowerment: Cross-Disciplinary Perspectives," Feb. 4–5, 2003. Available at http://siteresources.worldbank.org/INTEMPOWERMENT/-Resources/486312-1095970750368/529763-1095970803335/diener.pdf.

———. "Will Money Increase Subjective Well-Being?" *Social Indicators Research* 57 (2002): 119–69.

Diener, Ed, and Martin E. P. Seligman. "Beyond Money: Toward an Economy of Well-Being." *Psychological Science in the Public Interest* 5:1 (2004): 1–31.

Divorce Magazine.com (Web site). http://www.divorcemag.com/statistics/statsWorld.sht.

Dominguez, Joe, and Vicki Robin. *Your Money or Your Life.* New York: Penguin, 1999.

Draganski, Bogdan, Christian Gaser, Volker Busch, et al. "Neuroplasticity: Changes in Grey Matter Induced by Training." *Nature* 427 (2004): 311–12.

The Economist. "Economics Discovers Its Feelings" (unsigned article). December 23, 2006.

———. "The Economist Intelligence Unit's Quality-of-Life Index." (2005) http://economist.com/media/pdf/QUALITY_OF_LIFE.pdf.

Edwards, V. J., G. W. Holden, V. J. Felitti, and R. F. Anda. "Relationship Between Multiple Forms of Childhood Maltreatment and Adult Mental Health in Community

Respondents: Results from the Adverse Childhood Experiences Study." *American Journal of Psychiatry* 160:8 (2003): 1453–60.

Eid, Michael and Ed Diener. "Norms for Experiencing Emotions in Different Cultures: Inter- and Intranational Differences." *Journal of Personality and Social Psychology* 81 (2001): 869–85.

Ekman, Paul. *Emotions Revealed*. New York: Times Books, 2003.

Elbert, Thomas, Christo Pantev, Christian Wienbruch, Brigitte Rockstroh, and Edward Taub. "Increased Cortical Representation of the Fingers of the Left Hand in String Players." *Science* 270 (1995): 305–07.

Ellis, Alfred, and Catharine Maclaren. *Rational Emotive Behavior Therapy*. New York: Impact Publishers, 2005.

Ellison, Harlan. "Strange Wine." In Harlan Ellison, *Strange Wine*. New York: Warner Books, 1978.

Emmons, Robert A., and Michael E. McCullough. "Counting Blessings Versus Burdens: An Experimental Investigation of Gratitude and Subjective Well-Being in Daily Life." *Journal of Personality and Social Psychology* 84:2 (2005): 377–89.

Engert, Florian, and Tobias Bonhoeffer. "Dendritic Spine Changes Associated with Hippocampal Long-Term Synaptic Plasticity." *Nature* 399 (1999): 66–70.

Epstein, Mark. *Going to Pieces Without Falling Apart*. New York: Broadway Books, 1998.

Eriksson, Peter S., Ekaterina Perfilieva, Thomas Bjork-Erisson, Ann-Marie Alborn, Claes Nordborg, Daniel A. Peterson, and Fred H. Gage. "Neurogenesis in the Adult Human Hippocampus." *Nature Medicine* 4:11 (1998): 1313–17.

Ewing, Reid, Tom Schmid, Richard Killingsworth, Amy Zlot, and Steven Raudenbush. "Relationship Between Urban Sprawl and Physical Activity, Obesity, and Morbidity." *American Journal of Health Promotion* (2003, Sept.–Oct.): 47–57.

Felitti, Vincent J. "Reverse Alchemy in Childhood: Turning Gold into Lead." *Family Violence Prevention Fund Health Alert* 8:1 (2001): 1–8.

Felitti, Vincent J., Robert F. Anda, Dale Nordenberg, David F. Williamson, Alison M. Spitz, Valeri Edwards, Mary P. Koss, and James S. Marks. "Relationship of Childhood Abuse and Household Dysfunction to Many of the Leading Causes of Death in Adults: The Adverse Childhood Experiences (ACE) study." *American Journal of Preventive Medicine* 14:4 (1998): 245–58.

Field, Tiffany. "Stimulation of Preterm Infants." *Pediatric Review* 24:1 (2003): 4–11.

Fiorino, Dennis F., Ariane Coury, and Anthony G. Phillips. "Dynamic Changes in Nucleus Accumbens Dopamine Efflux During the Coolidge Effect in Male Rats." *Journal of Neuroscience* 17:12 (1997): 4849–50.

Fisher, Anne. "Does Your Employer Help You Stay Healthy?" *Fortune* (July 12, 2005): 60.

Fleeson, William, Adrian B. Malanos, and Noelle M. Achille. "An Intraindividual Process Approach to the Relationship Between Extraversion and Positive Affect: Is Acting Extraverted as 'Good' as Being Extraverted?" *Journal of Personality and Social Psychology* 83:6 (2002): 1409–22.

Fordyce, Michael W. "A Program to Increase Happiness: Further Studies." *Journal of Counseling Psychology* 30:4 (1983): 483–98.

Fox, Nathan A., and Richard Davidson. "Taste-Elicited Changes in Facial Signs of Emotion and the Asymmetry of Brain Electrical Activity in Human Newborns." *Neuropsychologia* 24 (1986): 417–22.

Francis, Darlene, Josie Diorio, Dong Liu, and Michael J. Meaney. "Nongenomic Transmission Across Generations of Maternal Behavior and Stress Responses in the Rat." *Science* 286:5442 (1999): 1155–59.

Frankl, Viktor. *Man's Search for Meaning.* New York: Washington Square Press, 1967.

Frederick, Shane, and George Loewenstein. "Hedonic Adaptation." In Daniel Kahneman, Ed Diener, and Norbert Schwarz, eds., *Well-Being: The Foundations of Hedonic Psychology.* New York: Russell Sage, 1999.

Fredrickson, Barbara. "The Role of Positive Emotions in Positive Psychology." *American Psychologist* 56:3 (March 2001): 218–26.

Fujita, Frank, and Ed Diener. "Life Satisfaction Set Point: Stability and Change." *Journal of Personality and Social Psychology* 88:1 (2005): 158–64.

Fullerton, Carol S., Robert J. Ursano, and Leming Wang. "Acute Stress Disorder, Posttraumatic Stress Disorder, and Depression in Disaster or Rescue Workers." *American Journal of Psychiatry* 161:8 (2004): 1370–76.

Gilbert, Daniel. *Stumbling on Happiness.* New York: Knopf, 2006.

Gilbert, Daniel. "The Pleasure Paradox." *Tricycle: The Buddhist Review.* Fall 2005.

Goldenberg, Don L., Kenneth H. Kaplan, Maureen Galvin-Nadeau, et al. "A Controlled Study of a Stress-Reduction, Cognitive-Behavioral Treatment Program in Fibromyalgia." *Journal of Musculoskeletal Pain* 2 (1994): 53–66.

Goleman, Daniel. *Emotional Intelligence.* New York: Bantam, 1995.

Greenhouse, Steven. "Report Shows Americans Have More 'Labor Days.'" *New York Times* (Sept. 1, 2001).

———. "Worked Over and Overworked." *New York Times* (April 11, 2008).

Grossman, Paul, Ludger Niemann, Stefan Schmidt, and Harald Walach. "Mindfulness-Based Stress Reduction and Health Benefits: A Meta-Analysis." *Journal of Psychosomatic Research* 57 (2004): 35–43.

Guardian. "Fast Forward into Trouble" (unsigned article). June 14, 2003. http://www.guardian.co.uk/weekend/story/0,3605,975769,00.html

Haidt, Jonathan. *The Happiness Hypothesis.* New York: Basic Books, 2006.

Handler, R. "20 Weeks to Happiness." *Psychotherapy Networker* (Jan./Feb. 2006).

Harmer, Catherine J., Nicholas C. Shelley, Philip J. Cowen, and Guy M. Goodwin. "Increased Positive Versus Negative Perception and Memory in Healthy Volunteers Following Selective Serotonin and Norepinephrine Reuptake Inhibition." *American Journal of Psychiatry* 161 (2004): 1256–63.

Hayes, Steven C., Kirk D. Strosahl, and Kelly G. Wilson. *Acceptance and Commitment Therapy: An Experiential Approach to Behavior Change.* New York: Guilford, 1999.

Henderson, Mark. "Modern Life: It's One Step at a Time, Only Much Quicker." *Times* (London) (May 2, 2007).

Henwood, D. *Wall Street: How It Works and for Whom.* New York: Verso, 1998.

Herman, Judith. *Trauma and Recovery.* New York: Basic Books, 1992.

Hirsch, Alan R. "Effects of Garlic Bread on Family Interactions." Poster presented at the 58th annual meeting of the American Psychosomatic Society, March 1, 2000.

Hirshleifer, David, and Tyler Shumway. "Good Day Sunshine: Stock Returns and the Weather." *The Journal of Finance* 58:3 (2003): 1009–32.

Hodgkinson, Tom. *How to Be Idle.* New York: HarperCollins, 2005.

Isen, Alice M. "Positive Affect as a Source of Human Strength." In L. G. Aspinwall and U. M. Staudinger, eds., *A Psychology of Human Strengths: Fundamental Questions and Future Directions for a Positive Psychology.* Washington, D.C.: American Psychological Association, 2003.

Isen, A. M., K. A. Daubman, and G. P. Nowicki. "Positive Affect Facilitates Creative Problem Solving." *Journal of Personality and Social Psychology* 52:6 (1987): 1122–31.

James, William. *Principles of Psychology.* New York: Henry Holt, 1890.

Kabat-Zinn, Jon, Ann O. Massion, Jean Kristeller, Linda Gay Peterson, et al. "Effectiveness of a Meditation-Based Stress Reduction Program in the Treatment of Anxiety Disorders." *American Journal of Psychiatry* 149 (1992): 936–43.

Kabat-Zinn, Jon, Elizabeth Wheeler, Timothy Light, Anne Skillings, et al. "Influence of a Mindfulness-Based Stress Reduction Intervention on Rates of Skin Clearing in Patients with Moderate to Severe Psoriasis Undergoing Phototherapy UVB and Photochemotherapy PUVA." *Psychosomatic Medicine* 50 (1998): 625–32.

Kabat-Zinn, Jon. "An Outpatient Program in Behavioral Medicine for Chronic Pain Patients Based on the Practice of Mindfulness Meditation: Theoretical Considerations and Preliminary Results." *General Hospital Psychiatry* 4 (1982): 33–47.

Kadison, Richard. "The Mental Health Crisis: What Colleges Must Do." *Chronicle of Higher Education* 51:16 (2004): B20.

Kahneman, Daniel, Alan B. Krueger, David Schkade, Norbert Schwarz, and Arthur A. Stone. "Would You Be Happier if You Were Richer? A Focusing Illusion." *Science* 312 (2006): 1908–10.

Kahneman, Daniel, and Alan B. Krueger. "Developments in the Measurement of Subjective Well-Being." *Journal of Economic Perspectives* 20:1 (2006): 3–24.

Kahneman, Daniel. "Experienced Utility and Objective Happiness: A Moment-Based Approach." In Daniel Kahneman and Amos Tversky, eds., *Choices, Values, and Frames.* New York: Cambridge University Press, 2000.

Karen, Robert. *Becoming Attached.* New York: Warner Books, 1994.

Kasser, Tim. *The High Price of Materialism.* Cambridge, MA: MIT Press, 2002.

Kasser, Tim, and Kirk W. Brown. "On Time, Happiness, and Ecological Footprints." In J. de Graaf, ed., *Take Back Your Time: Fighting Overwork and Time Poverty in America* (107–112). San Francisco, CA: Berrett-Koehler, 2003.

Kasser, Tim, and Kennon M. Sheldon. "Time Affluence as a Path Towards Personal Happiness and Ethical Business Practice." *Journal of Business Ethics,* in press.

Kessler, Ronald C., Amanda Sonnega, Evelyn Bromet, M. Hughes, et al. "Posttraumatic Stress Disorder in the National Comorbidity Survey." *Archives of General Psychiatry* 52:12 (1995): 1048–60.

Kiecolt-Glaser, Janice K., Lynanne McGuire, Theodore F. Robles, and Ronald Glaser. "Psychoneuroimmunology: Psychological Influences on Immune Function and Health." *Journal of Consulting and Clinical Psychology* 70:3 (2002): 537–47.

Kipfer, Barbara Ann. *14,000 Things to be Happy About.* Rev. ed. New York: Workman, 2007.

Klein, Stefan. *The Science of Happiness.* New York: Marlowe 2006.

Knutson, Brian, Owen M. Wolkowitz, Steve W. Cole, Theresa Chan, et al. "Selective Alteration of Personality and Social Behavior by Serotonergic Intervention." *American Journal of Psychiatry* 155 (1998): 373–79.

Kramer, Peter. *Listening to Prozac.* New York: Penguin, 1998.

Kristeller, Jean, and Brendan Hallett. "An Exploratory Study of a Meditation-Based Intervention for Binge Eating Disorder." *Journal of Health Psychology* 4 (1999): 357–63.

Kubey, Robert, and Mihaly Csikszentmihalyi. "Television Addiction is No Mere Metaphor." *Scientific American,* February 2002.

Kübler-Ross, Elisabeth. *On Death and Dying.* New York: Scribner, 1997.

Kulka, Richard A., William E. Schlenger, John A. Fairbank, Richard L. Hough, et al. *Trauma and the Vietnam War Generation: Report of Findings from the National Vietnam Veterans Readjustment Study.* New York: Brunner/Mazel, 1990.

Kutz, Ilan, Jane Leserman, Claudia Dorrington, Catherine Morrison, Joan Borysenko, and Herbert Benson. "Meditation as an Adjunct to Psychotherapy." *Psychotherapy and Psychosomatics* 43 (1985): 209–18.

Lamott, Anne. "Scattering the Present." http://archive.salon.com/mwt/col/lamott/2003/08/01/ashes/index.html. 2003.

Lane, Robert E. *The Loss of Happiness in Market Democracies.* New Haven: Yale University Press, 2000.

Langer, Ellen J., and M. Moldoveanu. "The Construct of Mindfulness." *Journal of Social Issues* 56 (2000): 1–9.

Langer, Ellen. *Mindfulness.* Cambridge, MA: Perseus Books, 1989.

Langer, Ellen. *On Becoming an Artist.* New York: Ballantine Books, 2005.

Larsen, Jeff T., Scott H. Hemenover, Catherine J. Norris, and John T. Cacioppo. "Turning Adversity to Advantage: On the Virtues of the Coactivation of Positive and Negative Emotions." In Lisa G. Aspinwall and Ursula M. Staudinger, eds., *A Psychology of Human Strengths: Fundamental Questions and Future Directions for a Positive Psychology.* Washington, D.C.: American Psychological Association, 2003.

Layard, Richard. *Happiness: Lessons from a New Science.* New York: Penguin, 2005.

Lazar, Sara W., Catherine E. Kerr, Rachel H. Wasserman, et al. "Meditation Experience Is Associated with Increased Cortical Thickness." *Neuroreport* 16:17 (2005): 1893–97.

LeDoux, Joseph. *The Emotional Brain: The Mysterious Underpinnings of Emotional Life.* New York: Touchstone, 1996.

Lee, Richard. "What Hunters Do for a Living or How to Make Out on Scarce Resources." In Richard Lee and Irven Devore, *Man the Hunter.* New York: Aldine, 1984.

Linehan, Marsha. *Cognitive-Behavioral Treatment of Borderline Personality Disorder.* New York: Guilford, 1992.

Louv, Richard. *Last Child in the Woods.* New York: Algonquin Books, 2006.

Lykken, David, and Auke Tellegen. "Happiness Is a Stochastic Phenomenon." *Psychological Science* 7 (1996): 186–89.

Lykken, David. *Happiness: The Nature and Nurture of Joy and Contentment.* New York: St. Martin's Griffin, 1999.

Lyubomirsky, Sonja, Kennon M. Sheldon, and David Schkade. "Pursuing Happiness: The Architecture of Sustainable Change." *Review of General Psychology* 9:2 (2005): 111–31.

Lyubomirsky, Sonja, Laura King, and Ed Diener. "The Benefits of Frequent Positive Affect: Does Happiness Lead to Success?" *Psychological Bulletin* 131:6 (2005): 803–55.

Lyubomirsky, Sonja, Lorie Sousa, and Rene Dickerhoof. "The Costs and Benefits of Writing, Talking, and Thinking about Life's Triumphs and Defeats." *Journal of Personality and Social Psychology* 90:4 (2006): 692–708.

Magid, Barry. *Ordinary Mind: Exploring the Common Ground of Zen and Psychotherapy.* Boston: Wisdom Publications, 2002.

Maguire, Eleanor A., David G. Gadian, Ingrid S. Johnsrude, Catriona D. Good, et al. "Navigation-Related Structural Change in the Hippocampi of Taxi Drivers." *Proceedings of the National Academy of Sciences* 97 (2000): 4398–403.

Marmot, Michael. *The Status Syndrome.* New York: Henry Holt, 2005.

McEwen, Bruce S., with E. N. Lasley. *The End of Stress as We Know It.* Washington, DC: Dana Press/Joseph Henry Press, 2002.

McPherson, Miller, Lynn Smith-Lovin, and Matthew E. Brashears. "Social Isolation in America: Changes in Core Discussion Networks over Two Decades." *American Sociological Review* 71 (2006): 353–75.

Medvec, Victoria H., Scott F. Madey, and Thomas Gilovich. "When Less Is More: Counterfactual Thinking and Satisfaction Among Olympic Medalists." *Journal of Personality and Social Psychology.* 69:4 (Oct. 1995): 603–10.

Melchior, Maria, Avshalom Caspi, Barry J. Milne, Andrea Danese, Richie Poulton and Terrie E. Moffitt. "Work Stress Precipitates Depression and Anxiety in Young, Working Women and Men." *Psychological Medicine* 37:8 (Aug. 2007): 1119–29.

Michigan, University of. Press release. http://www.umich.edu/news/index.html?Releases/2004/Dec04/r120204c.

Miller, Timothy. *How to Want What You Have.* New York: Avon, 1995.

Mipham, Sayong. *Turning the Mind into an Ally.* New York: Riverhead, 2004.

Moncrieff, Joanna, and David Cohen. "Do Antidepressants Cure or Create Abnormal Brain States?" *PLoS Med* 3:7 (2006): e240 doi:10.1371/journal.pmed.0030240.

Murray, Christopher J. L., and Alan D. Lopez, ed. *The Global Burden of Disease. A Comprehensive Assessment of Mortality and Disability From Disease, Injuries, and Risk Factors in 1990 and Projected to 2020.* World Health Organization, World Bank, Harvard University, 2006.

Myers, David G. *The Pursuit of Happiness.* New York: Avon, 1992.

Nesse, Randolph M. "Natural Selection and the Elusiveness of Happiness." *Philosophical Transactions of the Royal Society B: Biological Sciences,* 359:1449 (Sept 29, 2004): 1333–47.

Nettle, Daniel. *Happiness: The Science Behind Your Smile.* Oxford (UK): Oxford University Press, 2005.

O'Connor, Richard. *Undoing Depression: What Therapy Doesn't Teach You and Medication Can't Give You.* New York: Little, Brown, 1997.

———. *Active Treatment of Depression.* New York: Norton, 2001.

———. *Undoing Perpetual Stress.* New York: Berkley, 2005.

O'Hanlon, Bill. *Thriving Through Crisis.* New York: Perigee, 2005.

Opbroek, Adam, Pedro L. Delgado, Cindi Laukes, et al. "Emotional Blunting Associated with SSRI-Induced Sexual Dysfunction. Do SSRIs Inhibit Emotional Responses?" *International Journal of Neuropsychopharmacology* 5 (2002): 147–51.

Orsillo, Susan M., Lizabeth Roemer, Jennifer Block Lerner, and Matthew T. Tull. "Acceptance, Mindfulness, and Cognitive-Behavioral Therapy: Comparisons, Contrasts, and Application to Anxiety." In Steven C. Hayes, Victoria M. Follette, and Marsha M. Linehan, eds., *Mindfulness and Acceptance: Expanding the Cognitive-Behavioral Tradition.* New York: Guilford, 2004.

Pascual-Leone, Alvaro, Amir Amedi, Felipe Fregni, and Lotfi B. Merabet. "The Plastic Human Brain Cortex." *Annual Review of Neuroscience* 28 (2005): 377–401.

Pennebaker, James W. *Opening Up: The Healing Power of Expressing Emotions.* New York: Guilford, 1990.

Pennebaker, James W., Tracy J. Mayne, and Martha E. Francis. "Linguistic Predictors of Adaptive Bereavement." *Journal of Personality and Social Psychology* 72 (1997): 863–67.

Peterson, Christopher. *A Primer in Positive Psychology.* New York: Oxford, 2006.

Peterson, Christopher, Steven F. Maier, and Martin E. P. Seligman. *Learned Helplessness.* New York: Oxford, 1995.

Plassman, Hilke, John O'Doherty, Baba Shiv, and Antonio Rangel. "Marketing Actions Can Modulate Neural Representations of Experienced Pleasantness." *Proceedings of the National Academy of Sciences* 105 (2008): 1050–54.

Polivy, Janet, and C. Peter Herman. "If at First You Don't Succeed: False Hopes of Self-Change." *American Psychologist* 57:9 (Sept. 2002): 677–89.

Prelec, Drazen, and Duncan Simester. "Always Leave Home Without It: A Further Investigation of the Credit-Card Effect on Willingness to Pay." *Marketing Letters* 12:1 (Feb. 2001): 5–12.

Psychotherapy Networker (unsigned article). "The Top Ten," March/April 2007.

Putnam, Robert D. *Bowling Alone.* New York: Simon & Schuster, 2000.

Redelmeier, Donald A., and Sheldon M. Singh. "Survival in Academy Award-Winning Actors and Actresses." *Annals of Internal Medicine* 134:10 (2001): 955–62.

Reis, Harry T., and Shelly Gable, "Toward a Positive Psychology of Relationships." In Corey L. M. Keyes and Jonathan Haidt, eds., *Flourishing: Positive Psychology and the Life Well-Lived.* Washington, DC: American Psychological Association, 2003.

Rencanzone, G. H., C. E. Schreiner, and M. M. Merzenich. "Plasticity in the Frequency Representation of Primary Auditory Cortex Following Discrimination Training in Adult Owl Monkeys." *Journal of Neuroscience* 13 (1993): 87–103.

Reuters Summit. "U.S. Executive Pay Still Out of Control." February 18, 2004. http://www.reuters.com/newsArticle.jhtml.

Rosenkranz, Melissa A., Daren C. Jackson, Kim M. Dalton, Isa Dolski, et al. "Affective Style and *In Vivo* Immune Response: Neurobehavioral Mechanisms." *Proceedings of the National Academy of Sciences* 100 (2003): 11148–52.

Rotundo, E. Anthony. *American Manhood.* New York: Basic Books, 1994.

Ryff, Carol D. "Happiness Is Everything, or Is It? Explorations on the Meaning of Psychological Well-Being." *Journal of Personality and Social Psychology* 57:6 (1989): 1069–81.

Ryff, Carol D., and Burton Singer. "The Role of Emotion on Pathways to Positive Health." In Richard Davidson, Klaus L. Scherer, and H. Hill Goldsmith, eds., *Handbook of Affective Science.* New York: Oxford University Press, 2003.

Sapolsky, Robert M. *Why Zebras Don't Get Ulcers.* New York: W. H. Freeman, 1998.

Schkade, David, and Daniel Kahneman. "Does Living in California Make People Happy?" *Psychological Science* 9:340 (1998): 340–46.

Schor, Juliet B. *The Overworked American.* New York: Basic Books, 1993.

———. *The Overspent American.* New York: Basic Books, 1998.

Schore, Allan N. *Affect Regulation and the Origin of the Self: The Neurobiology of Emotional Development.* Hillsdale, NJ: Erlbaum, 1994.

———. *Affect Deregulation and Disorders of the Self.* New York: Norton, 2003a.

———. *Affect Regulation and the Repair of the Self.* New York: Norton, 2003b.

Schumaker, John F. *In Search of Happiness.* Westport, CT: Praeger, 2007.

Schwartz, Barry, Andrew Ward, John Monterosso, Sonja Lyubomirsky, Katherine White, and Darrin R. Lehman. "Maximizing versus Satisficing: Happiness Is a Matter of Choice." *Journal of Personality and Social Psychology* 83:5 (2002): 1178–97.

Schwartz, Barry. *The Paradox of Choice: Why More Is Less.* New York: HarperCollins, 2004.

Schwartz, J. M., P. W. Stoessel, L. R. Baxter, K. M. Martin, and M. E. Phelps. "Systematic Changes in Cerebral Glucose Metabolic Rate After Successful Behavior Modification Treatment of Obsessive-Compulsive Disorder." *Archives of General Psychiatry* 53 (1996): 109–13.

Schwartz, Jeffrey, and Sharon Begley. *The Mind and the Brain: Neuroplasticity and the Power of Mental Force.* New York: HarperCollins, 2002.

Schwarz, Norbert, and Fritz Strack. "Reports of Subjective Well-Being: Judgmental Processes and their Methodological Implications." In Daniel Kahneman, Ed Diener, and Norbert Schwarz, eds., *Well-Being: The Foundations of Hedonic Psychology.* New York: Russell Sage, 1999.

Scott-Clark, Cathy, and Adrian Levy. "Fast Forward into Trouble." *The Guardian,* June 14, 2003.

Segal, Zindel V., John Teasdale, and Mark Williams. "Mindfulness-Based Cognitive-Behavioral Therapy: Theoretical Rationale and Empirical Status." In Steven C. Hayes, Victoria M. Follette, and Marsha M. Linehan, eds., *Mindfulness and Acceptance: Expanding the Cognitive-Behavioral Tradition.* New York: Guilford, 2004.

Segal, Zindel V., Mark Williams, and John Teasdale. *Mindfulness-Based Cognitive Therapy for Depression.* New York: Guilford, 2002.

Seligman, Martin E. P. *Authentic Happiness.* New York: Free Press, 2002.

Seligman, Martin E. P., Tracy A. Steen, Nansook Park, and Christopher Peterson. "Positive Psychology Progress: Empirical Validation of Interventions." *American Psychologist* 60 (2005): 410–21.

Servan-Schreiber, David. *The Instinct to Heal.* Emmaus, PA: Rodale, 2003.

Setlow, C. "Reinforce Shopping as a Leisure Activity." *DSN Retailing Today*, June 4, 2001.

Shapiro, Shauna L., Gary E. Schwartz, and Ginny Bonner. "Effects of Mindfulness-Based Stress Reduction on Medical and Premedical Students." *Journal of Behavioral Medicine* 21 (1998): 581–99.

Sheldon, Kennon M., Andrew J. Elliot, Youngmee Kim, and Tim Kasser. "What Is Satisfying about Satisfying Events? Testing Ten Candidate Psychological Needs." *Journal of Personality and Social Psychology* 80:2 (2001): 325–39.

Sheline, Yvette I., Po W. Wang, Mokhtar H. Gado, John G. Csernansky, and Michael W. Vannier. "Hippocampal Atrophy in Recurrent Major Depression." *Proceedings of the National Academy of Sciences* 93:9 (1996): 3908–13.

Siegel, Daniel J. *The Developing Mind*. New York: Guilford, 2001.

———. *The Mindful Brain*. New York: Norton, 2007.

Singh-Manoux, Archana, Michael G. Marmot, and Nancy E. Adler. "Does Subjective Social Status Predict Health and Change in Health Status Better Than Objective Status?" *Psychosomatic Medicine* 67 (2005): 855–61.

Slusher, Morgan P., and Craig A. Anderson. "Belief Perseverance and Self-Defeating Behavior." In Rebecca Curtis, ed., *Self-Defeating Behaviors: Experimental Research, Clinical Impressions, and Practical Implications*. New York: Plenum Press, 1989.

Solnick, S., and Hemenway, D. "Is More Always Better? A Survey on Positional Concerns." *Journal of Economic Behavior and Organization* 37 (1998): 373–83.

Speca, M., L. E. Carlson, E. Goodey, and M. Angen. "A Randomized, Wait-List Controlled Clinical Trial: The Effect of a Mindfulness Meditation-Based Stress Reduction Program on Mood and Symptoms of Stress in Cancer Outpatients." *Psychosomatic Medicine* 62 (2000): 613–22.

Steffen, Patrick R., Timothy B. Smith, Michael Larson, and Leon Butler. "Acculturation to Western Society as a Risk Factor for High Blood Pressure: A Meta-Analytic Review." *Psychosomatic Medicine* 68 (2006): 386–97.

Stevenson, Betsey, and Justin Wolfers. "The Paradox of Declining Female Happiness." 2007. Available at: http://bpp.wharton.upenn.edu/jwolfers/Papers/WomensHappiness .pdf.

Stone, Arthur A., Joseph E. Schwartz, David Schkade, Norbert Schwarz, Alan Krueger, and Daniel Kahneman. "A Population Approach to the Study of Emotion." *Emotion* 6:1 (2006): 139–49.

Stutzer, Alois. "The Role of Income Aspirations in Individual Happiness." *Journal of Economic Behavior and Organization* 54:1 (May 2004): 89–109.

Taylor, Shelley E. "On Healthy Illusions." *Daedalus*, Jan. 1, 2005.

———. *Positive Illusions*. New York: Basic Books, 1989.

Taylor, Shelley E., Margaret E. Kemeny, Geoffrey M. Reed, Julienne E. Bower, and Tara L. Gruenewald. "Psychological Resources, Positive Illusions, and Health." *American Psychologist* 55:1 (Jan. 2000): 99–109.

Ulrich, R. S. "View Through a Window May Influence Recovery From Surgery." *Science* 224 (1984): 420–21.

UNICEF Report Card 7. "Child Poverty in Perspective: An Overview of Child Well-Being in Rich Countries." Available at http://www.unicef-irc.org/cgi-bin/unicef/Lunga.sql?ProductID = 445. Feb. 14, 2007.

Vaillant, George E. *The Wisdom of the Ego.* Cambridge, MA: Harvard University Press, 1993.

Van Boven, Leaf, and George Loewenstein. "Social Projection of Transient Drive States." *Personality and Social Psychology Bulletin* 29 (2003): 1159–68.

Van der Kolk, Bessel A. "In Terror's Grip: Healing the Ravages of Trauma." *Cerebrum* 4:34–50. New York: The Dana Foundation, 2002.

Ventura, Michael. "Appointments with Yourself." *Psychotherapy Networker* Nov./Dec. 2006, 29–33.

Viorst, Judith. *Necessary Losses.* New York: Free Press, 1998.

Vitello, Paul. "Pressed for Time and Money, Americans are Giving Up Golf." *New York Times,* Feb. 21, 2008, A1.

Walker, W. Richard, John J. Skowronski, and Charles P. Thompson. "Life Is Pleasant—and Memory Helps to Keep It That Way!" *Review of General Psychology* 7:2 (2003): 203–10.

Wallace, B. Alan. *Genuine Happiness.* New York: Wiley, 2005.

Wallerstein, Judith S., and Sandra Blakeslee. *Second Chances: Men, Women, and Children a Decade after Divorce.* New York: Ticknor & Fields, 1989.

Wallis, Claudia. "The New Science of Happiness." *Time,* Jan. 17, 2005.

Weiner, Eric. *The Geography of Bliss.* New York: Twelve, 2008.

Williams, Mark, John Teasdale, Zindel Segal, and Jon Kabat-Zinn. *The Mindful Way Through Depression.* New York: Guilford, 2007.

Wilson, Kelly G., and Amy R. Murrell. "Values Work in Acceptance and Commitment Therapy: Setting a Course for Behavioral Treatment." In Steven C. Hayes, Victoria M. Follette, and Marsha M. Linehan, eds., *Mindfulness and Acceptance: Expanding the Cognitive-Behavioral Tradition.* New York: Guilford, 2004.

Wrzesniewski, Amy, Paul Rozin, and Gwen Bennett, "Working, Playing, and Eating: Making the Most of Most Moments." In Corey L. M. Keyes and Jonathan Haidt, eds., *Flourishing: Positive Psychology and the Life Well-Lived.* Washington, DC: American Psychological Association, 2003.

Zwieg, Jason. *Your Money and Your Brain.* New York: Simon & Schuster, 2007.

INDEX